MADE MEN

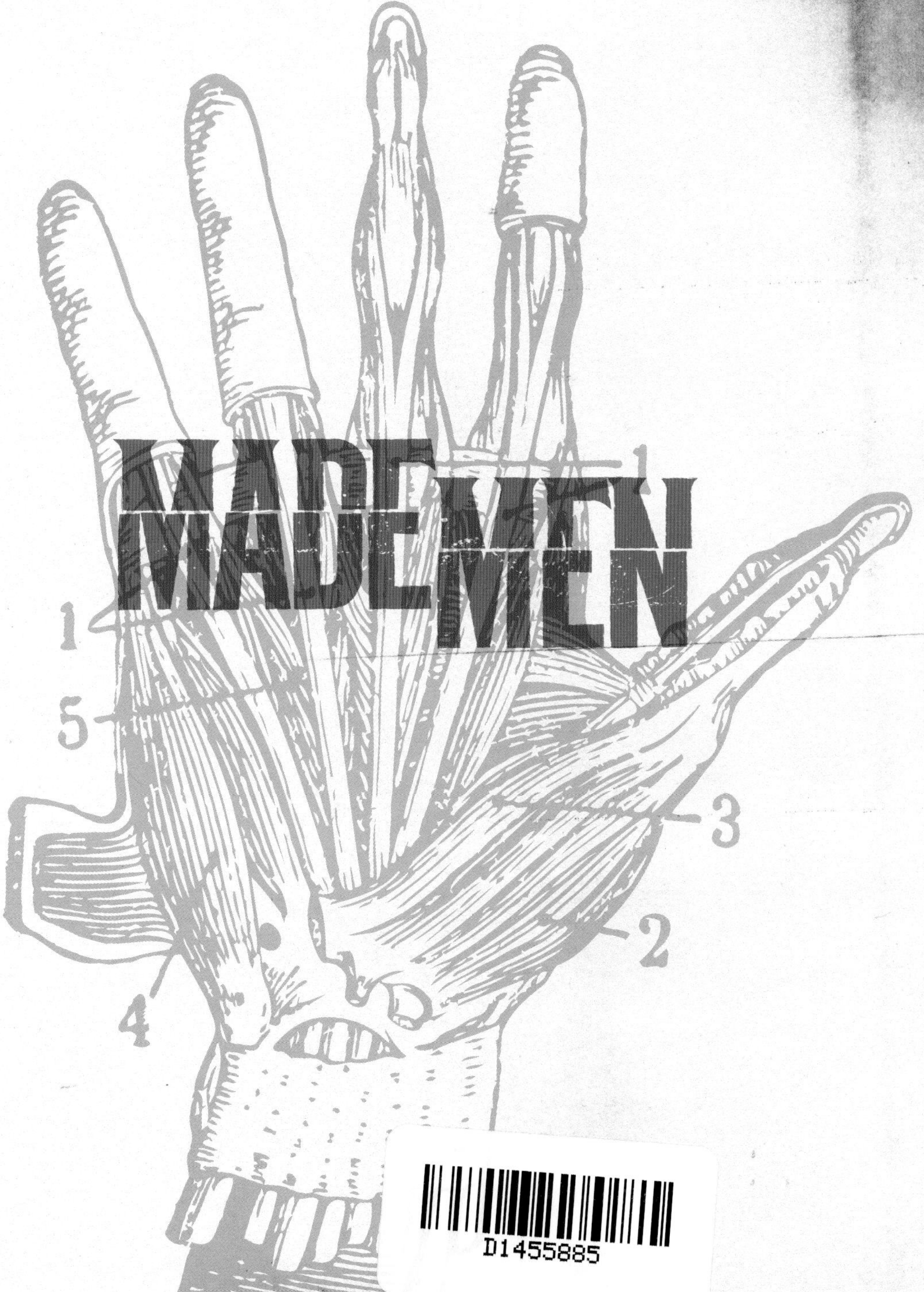

1
1
5
3
2
4

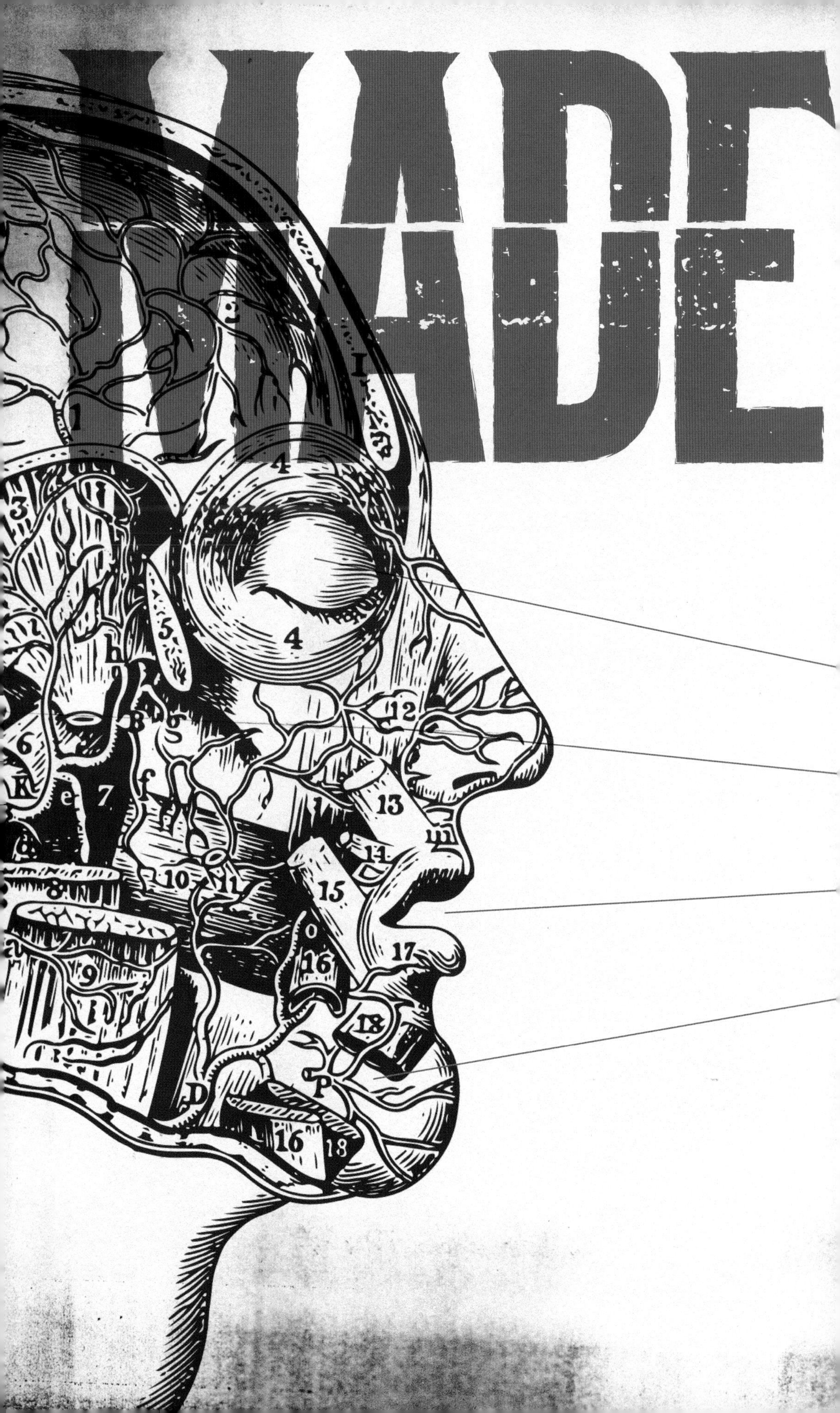
MADE
MADE

MEN

GETTING THE GANG BACK TOGETHER

WRITTEN BY PAUL TOBIN

ILLUSTRATED BY ARJUNA SUSINI

COLORED BY GONZALO DUARTE

LETTERED BY SAIDA TEMOFONTE

EDITED BY ROBIN HERRERA
DESIGNED BY DYLAN TODD

@PaulTobin / paultobin.net
@ArjunaSusini / arjunasusiniblog.blogspot.it
gonzaloduarte.com
@bigredrobot / bigredrobot.net

AN ONI PRESS PUBLICATION

PUBLISHED BY ONI PRESS, INC.

Joe Nozemack, **FOUNDER & CHIEF FINANCIAL OFFICER**
James Lucas Jones, **PUBLISHER**
Charlie Chu, **V.P. OF CREATIVE & BUSINESS DEVELOPMENT**
Brad Rooks, **DIRECTOR OF OPERATIONS**
Melissa Meszaros, **DIRECTOR OF PUBLICITY**
Margot Wood, **DIRECTOR OF SALES**
Rachel Reed, **MARKETING MANAGER**
Troy Look, **DIRECTOR OF DESIGN & PRODUCTION**
Hilary Thompson, **SENIOR GRAPHIC DESIGNER**
Kate Z. Stone, **JUNIOR GRAPHIC DESIGNER**
Sonja Synak, **JUNIOR GRAPHIC DESIGNER**
Angie Knowles, **DIGITAL PREPRESS LEAD**
Ari Yarwood, **EXECUTIVE EDITOR**
Robin Herrera, **SENIOR EDITOR**
Desiree Wilson, **ASSOCIATE EDITOR**
Alissa Sallah **ADMINISTRATIVE ASSISTANT**
Jung Lee, **LOGISTICS ASSOCIATE**

ONI PRESS, INC
1319 SE Martin Luther King, Jr. Blvd
Suite 240
Portland, OR 97214

onipress.com

🔘 facebook.com/onipress
🔘 twitter.com/onipress
🔘 onipress.tumblr.com
🔘 instagram.com/onipress

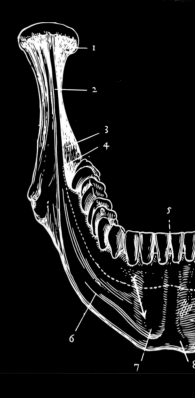

FIRST EDITION: JULY 2018

ISBN 978-1-62010-512-2
EISBN 978-1-62010-513-9

LIBRARY OF CONGRESS CONTROL NUMBER: 2017960733

1 2 3 4 5 6 7 8 9 10

PRINTED IN CHINA.

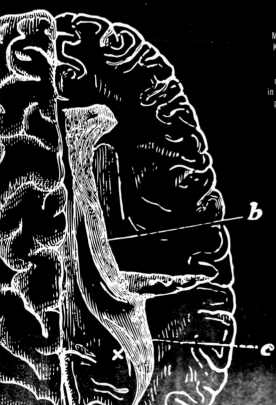

CHAPTER ONE

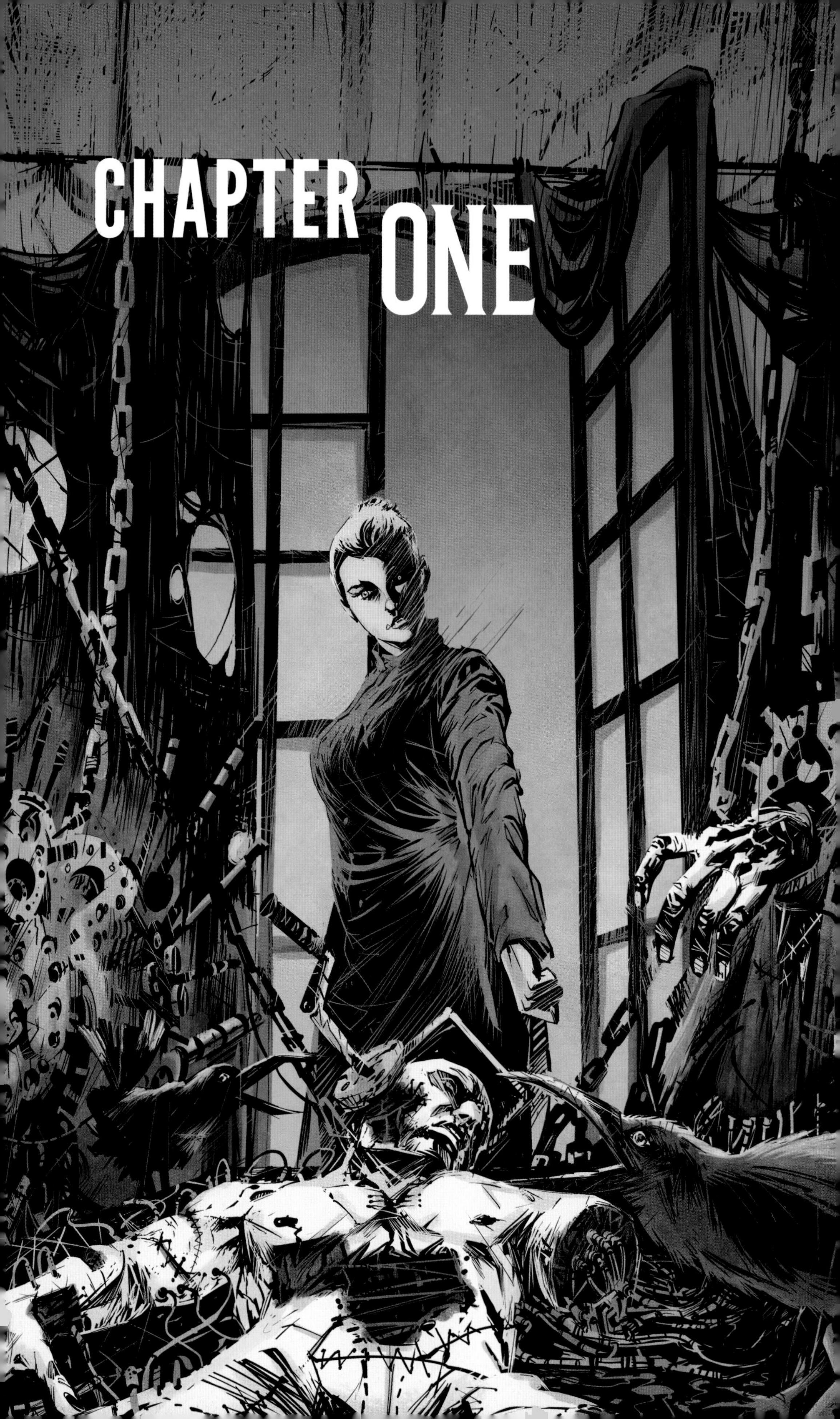

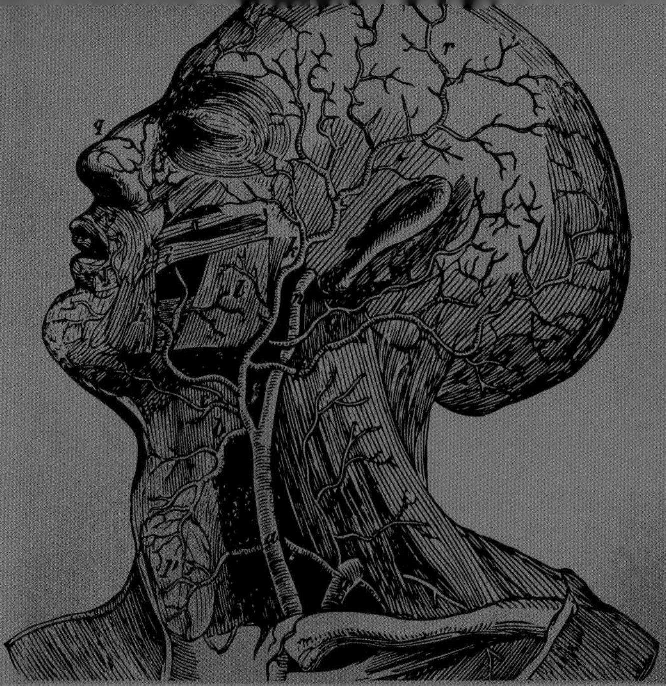

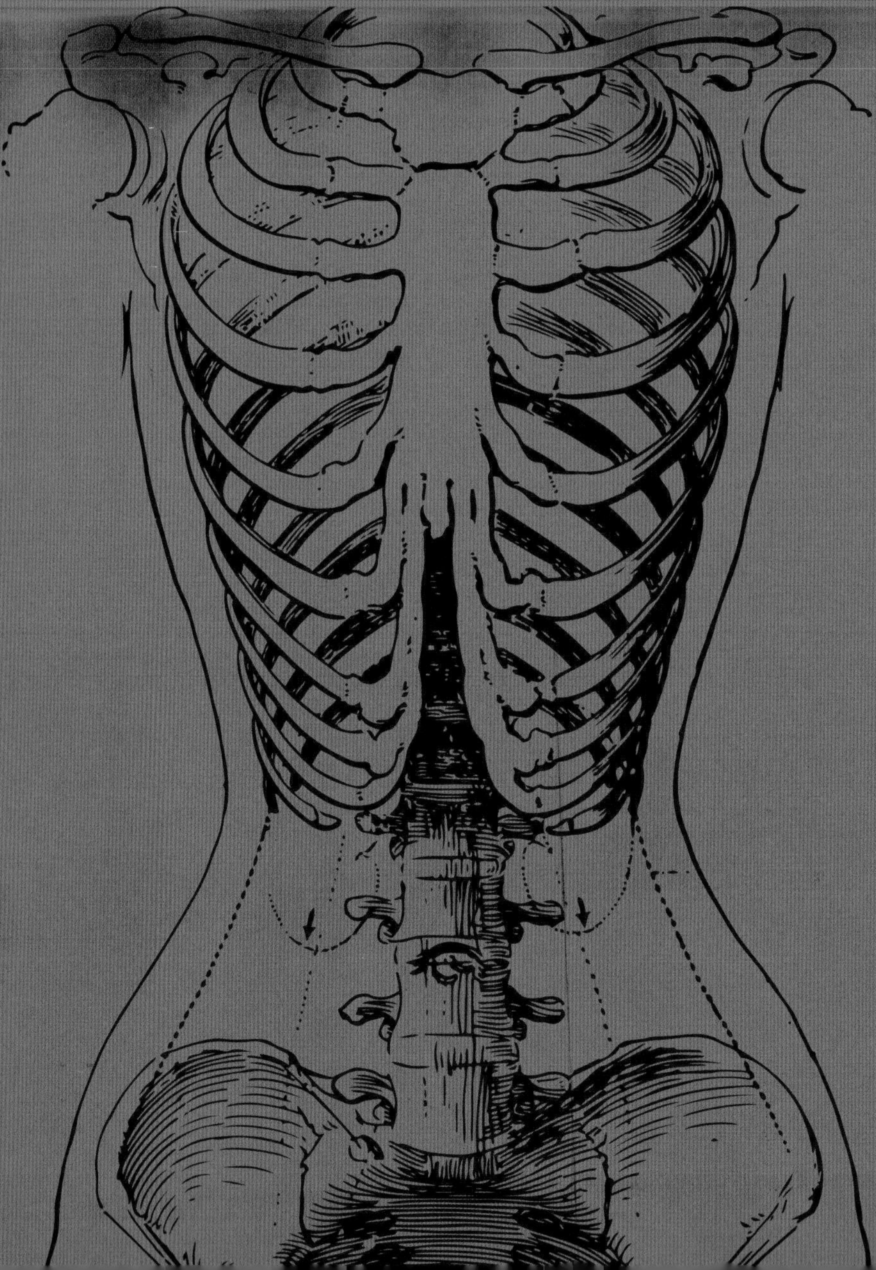

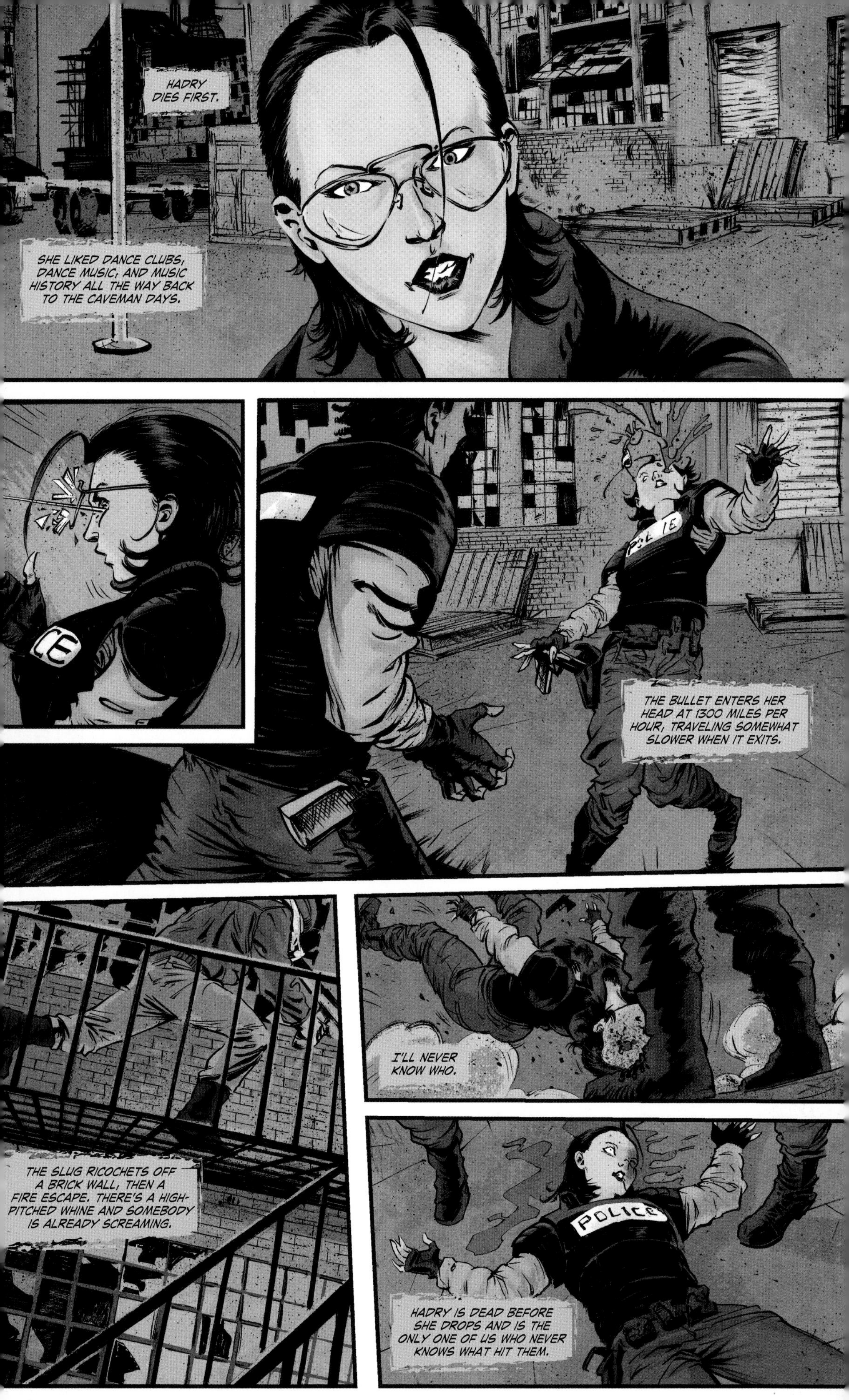

HADRY DIES FIRST.
SHE LIKED DANCE CLUBS, DANCE MUSIC, AND MUSIC HISTORY ALL THE WAY BACK TO THE CAVEMAN DAYS.
THE BULLET ENTERS HER HEAD AT 1300 MILES PER HOUR, TRAVELING SOMEWHAT SLOWER WHEN IT EXITS.
THE SLUG RICOCHETS OFF A BRICK WALL, THEN A FIRE ESCAPE. THERE'S A HIGH-PITCHED WHINE AND SOMEBODY IS ALREADY SCREAMING.
I'LL NEVER KNOW WHO.
POLICE
HADRY IS DEAD BEFORE SHE DROPS AND IS THE ONLY ONE OF US WHO NEVER KNOWS WHAT HIT THEM.

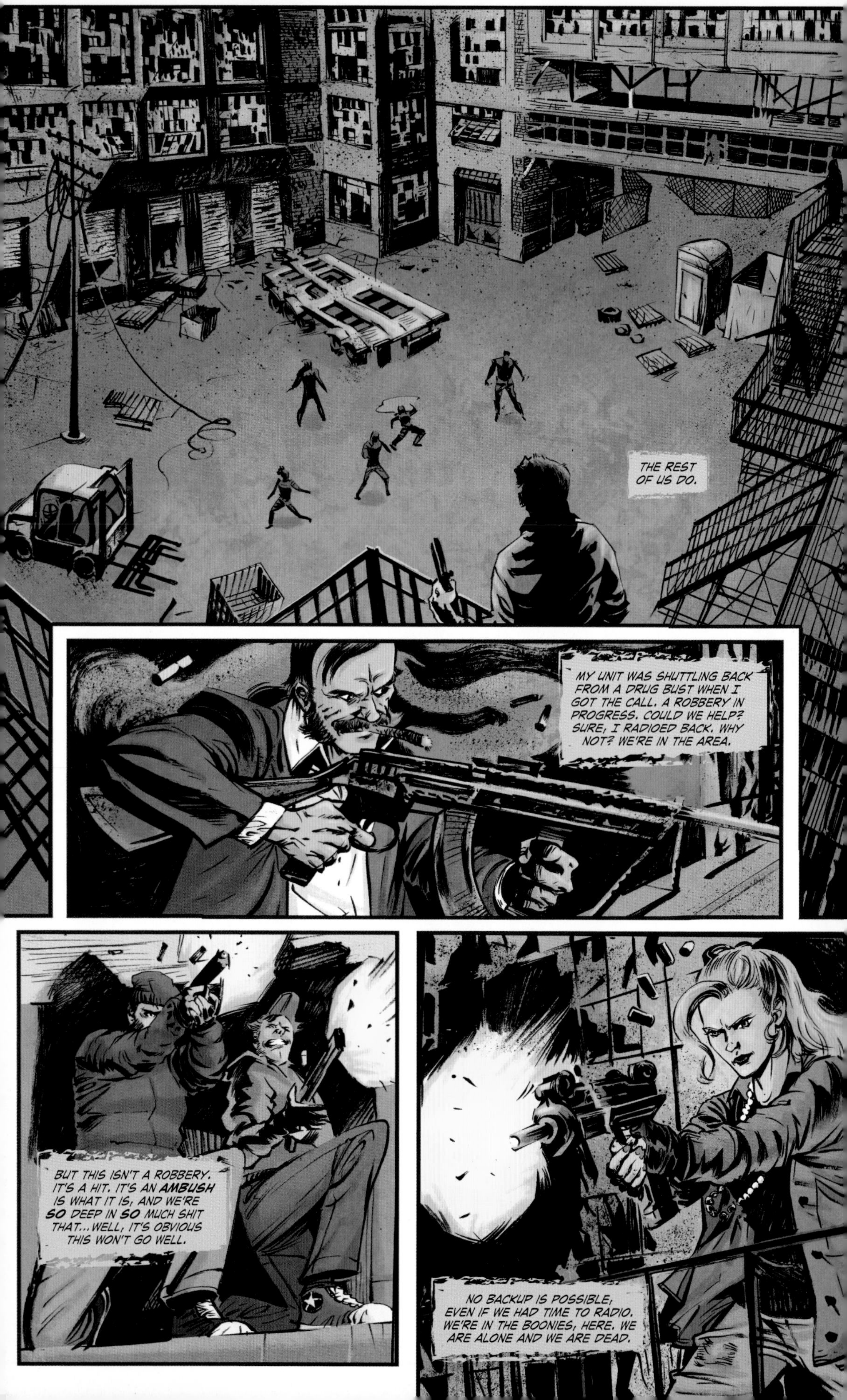
THE REST OF US DO.
MY UNIT WAS SHUTTLING BACK FROM A DRUG BUST WHEN I GOT THE CALL. A ROBBERY IN PROGRESS. COULD WE HELP? SURE, I RADIOED BACK. WHY NOT? WE'RE IN THE AREA.
BUT THIS ISN'T A ROBBERY. IT'S A HIT. IT'S AN AMBUSH IS WHAT IT IS, AND WE'RE SO DEEP IN SO MUCH SHIT THAT... WELL, IT'S OBVIOUS THIS WON'T GO WELL.
NO BACKUP IS POSSIBLE, EVEN IF WE HAD TIME TO RADIO. WE'RE IN THE BOONIES, HERE. WE ARE ALONE AND WE ARE DEAD.

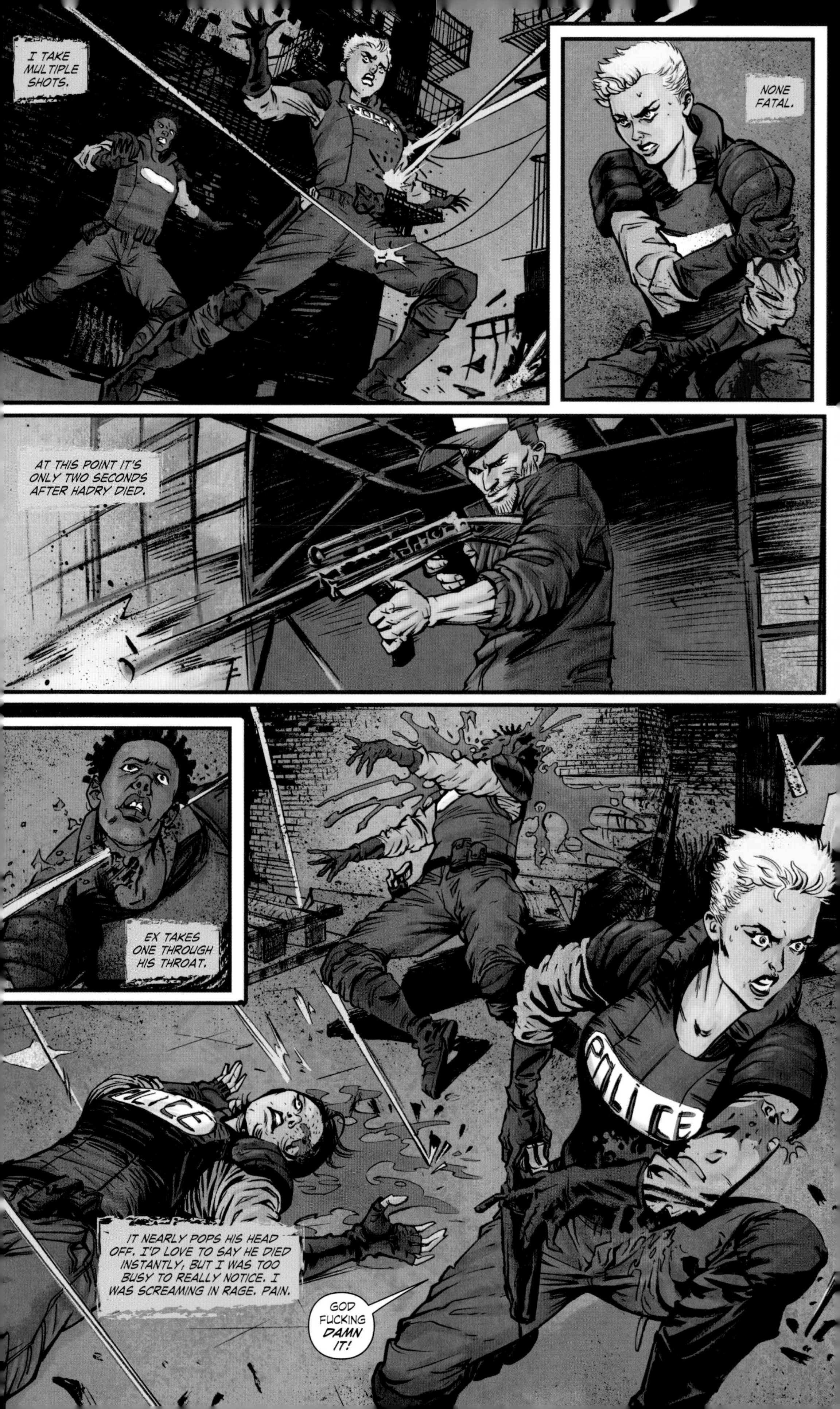
I TAKE MULTIPLE SHOTS.
NONE FATAL.
AT THIS POINT IT'S ONLY TWO SECONDS AFTER HADRY DIED.
EX TAKES ONE THROUGH HIS THROAT.
IT NEARLY POPS HIS HEAD OFF. I'D LOVE TO SAY HE DIED INSTANTLY, BUT I WAS TOO BUSY TO REALLY NOTICE. I WAS SCREAMING IN RAGE. PAIN.
GOD FUCKING DAMN IT!

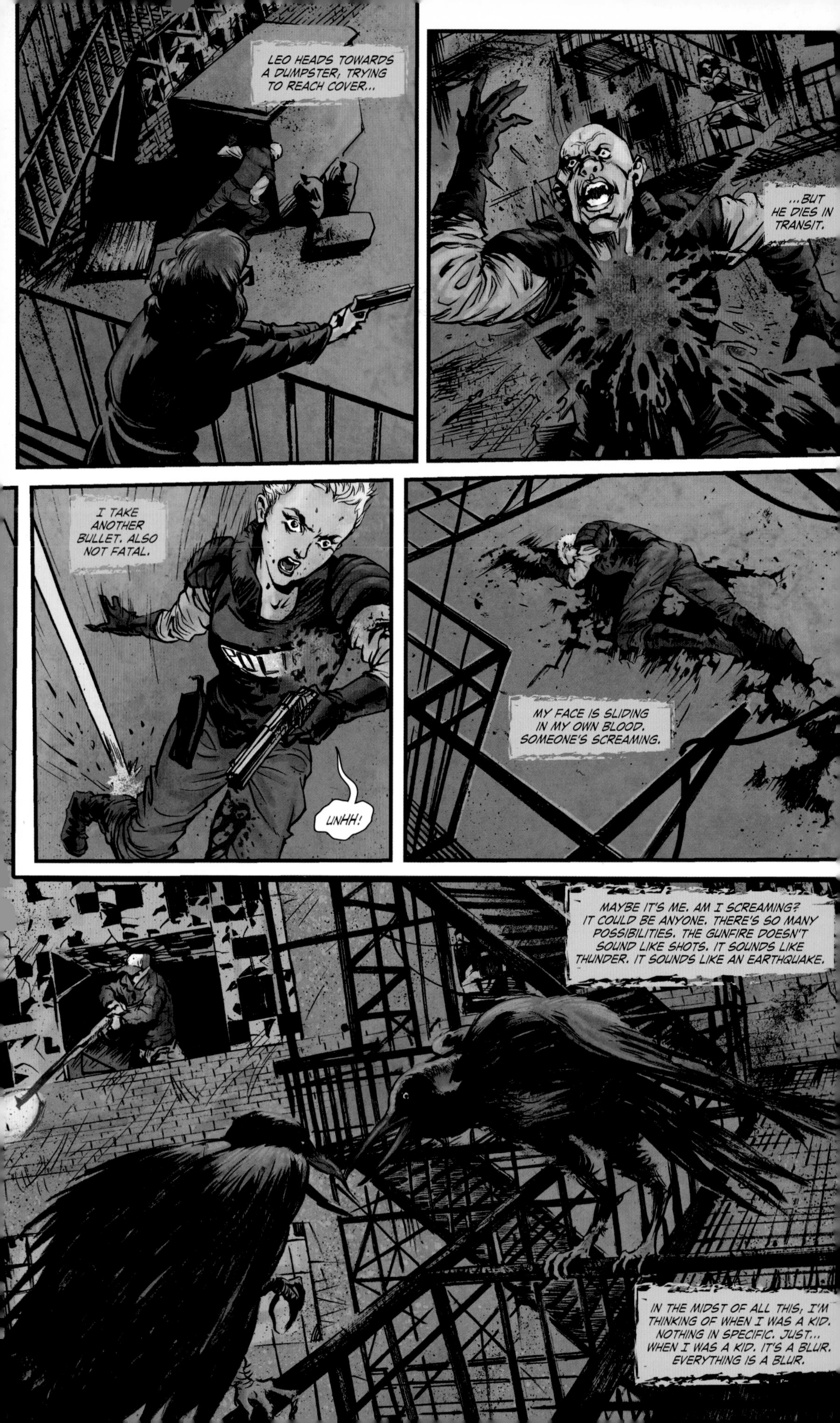
LEO HEADS TOWARDS A DUMPSTER, TRYING TO REACH COVER...
...BUT HE DIES IN TRANSIT.
I TAKE ANOTHER BULLET. ALSO NOT FATAL.
UNHH!
MY FACE IS SLIDING IN MY OWN BLOOD. SOMEONE'S SCREAMING.
MAYBE IT'S ME. AM I SCREAMING? IT COULD BE ANYONE. THERE'S SO MANY POSSIBILITIES. THE GUNFIRE DOESN'T SOUND LIKE SHOTS. IT SOUNDS LIKE THUNDER. IT SOUNDS LIKE AN EARTHQUAKE.
IN THE MIDST OF ALL THIS, I'M THINKING OF WHEN I WAS A KID. NOTHING IN SPECIFIC. JUST... WHEN I WAS A KID. IT'S A BLUR. EVERYTHING IS A BLUR.

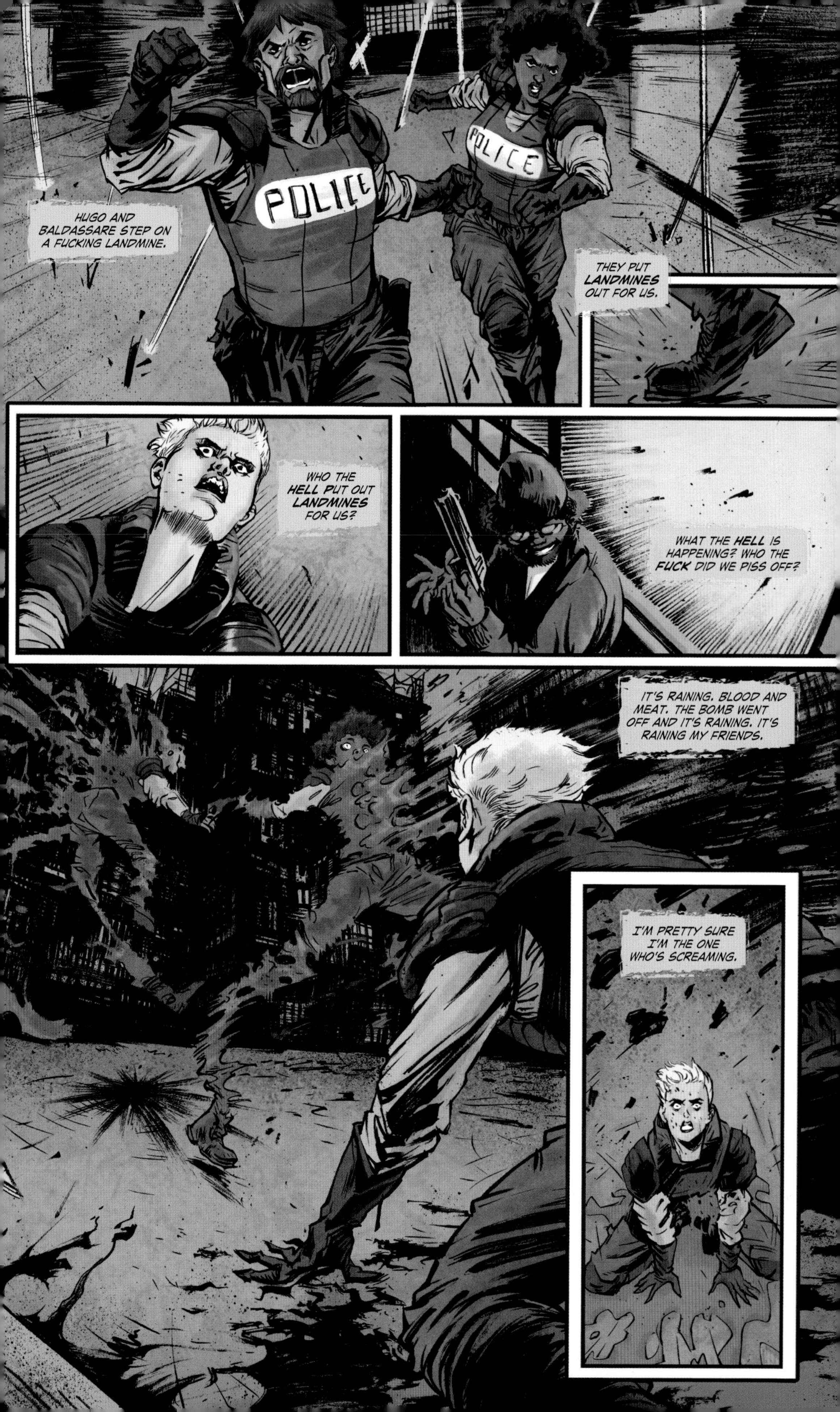
HUGO AND BALDASSARE STEP ON A FUCKING LANDMINE.
THEY PUT LANDMINES OUT FOR US.
WHO THE HELL PUT OUT LANDMINES FOR US?
WHAT THE HELL IS HAPPENING? WHO THE FUCK DID WE PISS OFF?
IT'S RAINING. BLOOD AND MEAT. THE BOMB WENT OFF AND IT'S RAINING. IT'S RAINING MY FRIENDS.
I'M PRETTY SURE I'M THE ONE WHO'S SCREAMING.

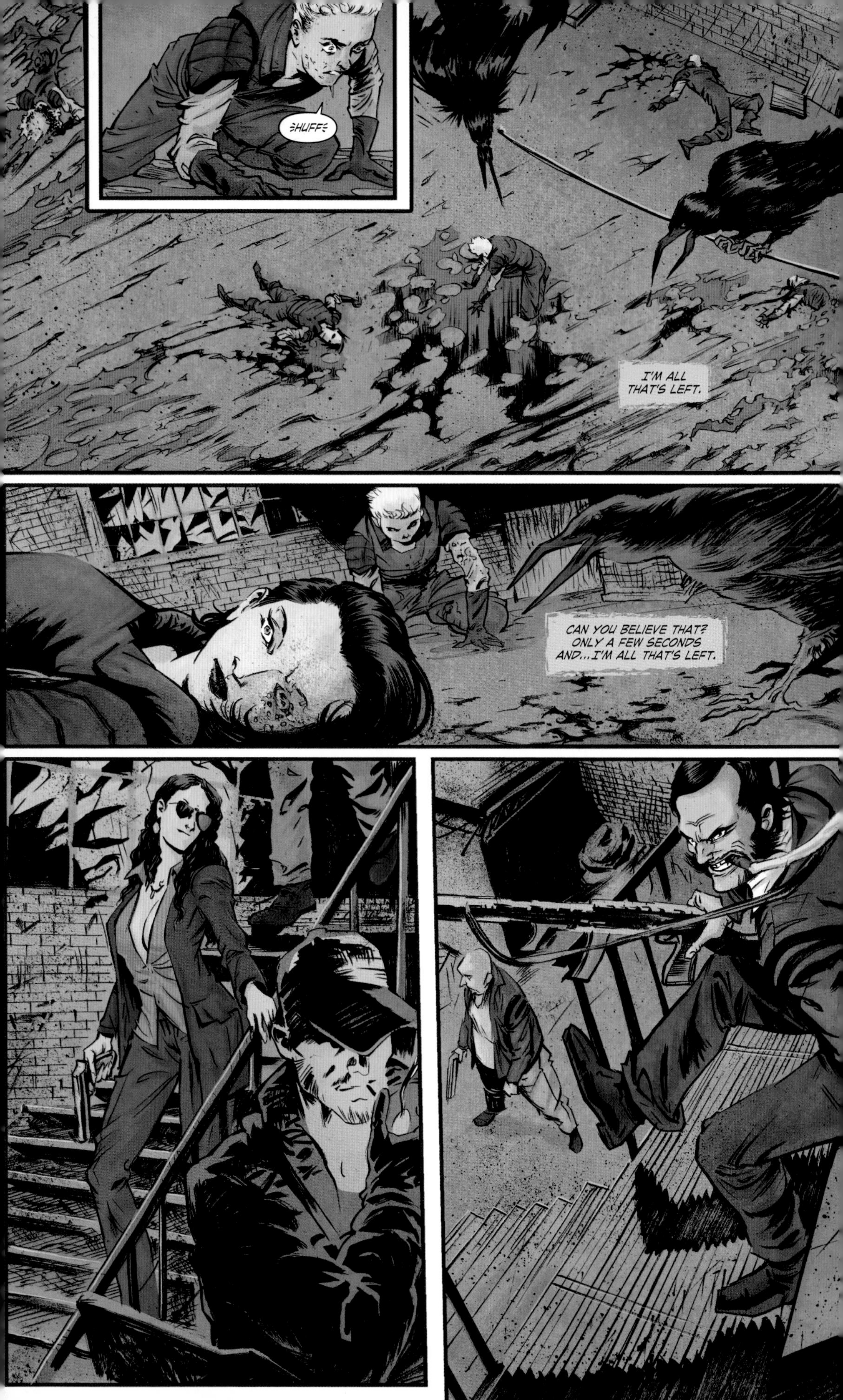
HUFF
I'M ALL THAT'S LEFT.
CAN YOU BELIEVE THAT? ONLY A FEW SECONDS AND... I'M ALL THAT'S LEFT.

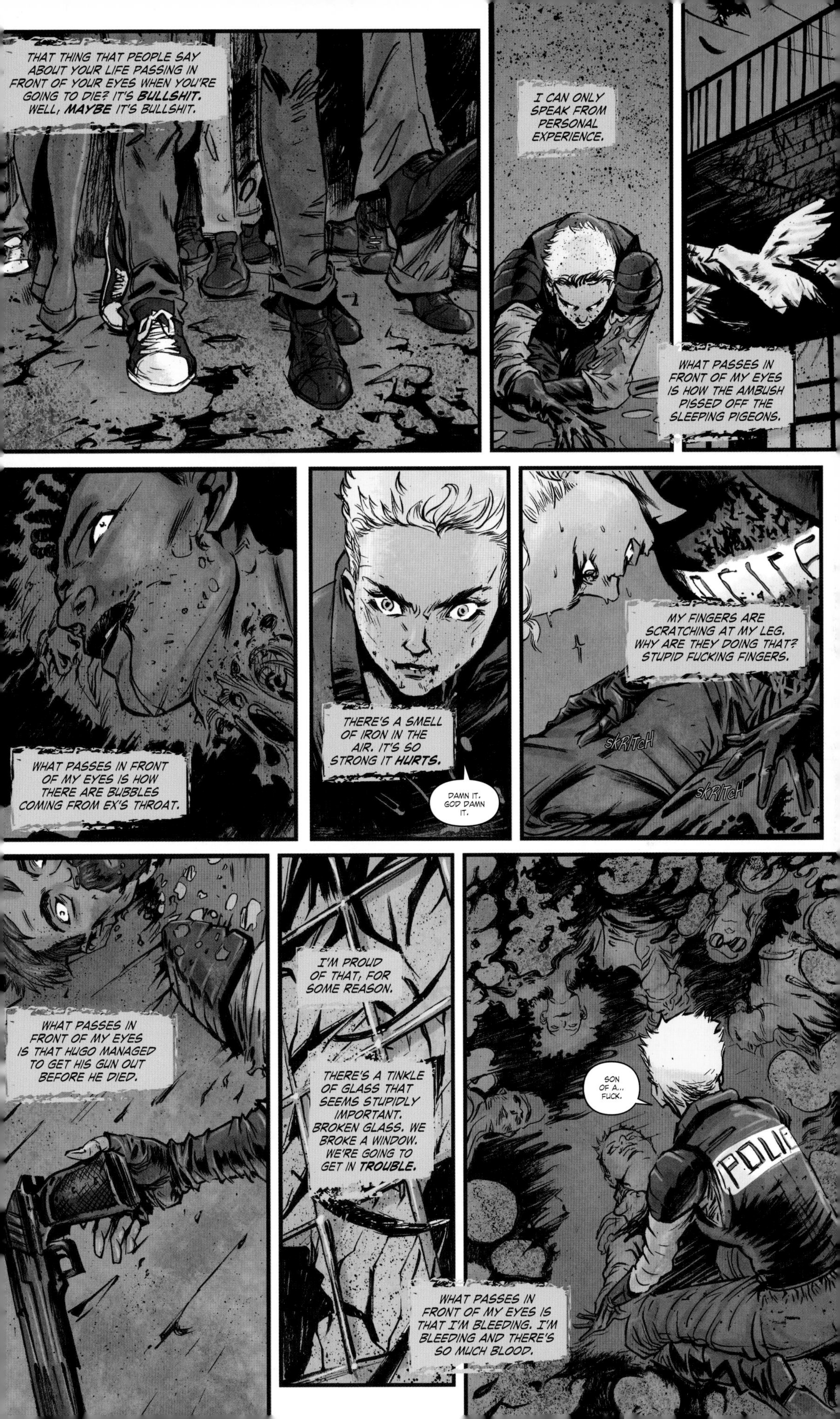
THAT THING THAT PEOPLE SAY ABOUT YOUR LIFE PASSING IN FRONT OF YOUR EYES WHEN YOU'RE GOING TO DIE? IT'S BULLSHIT. WELL, MAYBE IT'S BULLSHIT.
I CAN ONLY SPEAK FROM PERSONAL EXPERIENCE.
WHAT PASSES IN FRONT OF MY EYES IS HOW THE AMBUSH PISSED OFF THE SLEEPING PIGEONS.
WHAT PASSES IN FRONT OF MY EYES IS HOW THERE ARE BUBBLES COMING FROM EX'S THROAT.
THERE'S A SMELL OF IRON IN THE AIR. IT'S SO STRONG IT HURTS.
DAMN IT. GOD DAMN IT.
MY FINGERS ARE SCRATCHING AT MY LEG. WHY ARE THEY DOING THAT? STUPID FUCKING FINGERS.
SKRITCH
SKRITCH
WHAT PASSES IN FRONT OF MY EYES IS THAT HUGO MANAGED TO GET HIS GUN OUT BEFORE HE DIED.
I'M PROUD OF THAT, FOR SOME REASON.
THERE'S A TINKLE OF GLASS THAT SEEMS STUPIDLY IMPORTANT. BROKEN GLASS. WE BROKE A WINDOW. WE'RE GOING TO GET IN TROUBLE.
SON OF A... FUCK.
WHAT PASSES IN FRONT OF MY EYES IS THAT I'M BLEEDING. I'M BLEEDING AND THERE'S SO MUCH BLOOD.

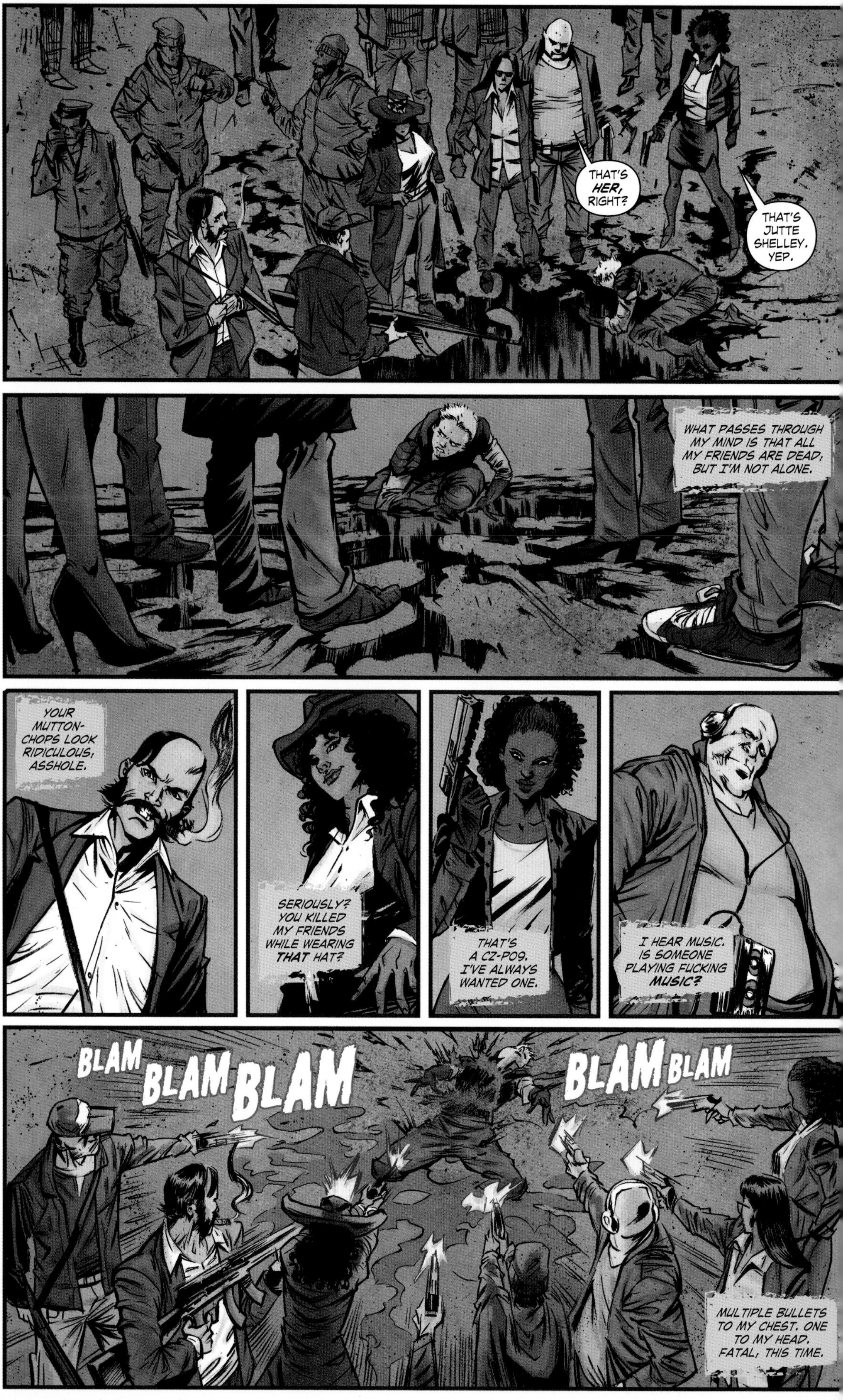
THAT'S *HER,* RIGHT?
THAT'S JUTTE SHELLEY. YEP.
WHAT PASSES THROUGH MY MIND IS THAT ALL MY FRIENDS ARE DEAD, BUT I'M NOT ALONE.
YOUR MUTTON-CHOPS LOOK RIDICULOUS, ASSHOLE.
SERIOUSLY? YOU KILLED MY FRIENDS WHILE WEARING *THAT* HAT?
THAT'S A CZ-P09. I'VE ALWAYS WANTED ONE.
I HEAR MUSIC. IS SOMEONE PLAYING FUCKING *MUSIC?*
BLAM BLAM BLAM
BLAM BLAM
MULTIPLE BULLETS TO MY CHEST. ONE TO MY HEAD. FATAL, THIS TIME.

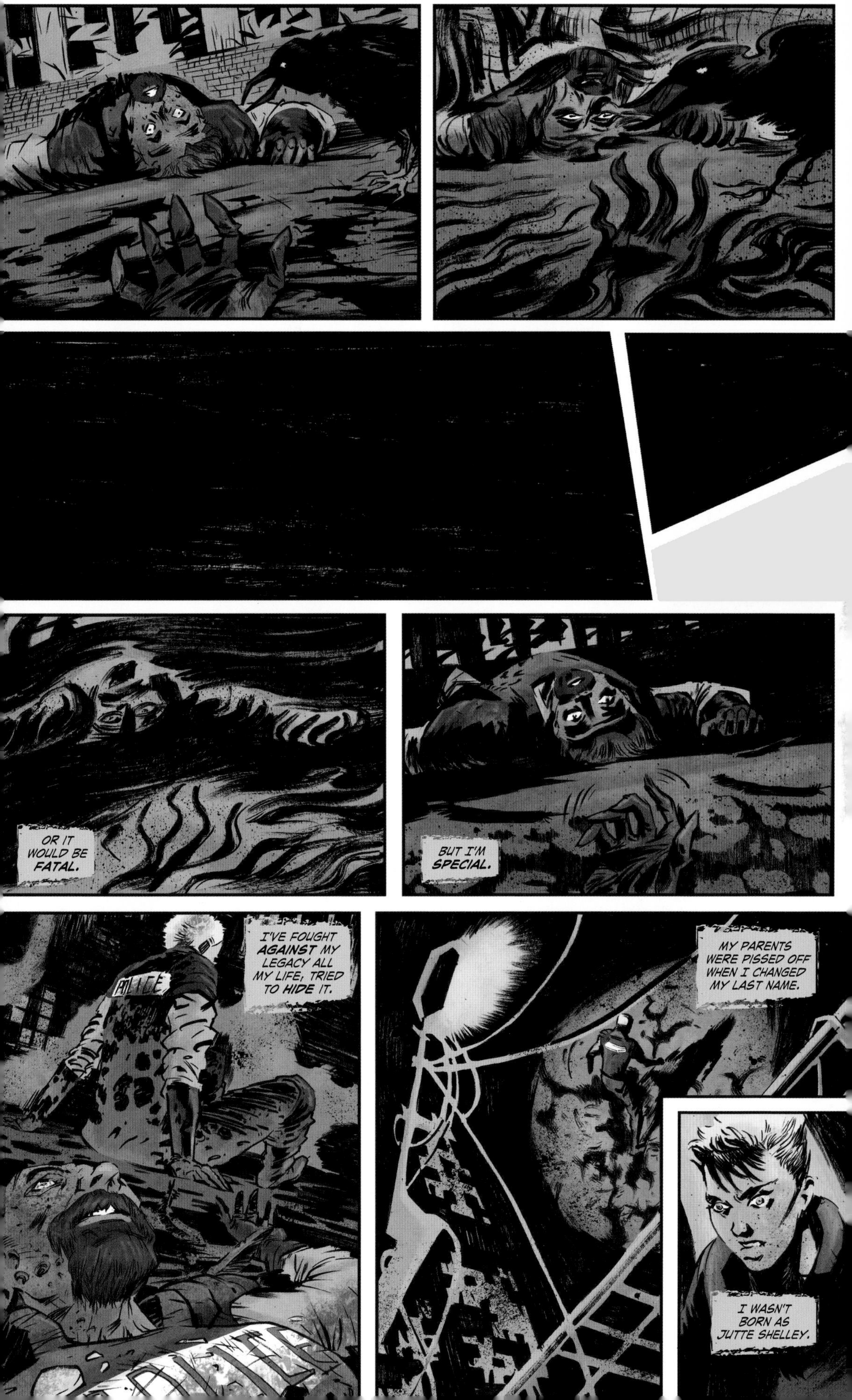
OR IT WOULD BE FATAL.
BUT I'M SPECIAL.
POLICE
I'VE FOUGHT AGAINST MY LEGACY ALL MY LIFE, TRIED TO HIDE IT.
MY PARENTS WERE PISSED OFF WHEN I CHANGED MY LAST NAME.
I WASN'T BORN AS JUTTE SHELLEY.

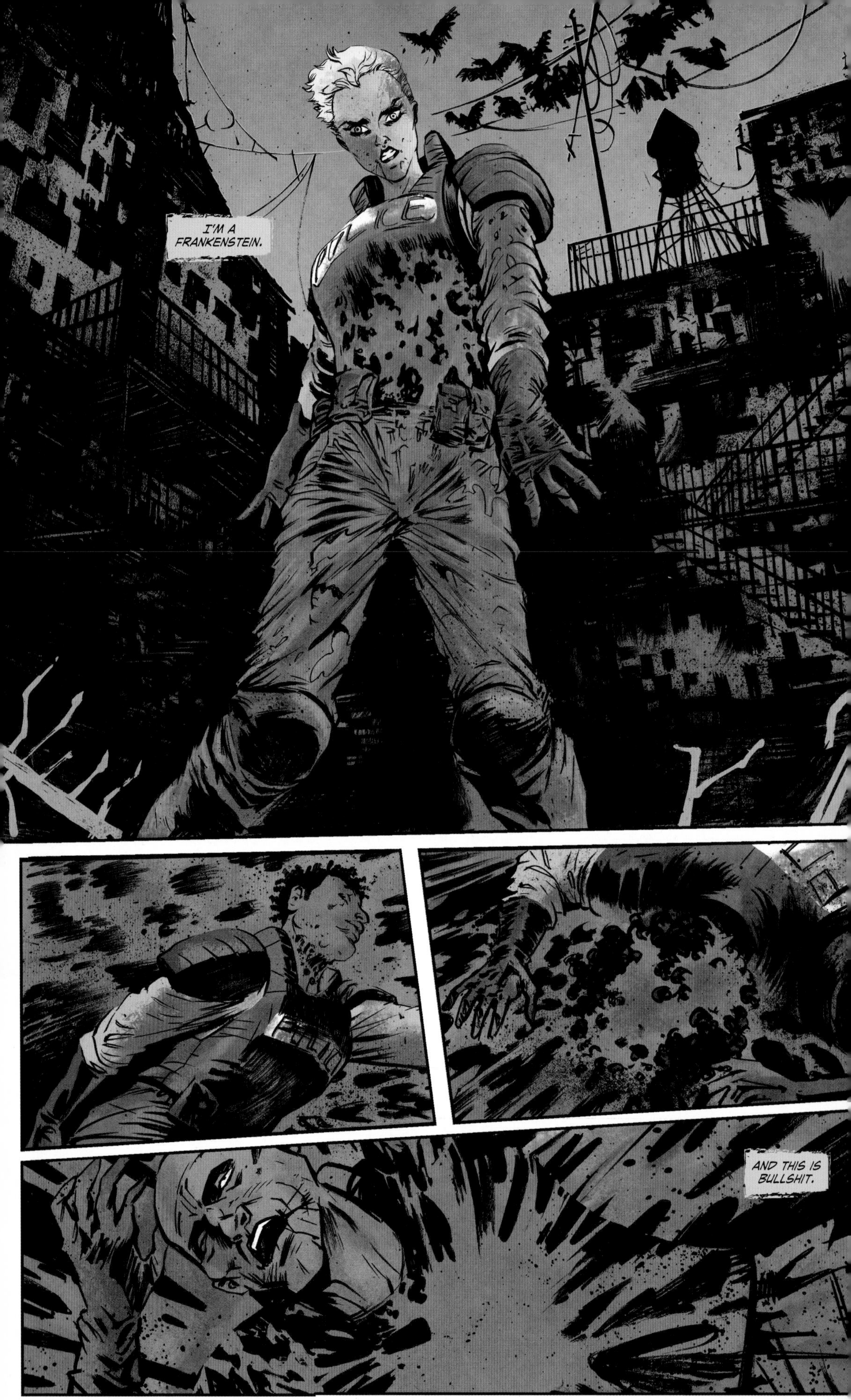
I'M A FRANKENSTEIN.
POLICE
AND THIS IS BULLSHIT.

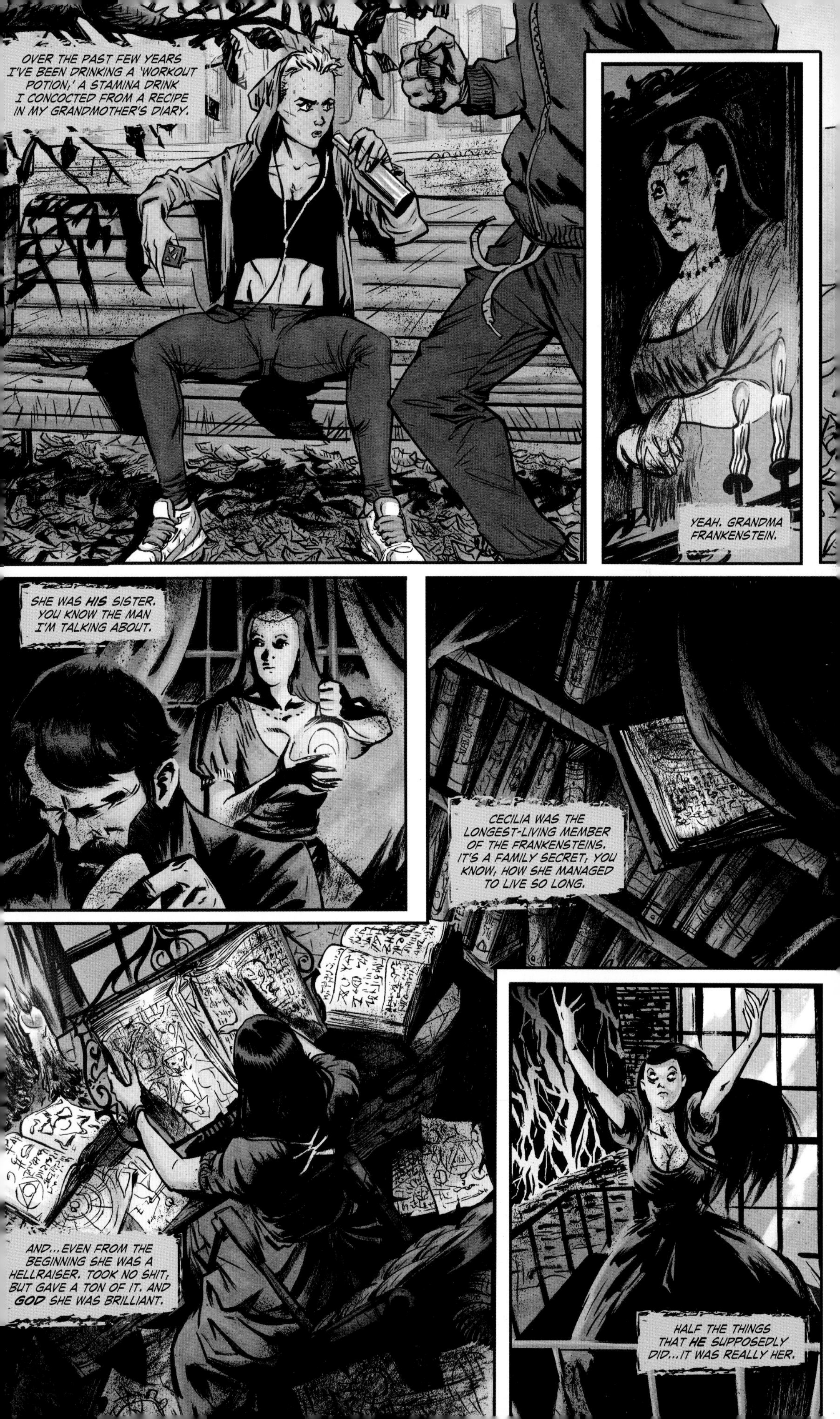
OVER THE PAST FEW YEARS I'VE BEEN DRINKING A 'WORKOUT POTION,' A STAMINA DRINK I CONCOCTED FROM A RECIPE IN MY GRANDMOTHER'S DIARY.
YEAH. GRANDMA FRANKENSTEIN.
SHE WAS **HIS** SISTER. YOU KNOW THE MAN I'M TALKING ABOUT.
CECILIA WAS THE LONGEST-LIVING MEMBER OF THE FRANKENSTEINS. IT'S A FAMILY SECRET, YOU KNOW, HOW SHE MANAGED TO LIVE SO LONG.
AND...EVEN FROM THE BEGINNING SHE WAS A HELLRAISER. TOOK NO SHIT, BUT GAVE A TON OF IT. AND **GOD** SHE WAS BRILLIANT.
HALF THE THINGS THAT **HE** SUPPOSEDLY DID...IT WAS REALLY HER.

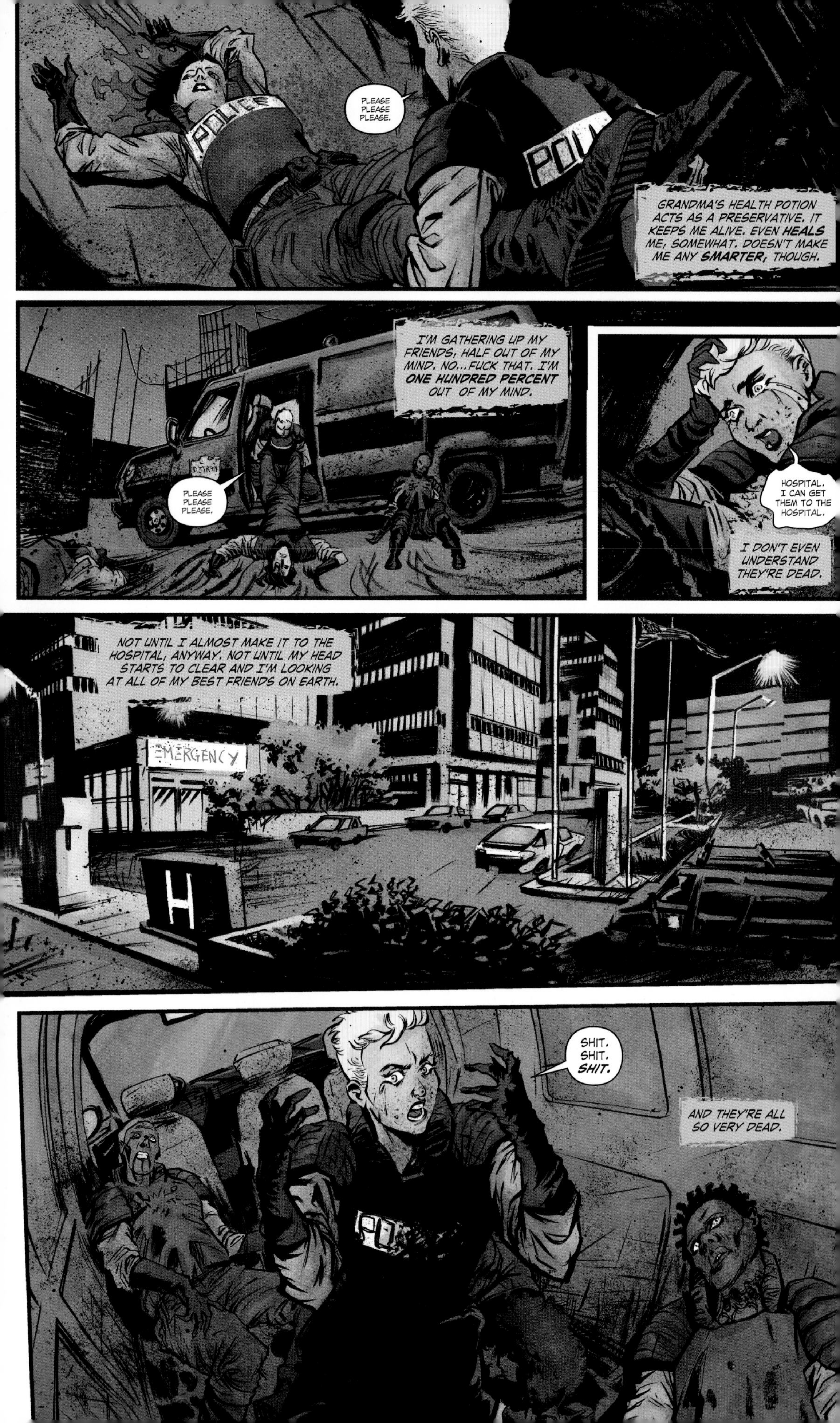
PLEASE PLEASE PLEASE.
GRANDMA'S HEALTH POTION ACTS AS A PRESERVATIVE. IT KEEPS ME ALIVE. EVEN HEALS ME, SOMEWHAT. DOESN'T MAKE ME ANY SMARTER, THOUGH.
I'M GATHERING UP MY FRIENDS, HALF OUT OF MY MIND. NO...FUCK THAT. I'M ONE HUNDRED PERCENT OUT OF MY MIND.
PLEASE PLEASE PLEASE.
HOSPITAL. I CAN GET THEM TO THE HOSPITAL.
I DON'T EVEN UNDERSTAND THEY'RE DEAD.
NOT UNTIL I ALMOST MAKE IT TO THE HOSPITAL, ANYWAY. NOT UNTIL MY HEAD STARTS TO CLEAR AND I'M LOOKING AT ALL OF MY BEST FRIENDS ON EARTH.
EMERGENCY
H
SHIT. SHIT. SHIT.
AND THEY'RE ALL SO VERY DEAD.

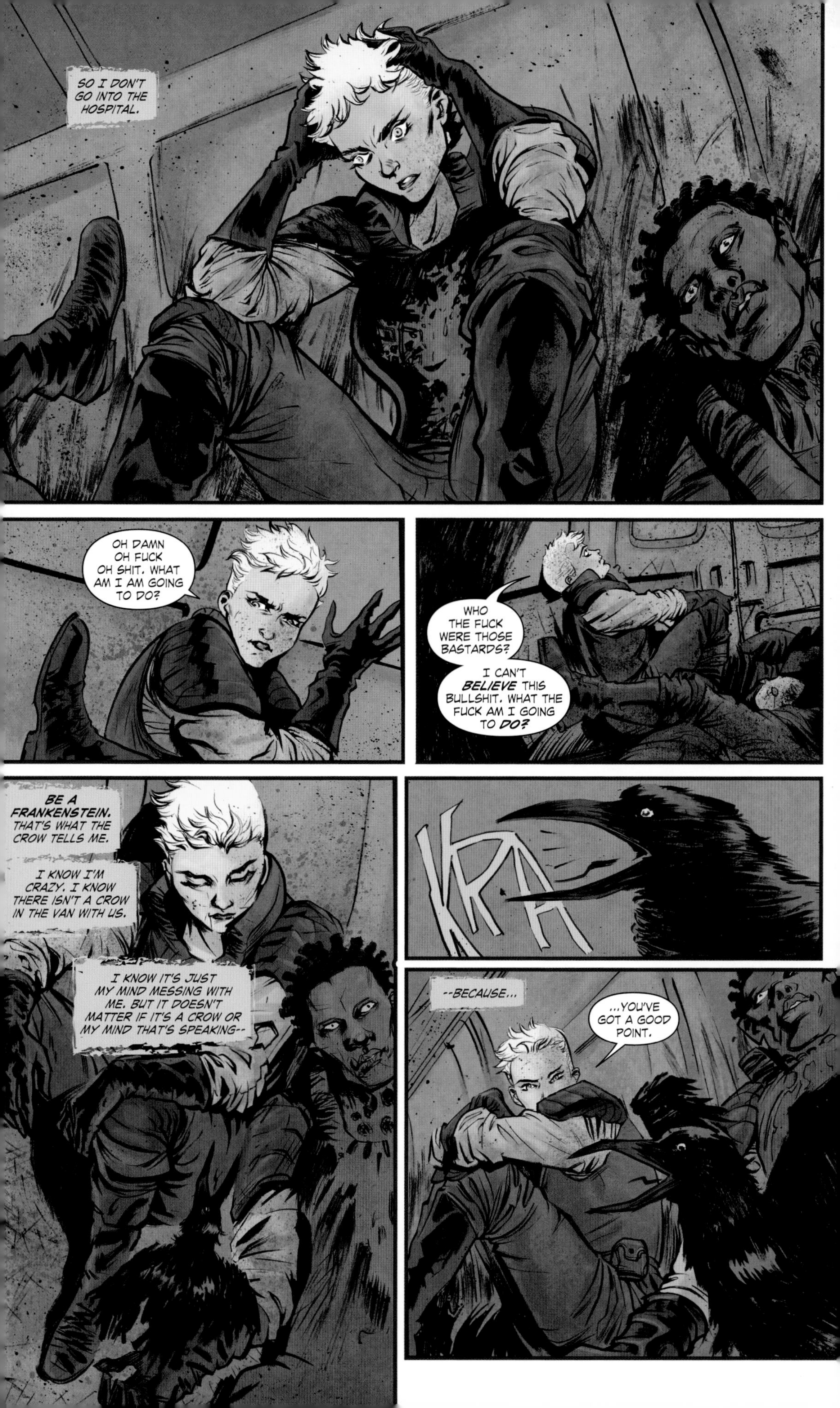
SO I DON'T GO INTO THE HOSPITAL.
OH DAMN OH FUCK OH SHIT. WHAT AM I AM GOING TO DO?
WHO THE FUCK WERE THOSE BASTARDS?
I CAN'T BELIEVE THIS BULLSHIT. WHAT THE FUCK AM I GOING TO DO?
BE A FRANKENSTEIN. THAT'S WHAT THE CROW TELLS ME.
I KNOW I'M CRAZY. I KNOW THERE ISN'T A CROW IN THE VAN WITH US.
I KNOW IT'S JUST MY MIND MESSING WITH ME. BUT IT DOESN'T MATTER IF IT'S A CROW OR MY MIND THAT'S SPEAKING--
KRA
--BECAUSE...
...YOU'VE GOT A GOOD POINT.

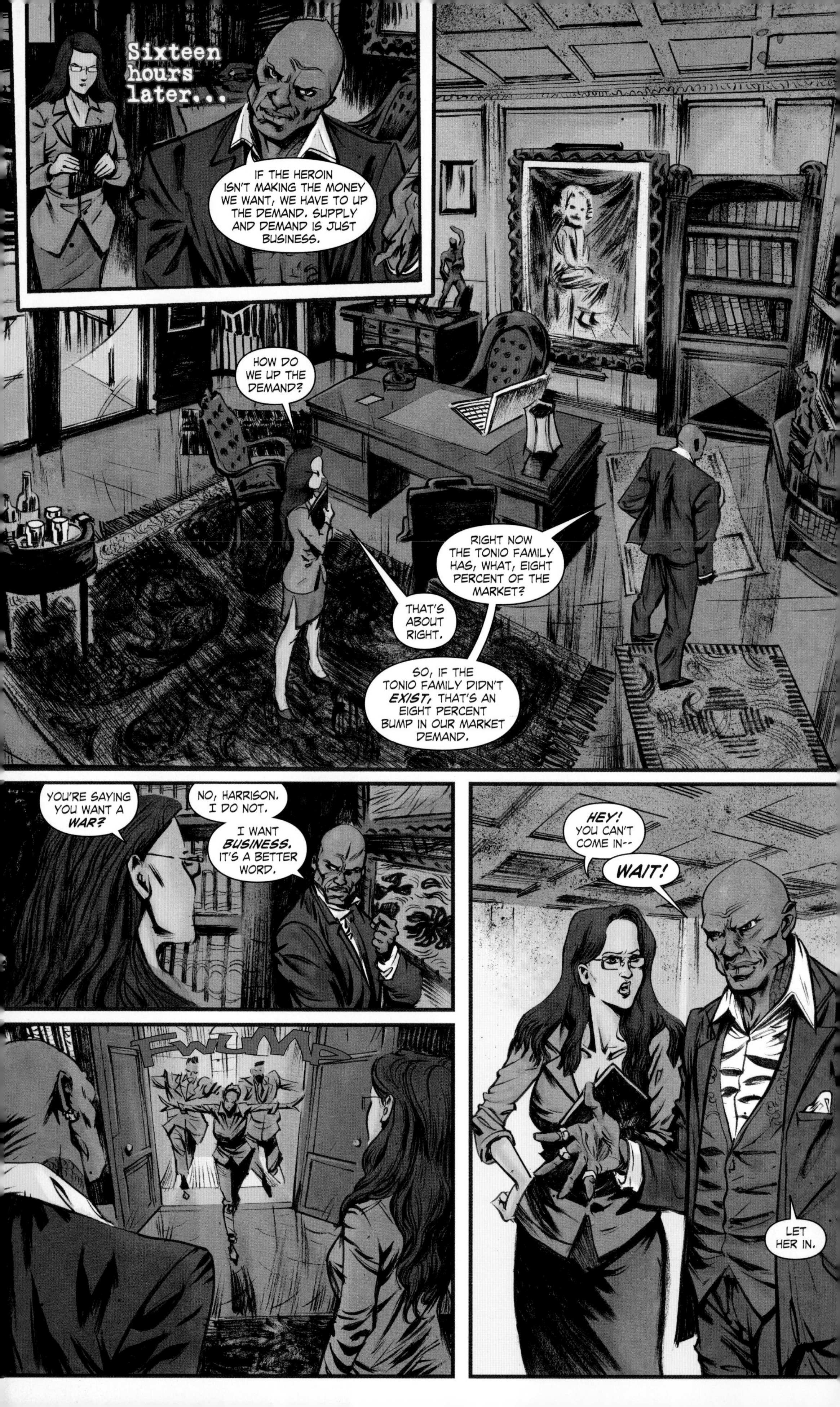

Sixteen hours later...
IF THE HEROIN ISN'T MAKING THE MONEY WE WANT, WE HAVE TO UP THE DEMAND. SUPPLY AND DEMAND IS JUST BUSINESS.
HOW DO WE UP THE DEMAND?
RIGHT NOW THE TONIO FAMILY HAS, WHAT, EIGHT PERCENT OF THE MARKET?
THAT'S ABOUT RIGHT.
SO, IF THE TONIO FAMILY DIDN'T *EXIST,* THAT'S AN EIGHT PERCENT BUMP IN OUR MARKET DEMAND.
YOU'RE SAYING YOU WANT A *WAR?*
NO, HARRISON. I DO NOT.
I WANT *BUSINESS.* IT'S A BETTER WORD.
FWUMP
HEY! YOU CAN'T COME IN--
WAIT!
LET HER IN.

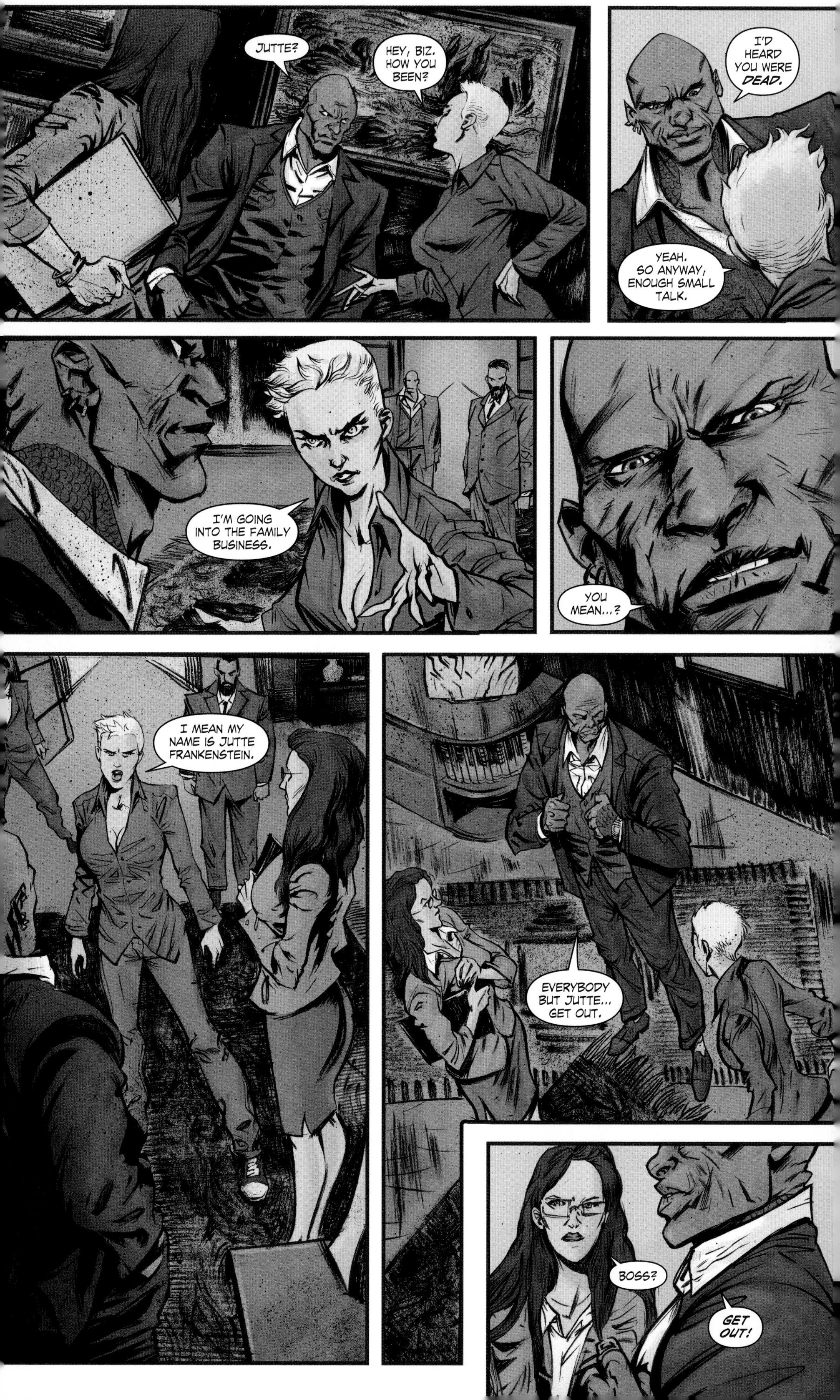
JUTTE?
HEY, BIZ. HOW YOU BEEN?
I'D HEARD YOU WERE *DEAD.*
YEAH. SO ANYWAY, ENOUGH SMALL TALK.
I'M GOING INTO THE FAMILY BUSINESS.
YOU MEAN...?
I MEAN MY NAME IS JUTTE FRANKENSTEIN.
EVERYBODY BUT JUTTE... GET OUT.
BOSS?
GET OUT!

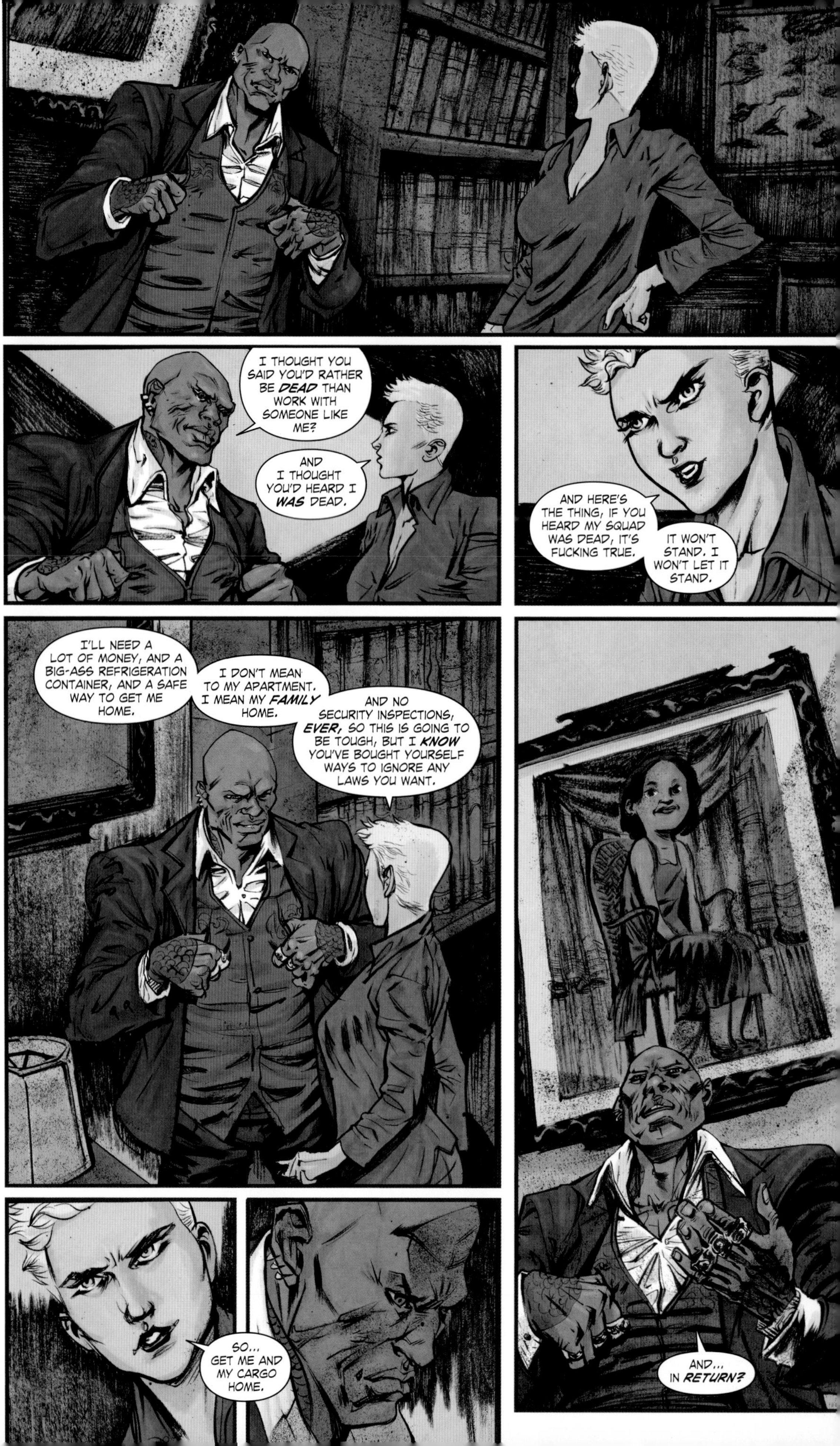
I THOUGHT YOU SAID YOU'D RATHER BE DEAD THAN WORK WITH SOMEONE LIKE ME?
AND I THOUGHT YOU'D HEARD I WAS DEAD.
AND HERE'S THE THING, IF YOU HEARD MY SQUAD WAS DEAD, IT'S FUCKING TRUE.
IT WON'T STAND. I WON'T LET IT STAND.
I'LL NEED A LOT OF MONEY, AND A BIG-ASS REFRIGERATION CONTAINER, AND A SAFE WAY TO GET ME HOME.
I DON'T MEAN TO MY APARTMENT. I MEAN MY FAMILY HOME.
AND NO SECURITY INSPECTIONS, EVER, SO THIS IS GOING TO BE TOUGH, BUT I KNOW YOU'VE BOUGHT YOURSELF WAYS TO IGNORE ANY LAWS YOU WANT.
SO... GET ME AND MY CARGO HOME.
AND... IN RETURN?

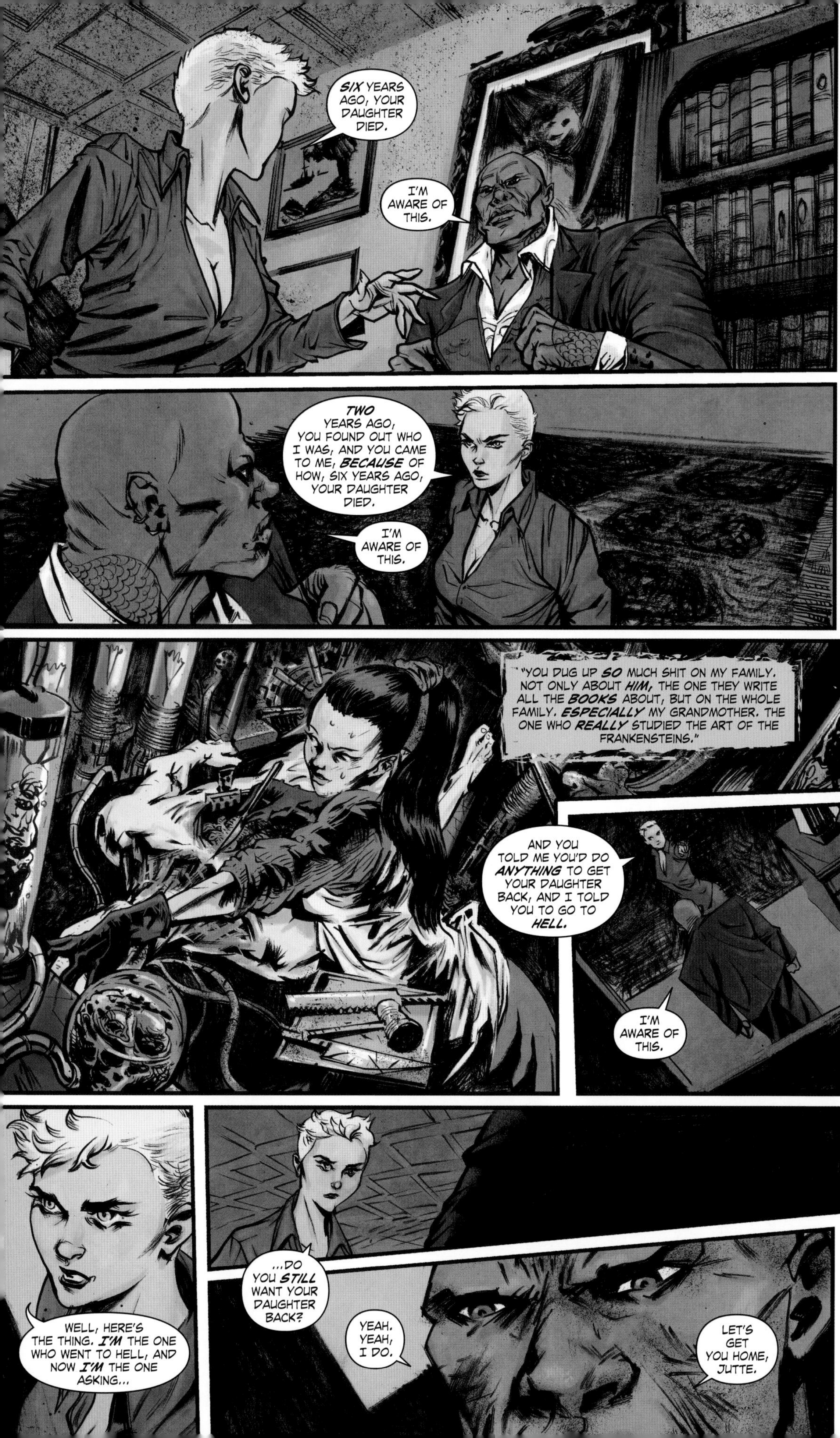
SIX YEARS AGO, YOUR DAUGHTER DIED.
I'M AWARE OF THIS.
TWO YEARS AGO, YOU FOUND OUT WHO I WAS, AND YOU CAME TO ME, BECAUSE OF HOW, SIX YEARS AGO, YOUR DAUGHTER DIED.
I'M AWARE OF THIS.
"YOU DUG UP SO MUCH SHIT ON MY FAMILY. NOT ONLY ABOUT HIM, THE ONE THEY WRITE ALL THE BOOKS ABOUT, BUT ON THE WHOLE FAMILY. ESPECIALLY MY GRANDMOTHER. THE ONE WHO REALLY STUDIED THE ART OF THE FRANKENSTEINS."
AND YOU TOLD ME YOU'D DO ANYTHING TO GET YOUR DAUGHTER BACK, AND I TOLD YOU TO GO TO HELL.
I'M AWARE OF THIS.
WELL, HERE'S THE THING. I'M THE ONE WHO WENT TO HELL, AND NOW I'M THE ONE ASKING...
...DO YOU STILL WANT YOUR DAUGHTER BACK?
YEAH. YEAH, I DO.
LET'S GET YOU HOME, JUTTE.

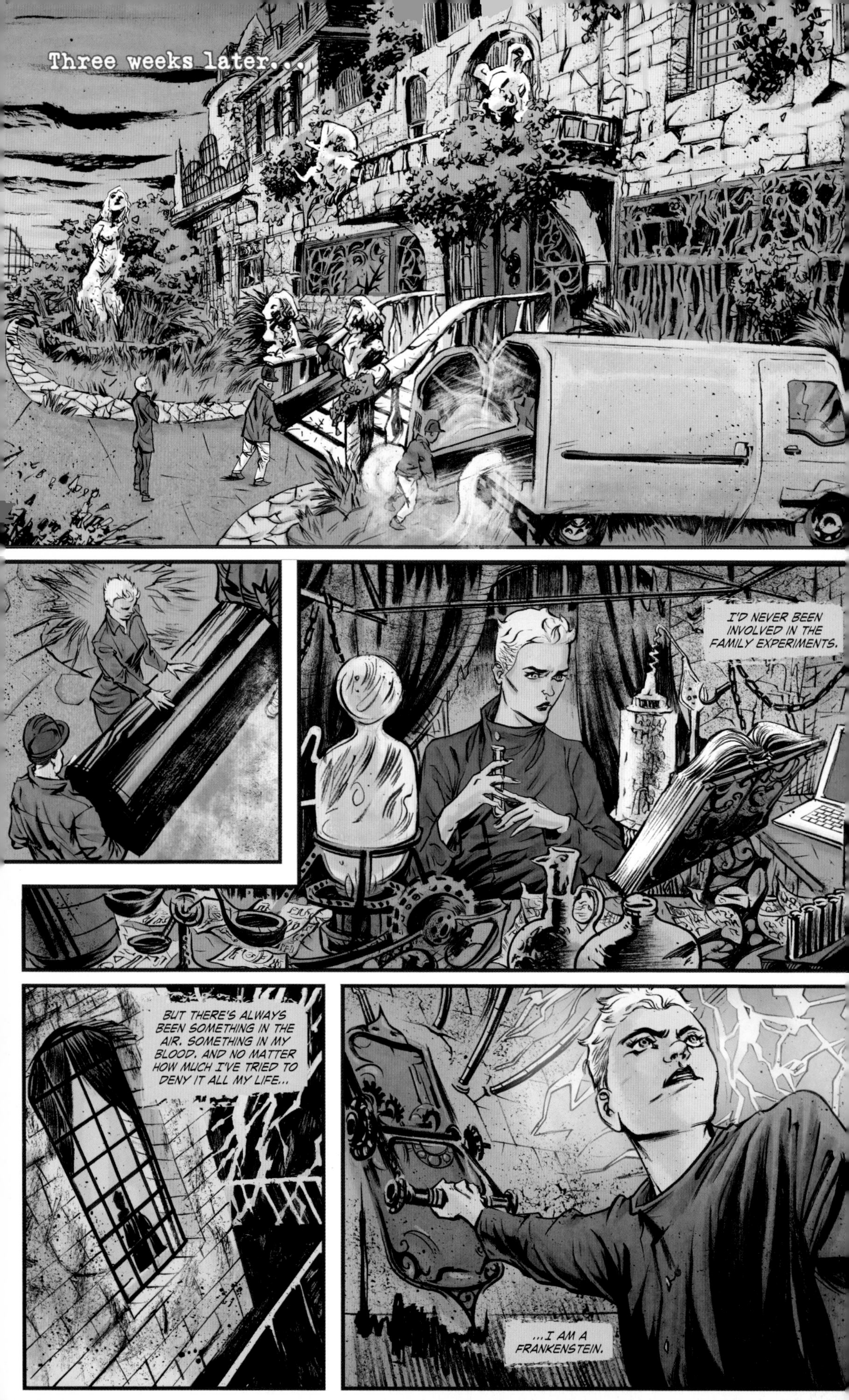
Three weeks later...
I'D NEVER BEEN INVOLVED IN THE FAMILY EXPERIMENTS.
BUT THERE'S ALWAYS BEEN SOMETHING IN THE AIR. SOMETHING IN MY BLOOD. AND NO MATTER HOW MUCH I'VE TRIED TO DENY IT ALL MY LIFE...
...I AM A FRANKENSTEIN.

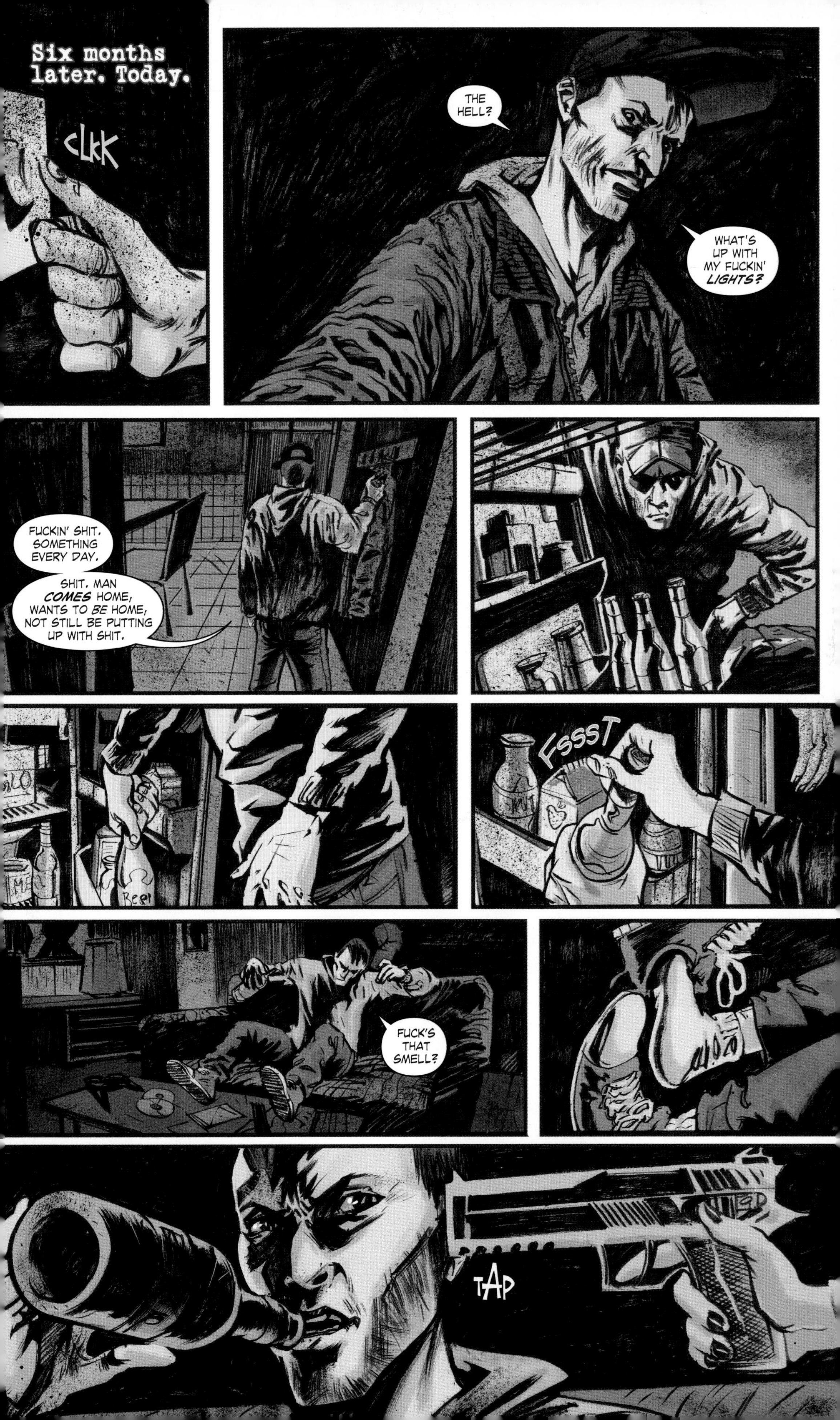
Six months later. Today.
CLKK
THE HELL?
WHAT'S UP WITH MY FUCKIN' LIGHTS?
FUCKIN' SHIT. SOMETHING EVERY DAY.
SHIT. MAN COMES HOME, WANTS TO BE HOME, NOT STILL BE PUTTING UP WITH SHIT.
FSSST
FUCK'S THAT SMELL?
TAP

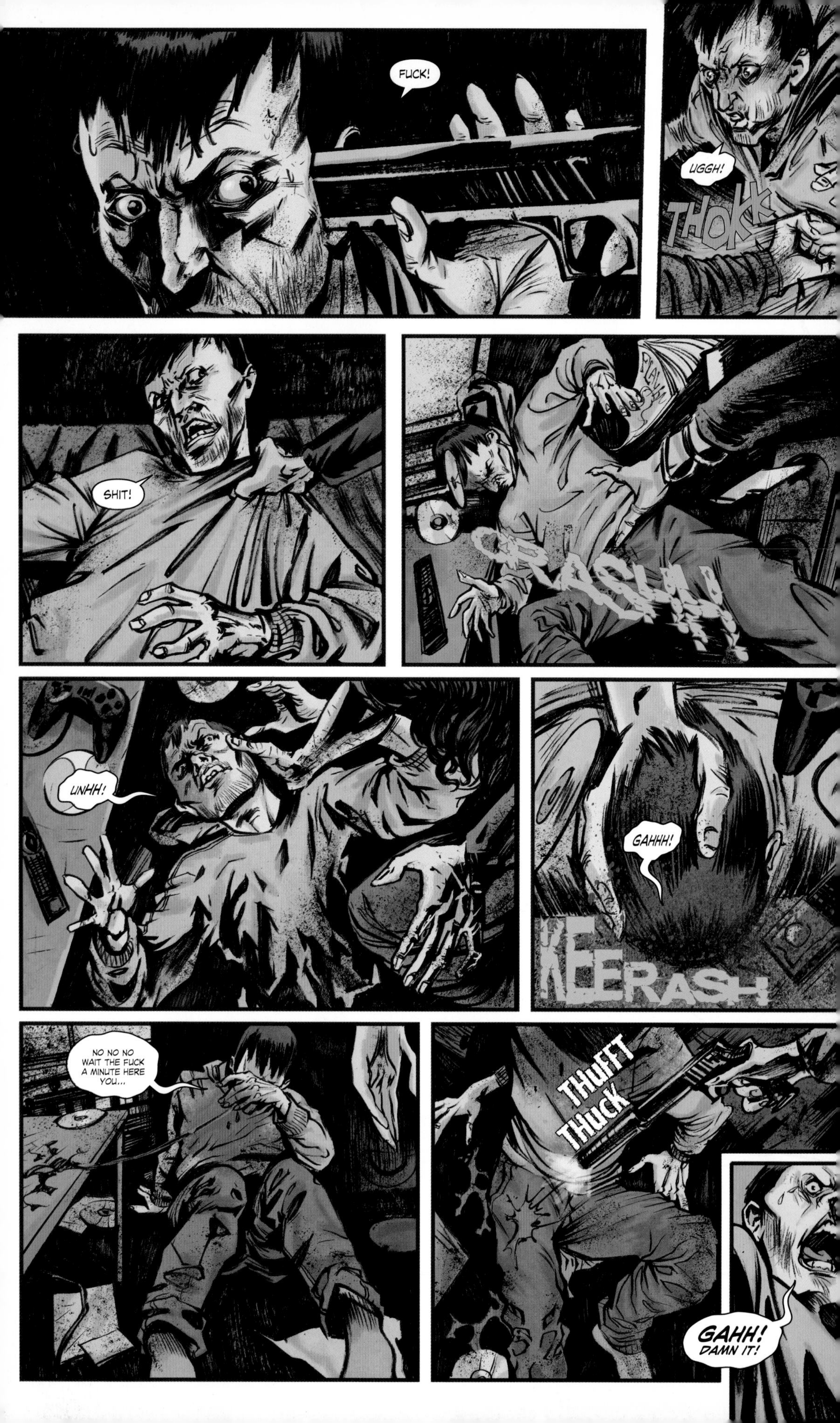
FUCK!
UGGH!
THOKK
SHIT!
CRASH!
UNHH!
GAHHH!
KEERASH
NO NO NO WAIT THE FUCK A MINUTE HERE YOU...
THUFFT
THUCK
GAHH! DAMN IT!

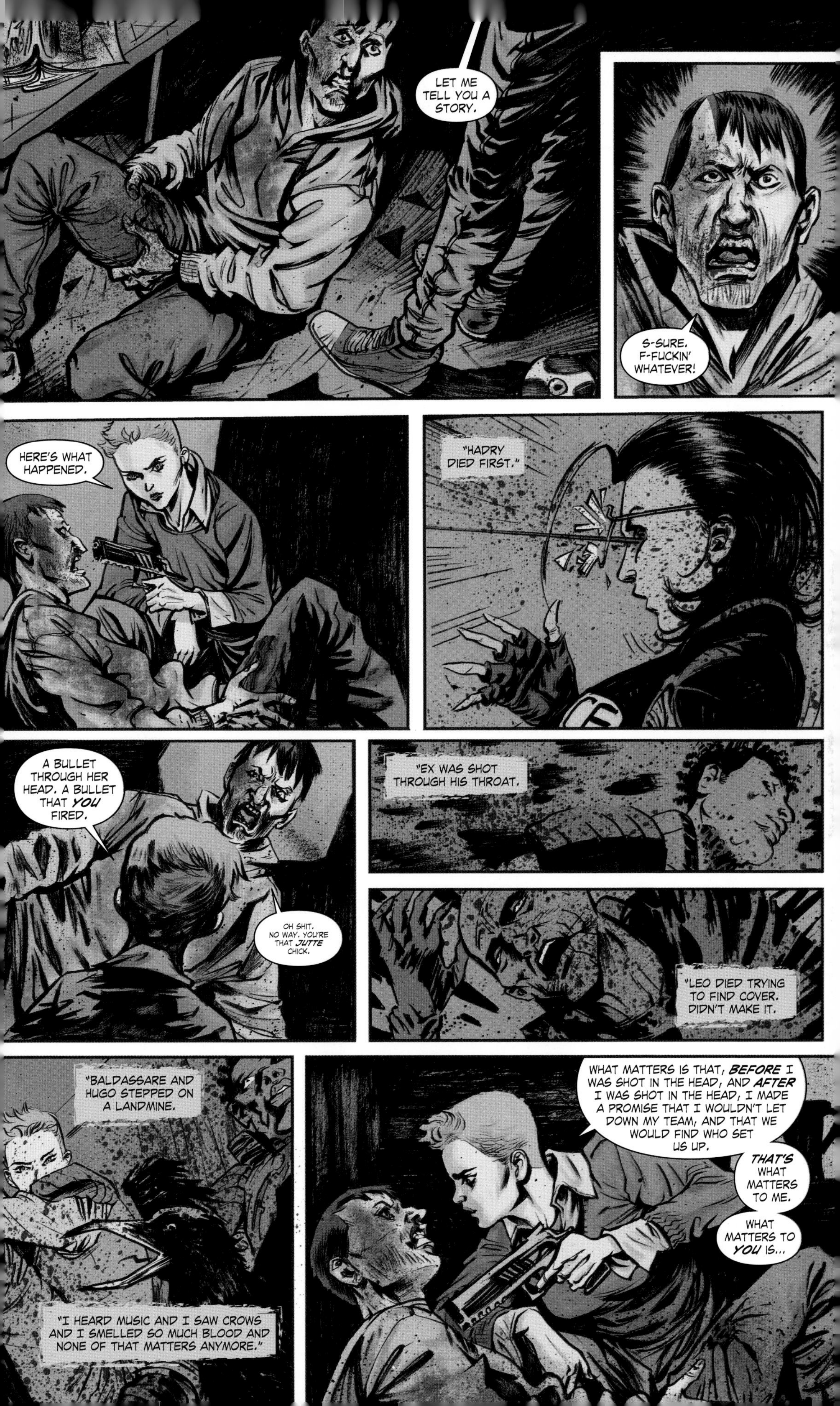
LET ME TELL YOU A STORY.
S-SURE. F-FUCKIN' WHATEVER!
HERE'S WHAT HAPPENED.
"HADRY DIED FIRST."
A BULLET THROUGH HER HEAD. A BULLET THAT YOU FIRED.
OH SHIT. NO WAY. YOU'RE THAT JUTTE CHICK.
"EX WAS SHOT THROUGH HIS THROAT.
"LEO DIED TRYING TO FIND COVER. DIDN'T MAKE IT.
"BALDASSARE AND HUGO STEPPED ON A LANDMINE.
"I HEARD MUSIC AND I SAW CROWS AND I SMELLED SO MUCH BLOOD AND NONE OF THAT MATTERS ANYMORE."
WHAT MATTERS IS THAT, BEFORE I WAS SHOT IN THE HEAD, AND AFTER I WAS SHOT IN THE HEAD, I MADE A PROMISE THAT I WOULDN'T LET DOWN MY TEAM, AND THAT WE WOULD FIND WHO SET US UP.
THAT'S WHAT MATTERS TO ME.
WHAT MATTERS TO YOU IS...

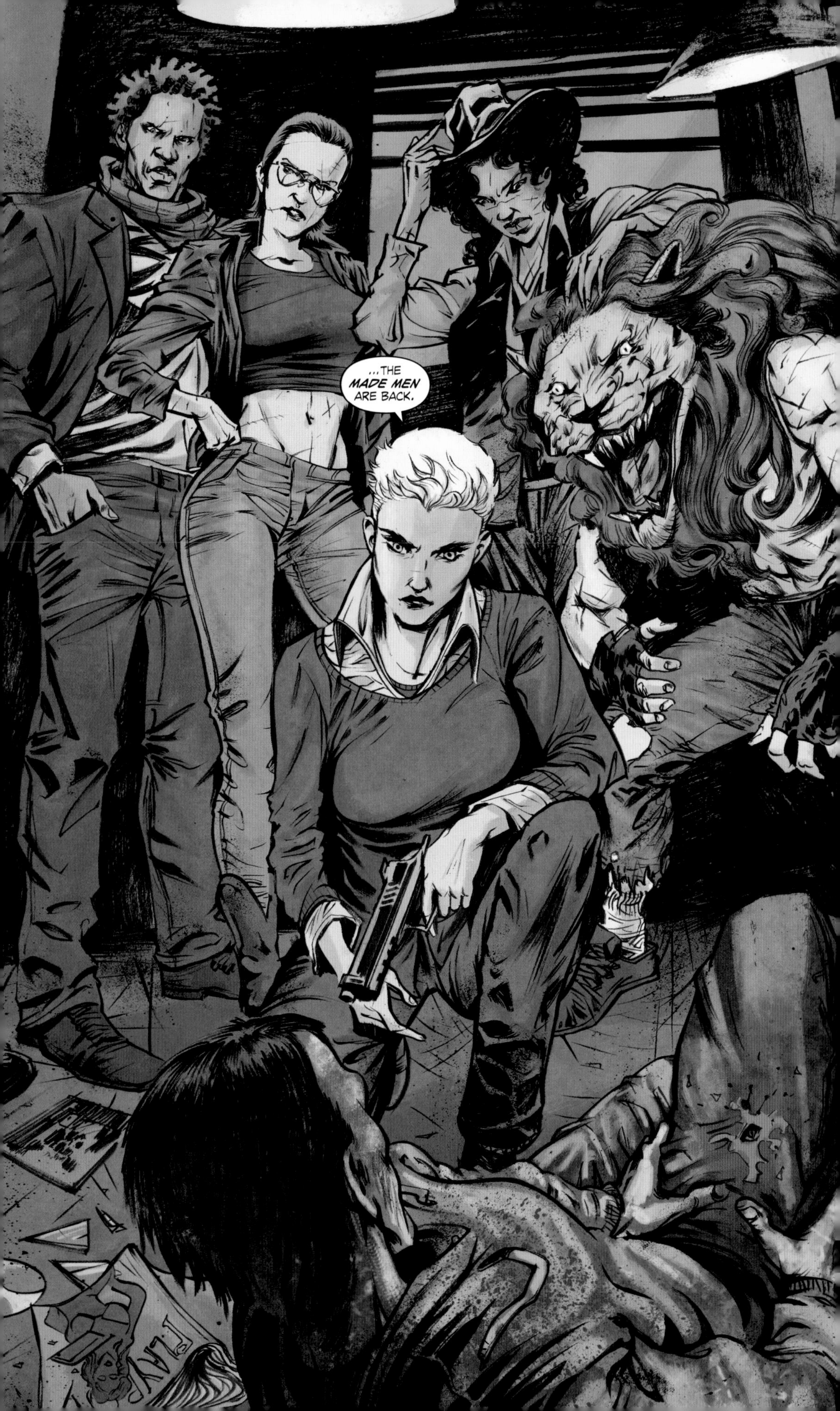
...THE MADE MEN ARE BACK.

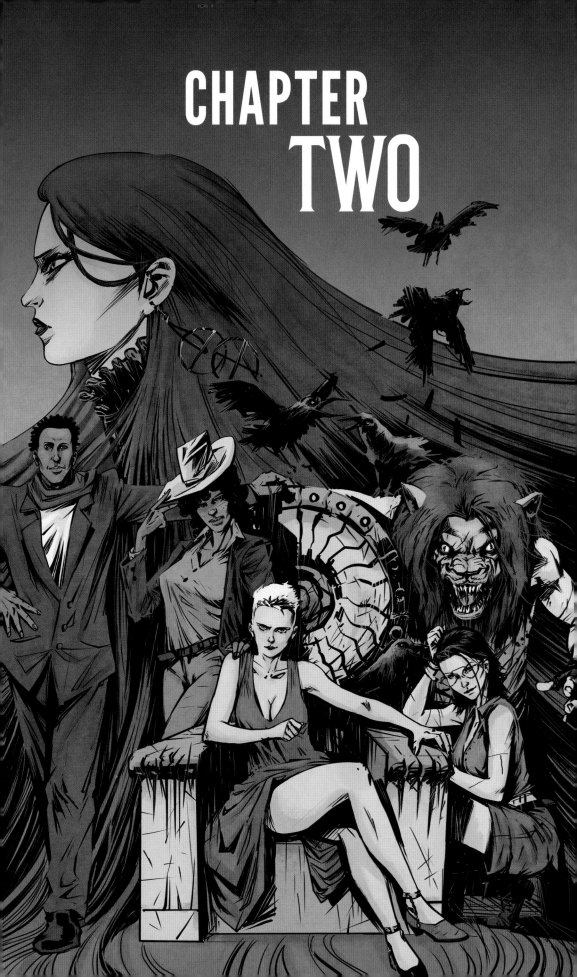

CHAPTER
TWO

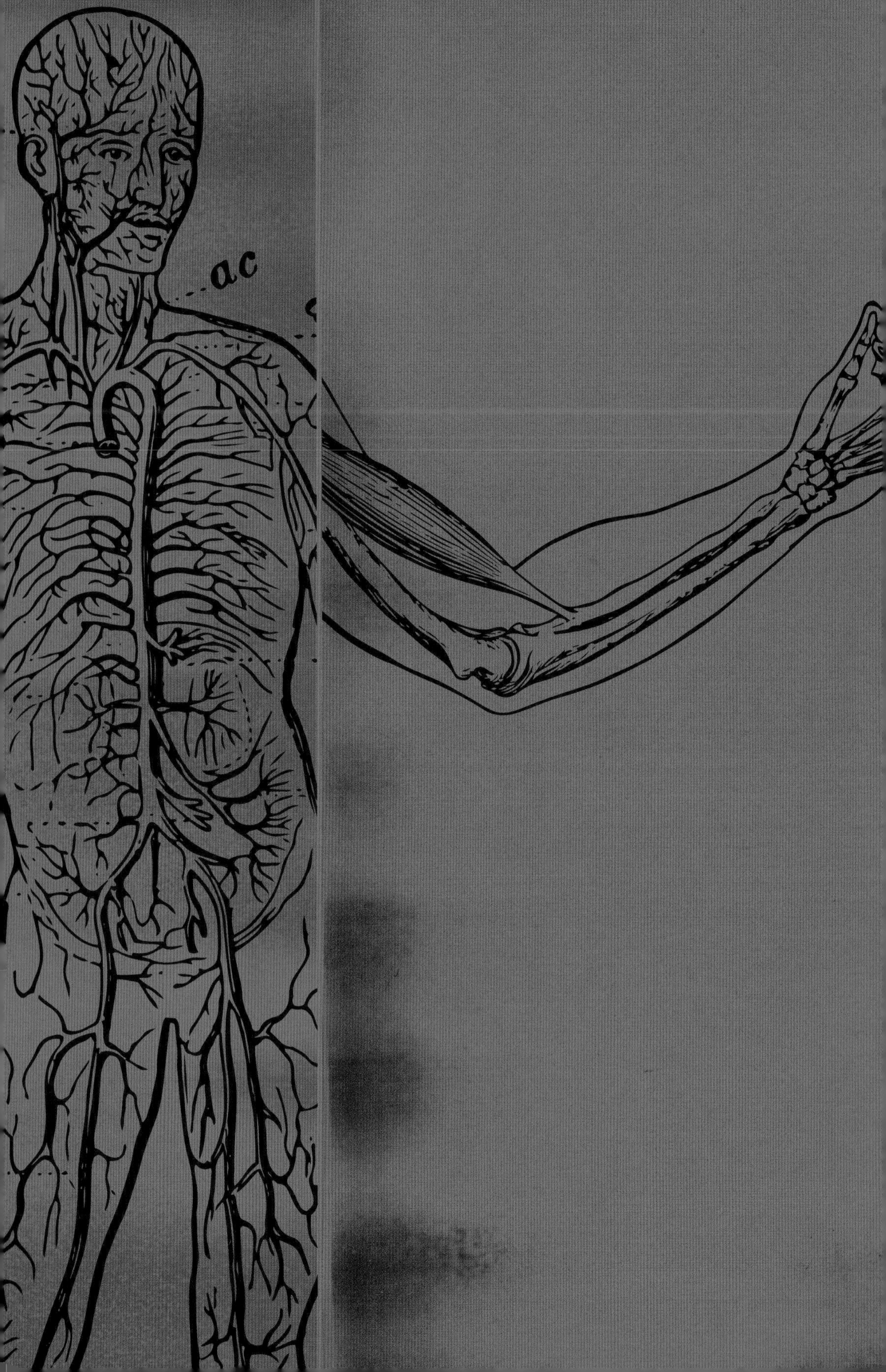
ac

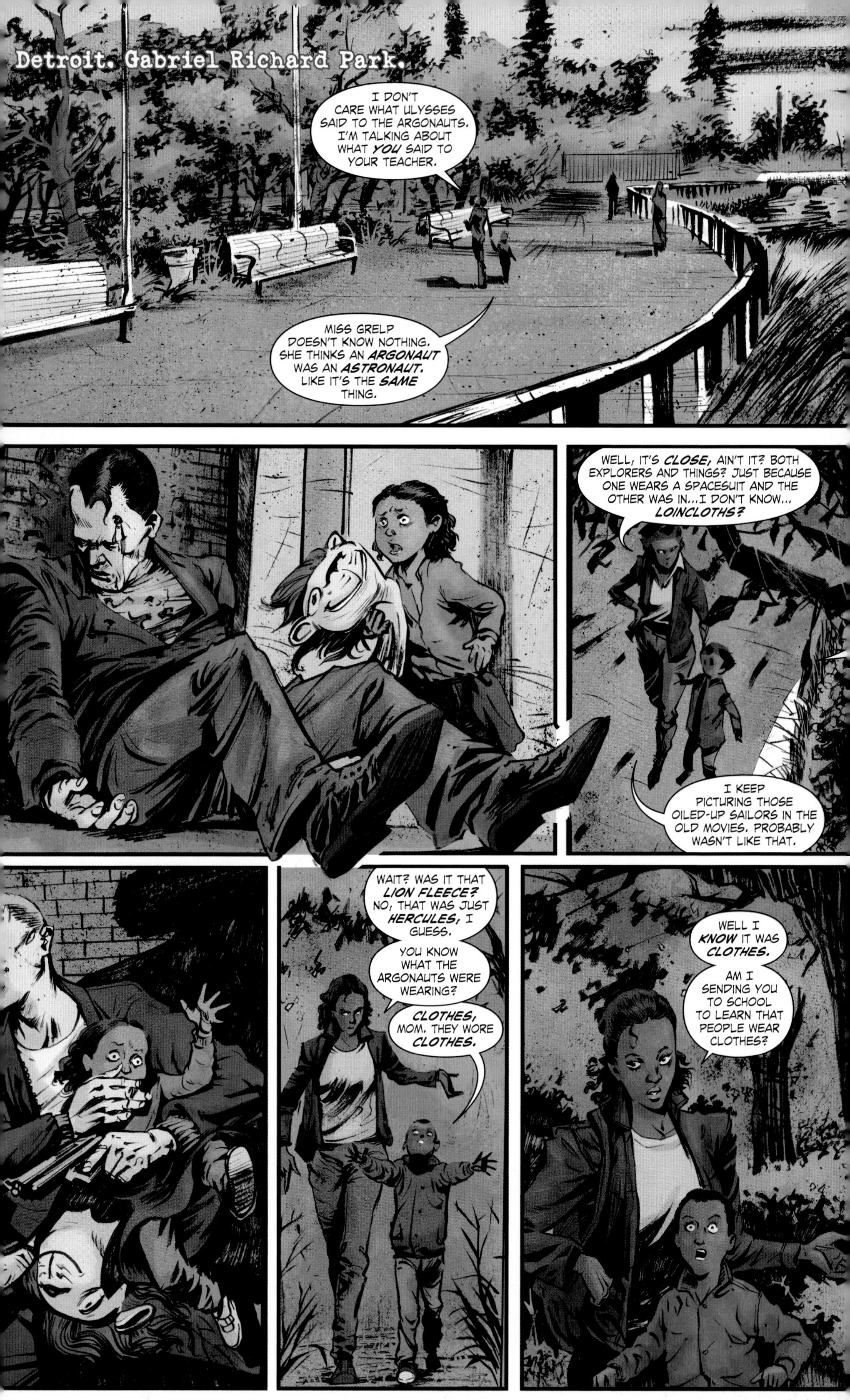

Detroit. Gabriel Richard Park.
I DON'T CARE WHAT ULYSSES SAID TO THE ARGONAUTS. I'M TALKING ABOUT WHAT *YOU* SAID TO YOUR TEACHER.
MISS GRELP DOESN'T KNOW NOTHING. SHE THINKS AN *ARGONAUT* WAS AN *ASTRONAUT.* LIKE IT'S THE *SAME* THING.
WELL, IT'S *CLOSE,* AIN'T IT? BOTH EXPLORERS AND THINGS? JUST BECAUSE ONE WEARS A SPACESUIT AND THE OTHER WAS IN...I DON'T KNOW... *LOINCLOTHS?*
I KEEP PICTURING THOSE OILED-UP SAILORS IN THE OLD MOVIES. PROBABLY WASN'T LIKE THAT.
WAIT? WAS IT THAT *LION FLEECE?* NO, THAT WAS JUST *HERCULES,* I GUESS.
YOU KNOW WHAT THE ARGONAUTS WERE WEARING?
CLOTHES, MOM. THEY WORE *CLOTHES.*
WELL I *KNOW* IT WAS *CLOTHES.*
AM I SENDING YOU TO SCHOOL TO LEARN THAT PEOPLE WEAR CLOTHES?

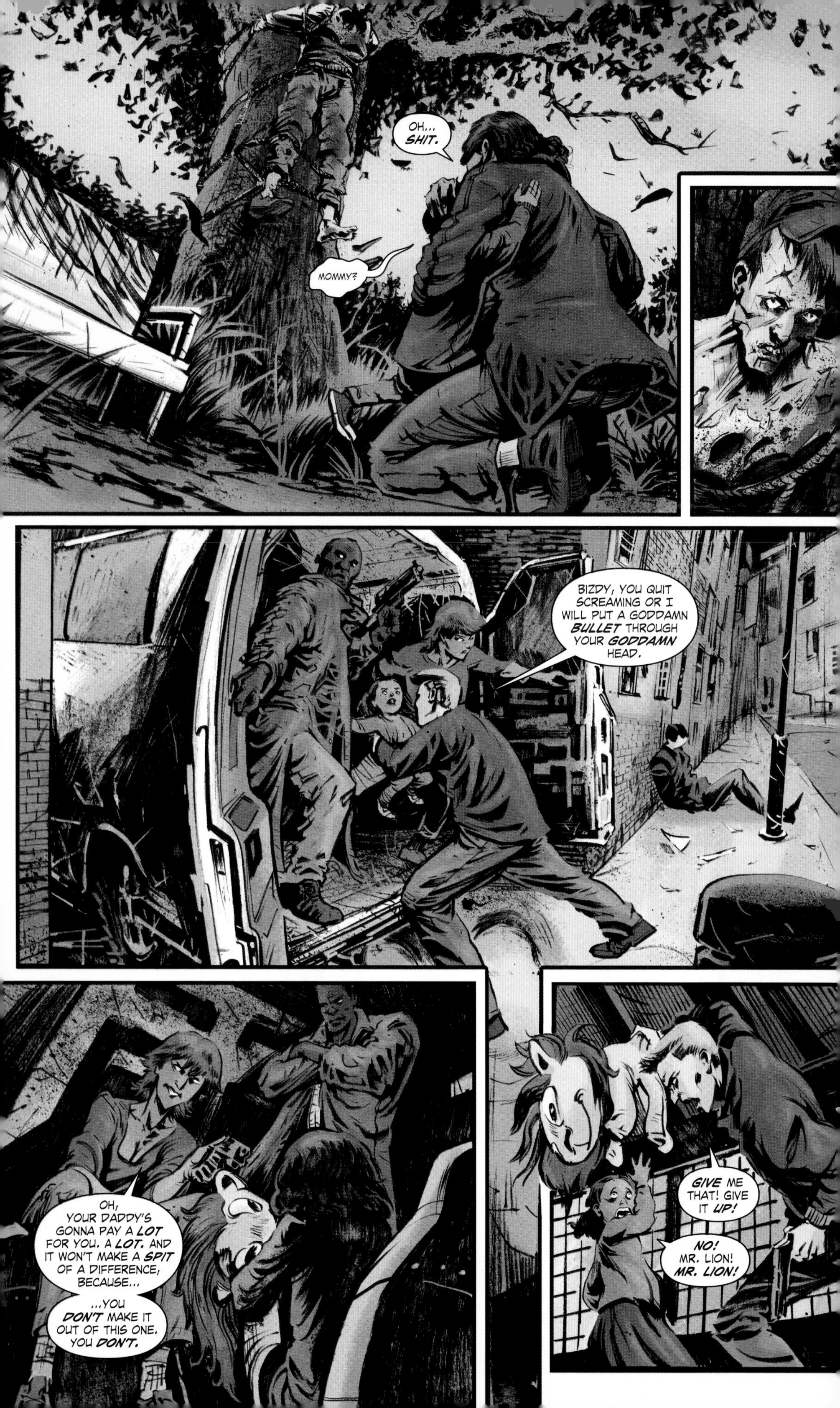
OH... SHIT.
MOMMY?
BIZDY, YOU QUIT SCREAMING OR I WILL PUT A GODDAMN BULLET THROUGH YOUR GODDAMN HEAD.
OH, YOUR DADDY'S GONNA PAY A LOT FOR YOU. A LOT. AND IT WON'T MAKE A SPIT OF A DIFFERENCE, BECAUSE...
...YOU DON'T MAKE IT OUT OF THIS ONE. YOU DON'T.
GIVE ME THAT! GIVE IT UP!
NO! MR. LION! MR. LION!

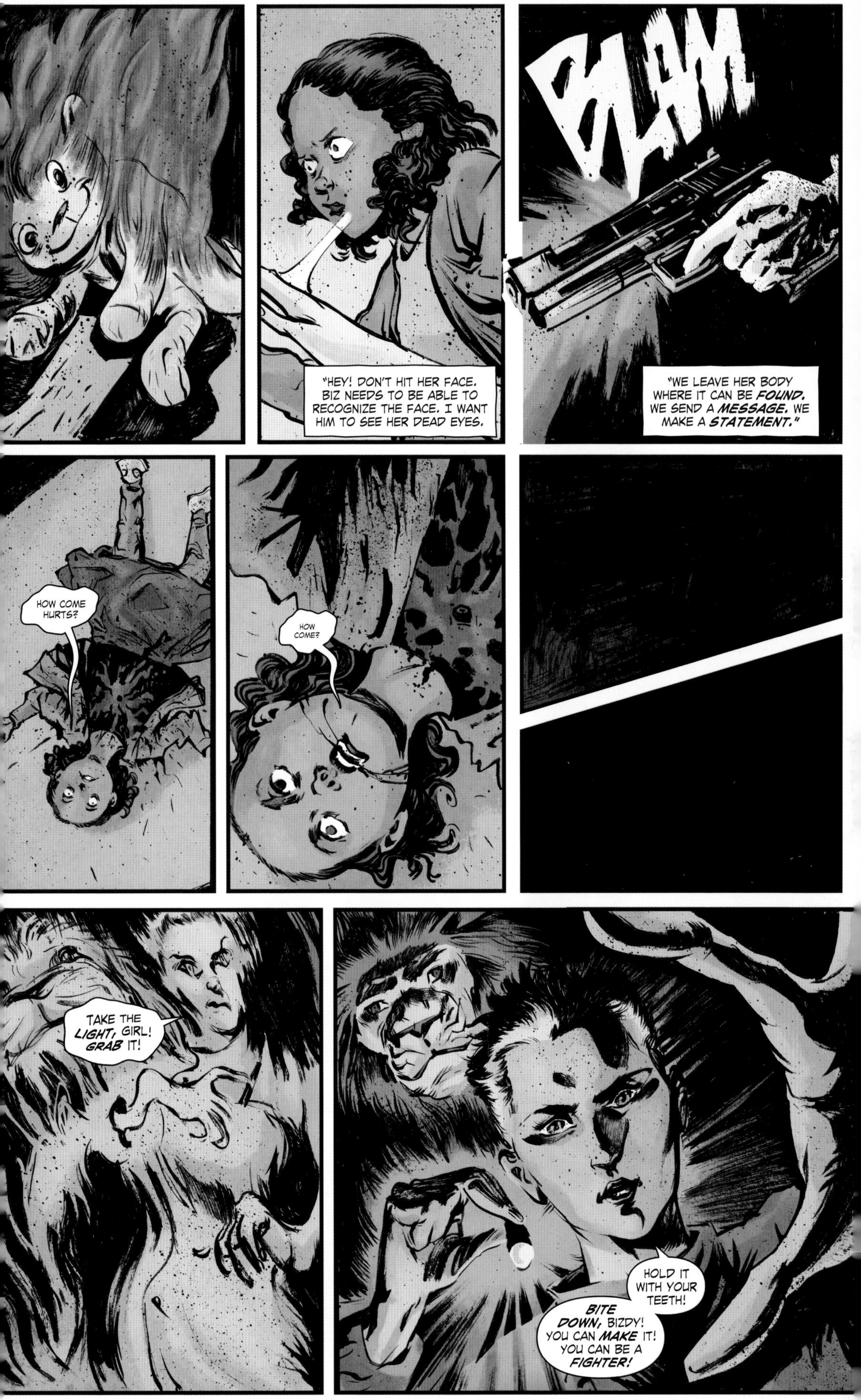
"HEY! DON'T HIT HER FACE. BIZ NEEDS TO BE ABLE TO RECOGNIZE THE FACE. I WANT HIM TO SEE HER DEAD EYES.
BLAM
"WE LEAVE HER BODY WHERE IT CAN BE FOUND. WE SEND A MESSAGE. WE MAKE A STATEMENT."
HOW COME HURTS?
HOW COME?
TAKE THE LIGHT, GIRL! GRAB IT!
HOLD IT WITH YOUR TEETH!
BITE DOWN, BIZDY! YOU CAN MAKE IT! YOU CAN BE A FIGHTER!

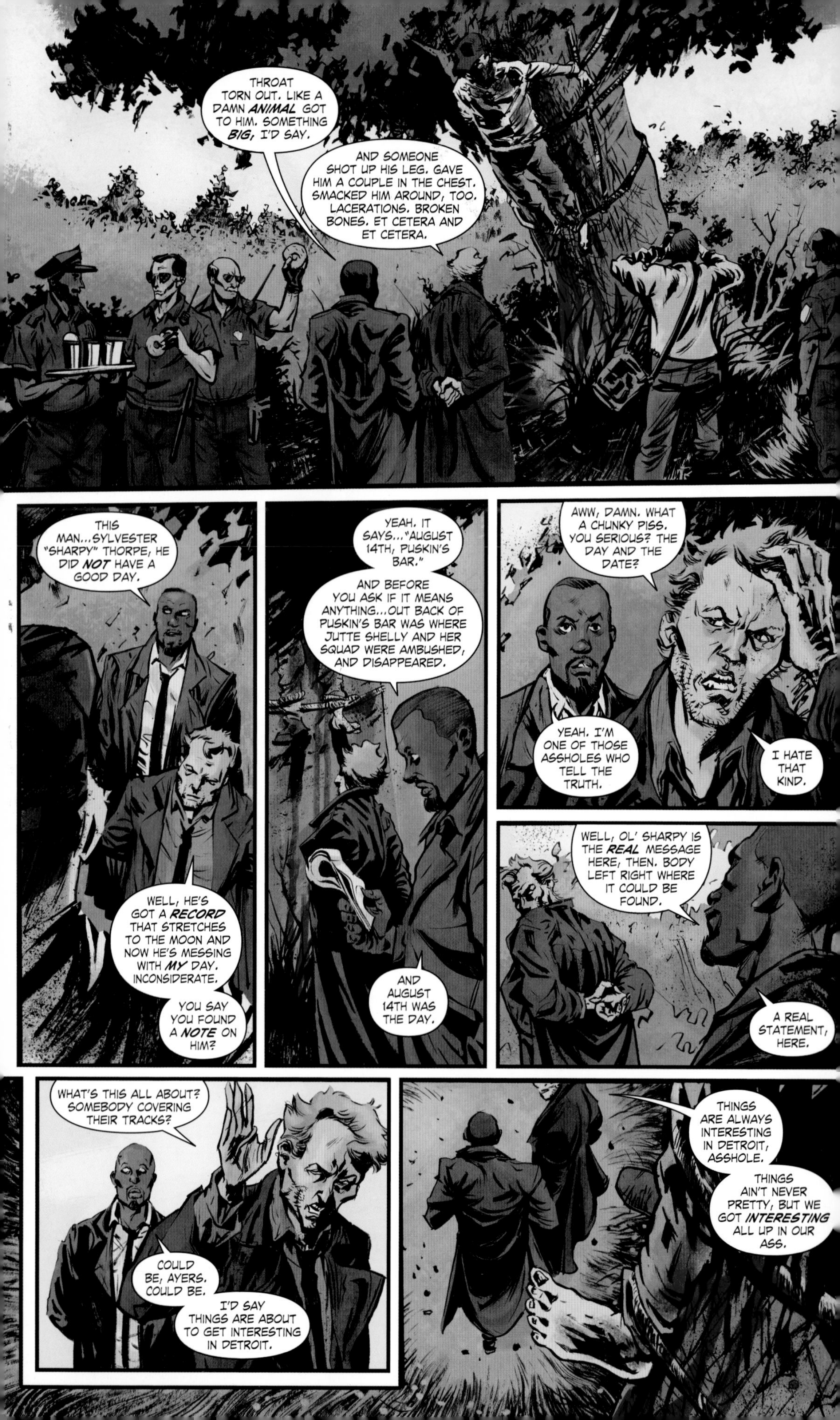
THROAT TORN OUT. LIKE A DAMN ANIMAL GOT TO HIM. SOMETHING BIG, I'D SAY.
AND SOMEONE SHOT UP HIS LEG. GAVE HIM A COUPLE IN THE CHEST. SMACKED HIM AROUND, TOO. LACERATIONS. BROKEN BONES. ET CETERA AND ET CETERA.
THIS MAN...SYLVESTER "SHARPY" THORPE, HE DID NOT HAVE A GOOD DAY.
WELL, HE'S GOT A RECORD THAT STRETCHES TO THE MOON AND NOW HE'S MESSING WITH MY DAY. INCONSIDERATE.
YOU SAY YOU FOUND A NOTE ON HIM?
YEAH. IT SAYS..."AUGUST 14TH, PUSKIN'S BAR."
AND BEFORE YOU ASK IF IT MEANS ANYTHING...OUT BACK OF PUSKIN'S BAR WAS WHERE JUTTE SHELLY AND HER SQUAD WERE AMBUSHED, AND DISAPPEARED.
AND AUGUST 14TH WAS THE DAY.
AWW, DAMN. WHAT A CHUNKY PISS. YOU SERIOUS? THE DAY AND THE DATE?
YEAH. I'M ONE OF THOSE ASSHOLES WHO TELL THE TRUTH.
I HATE THAT KIND.
WELL, OL' SHARPY IS THE REAL MESSAGE HERE, THEN. BODY LEFT RIGHT WHERE IT COULD BE FOUND.
A REAL STATEMENT, HERE.
WHAT'S THIS ALL ABOUT? SOMEBODY COVERING THEIR TRACKS?
COULD BE, AYERS. COULD BE.
I'D SAY THINGS ARE ABOUT TO GET INTERESTING IN DETROIT.
THINGS ARE ALWAYS INTERESTING IN DETROIT, ASSHOLE.
THINGS AIN'T NEVER PRETTY, BUT WE GOT INTERESTING ALL UP IN OUR ASS.

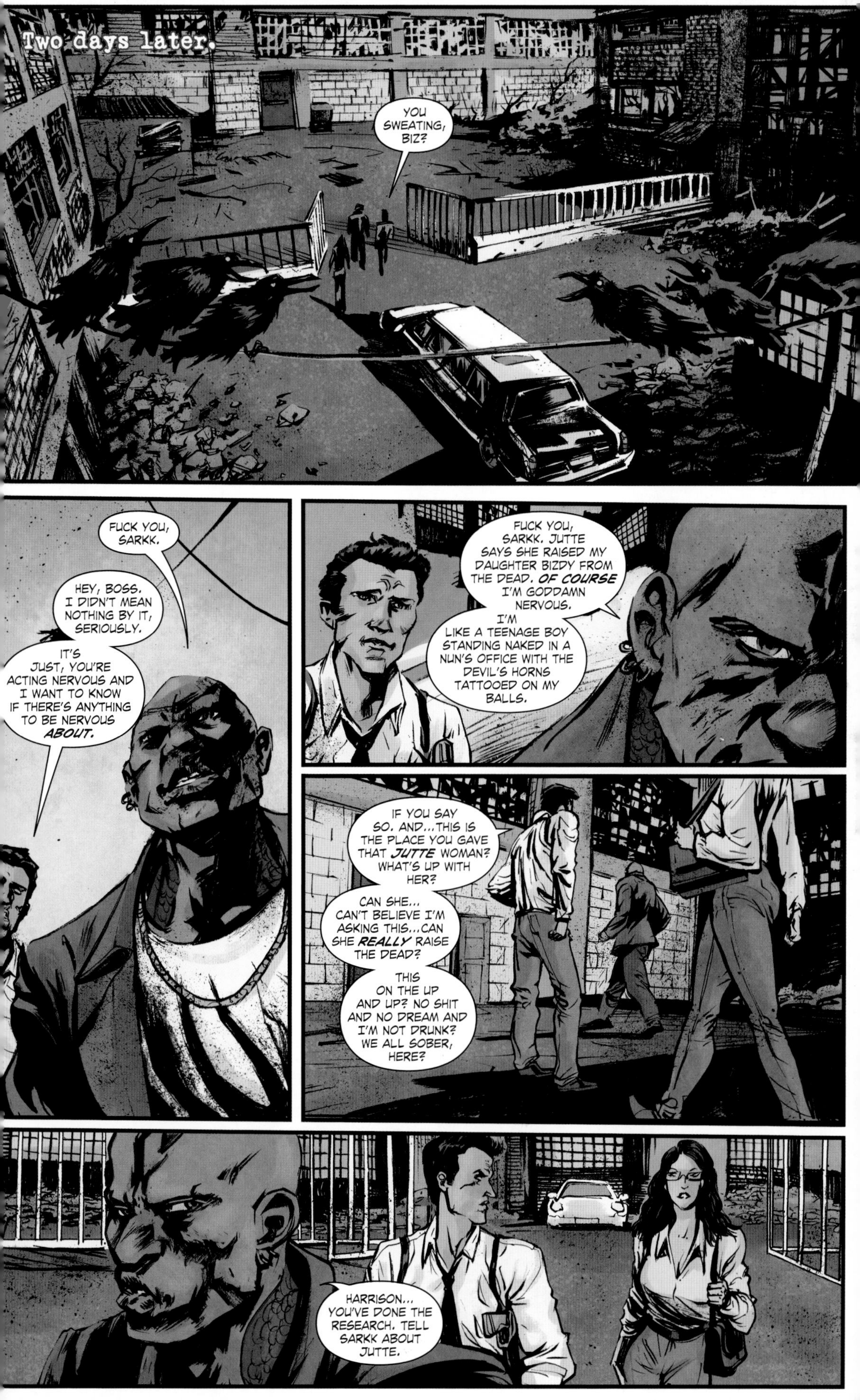
Two days later.
YOU SWEATING, BIZ?
FUCK YOU, SARKK.
HEY, BOSS. I DIDN'T MEAN NOTHING BY IT, SERIOUSLY.
IT'S JUST, YOU'RE ACTING NERVOUS AND I WANT TO KNOW IF THERE'S ANYTHING TO BE NERVOUS *ABOUT.*
FUCK YOU, SARKK. JUTTE SAYS SHE RAISED MY DAUGHTER BIZDY FROM THE DEAD. *OF COURSE* I'M GODDAMN NERVOUS.
I'M LIKE A TEENAGE BOY STANDING NAKED IN A NUN'S OFFICE WITH THE DEVIL'S HORNS TATTOOED ON MY BALLS.
IF YOU SAY SO. AND...THIS IS THE PLACE YOU GAVE THAT *JUTTE* WOMAN? WHAT'S UP WITH HER?
CAN SHE... CAN'T BELIEVE I'M ASKING THIS...CAN SHE *REALLY* RAISE THE DEAD?
THIS ON THE UP AND UP? NO SHIT AND NO DREAM AND I'M NOT DRUNK? WE ALL SOBER, HERE?
HARRISON... YOU'VE DONE THE RESEARCH. TELL SARKK ABOUT JUTTE.

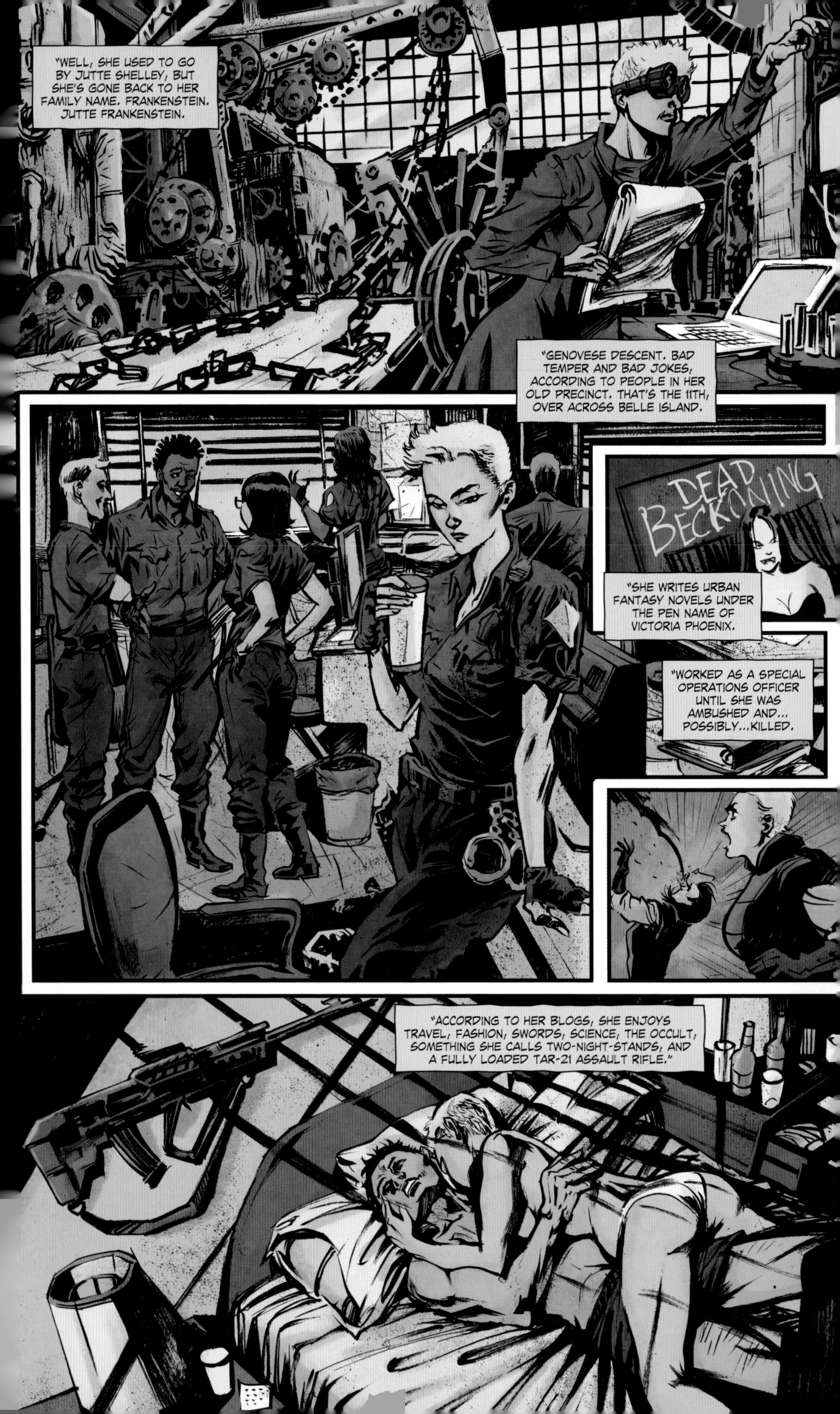
"WELL, SHE USED TO GO BY JUTTE SHELLEY, BUT SHE'S GONE BACK TO HER FAMILY NAME. FRANKENSTEIN. JUTTE FRANKENSTEIN.
"GENOVESE DESCENT. BAD TEMPER AND BAD JOKES, ACCORDING TO PEOPLE IN HER OLD PRECINCT. THAT'S THE 11TH, OVER ACROSS BELLE ISLAND.
DEAD BECKONING
"SHE WRITES URBAN FANTASY NOVELS UNDER THE PEN NAME OF VICTORIA PHOENIX.
"WORKED AS A SPECIAL OPERATIONS OFFICER UNTIL SHE WAS AMBUSHED AND... POSSIBLY...KILLED.
"ACCORDING TO HER BLOGS, SHE ENJOYS TRAVEL, FASHION, SWORDS, SCIENCE, THE OCCULT, SOMETHING SHE CALLS TWO-NIGHT-STANDS, AND A FULLY LOADED TAR-21 ASSAULT RIFLE."

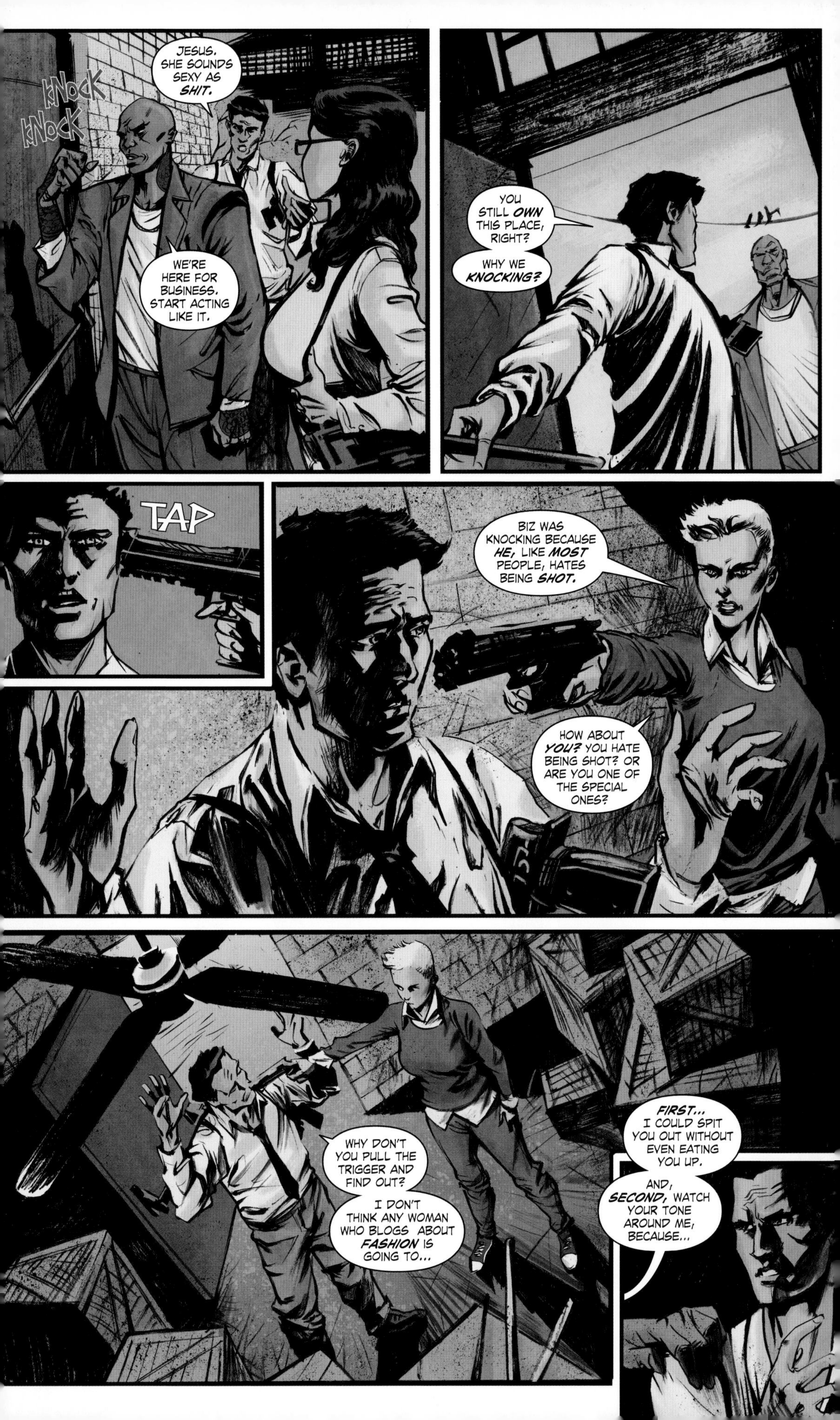
KNOCK KNOCK
JESUS. SHE SOUNDS SEXY AS SHIT.
WE'RE HERE FOR BUSINESS. START ACTING LIKE IT.
YOU STILL OWN THIS PLACE, RIGHT?
WHY WE KNOCKING?
TAP
BIZ WAS KNOCKING BECAUSE HE, LIKE MOST PEOPLE, HATES BEING SHOT.
HOW ABOUT YOU? YOU HATE BEING SHOT? OR ARE YOU ONE OF THE SPECIAL ONES?
WHY DON'T YOU PULL THE TRIGGER AND FIND OUT?
I DON'T THINK ANY WOMAN WHO BLOGS ABOUT FASHION IS GOING TO...
FIRST... I COULD SPIT YOU OUT WITHOUT EVEN EATING YOU UP.
AND, SECOND, WATCH YOUR TONE AROUND ME, BECAUSE...

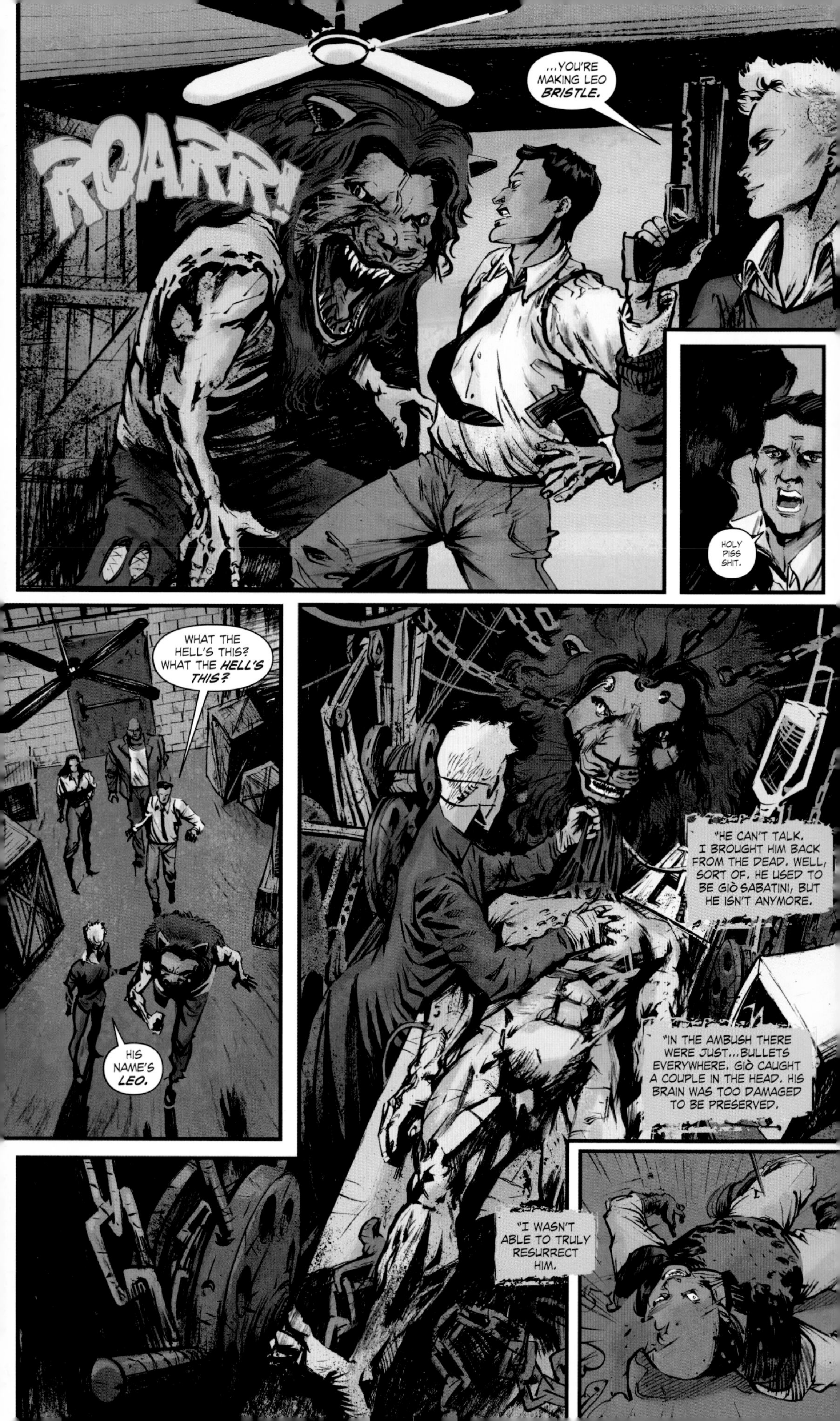
ROARR!
...YOU'RE MAKING LEO BRISTLE.
HOLY PISS SHIT.
WHAT THE HELL'S THIS? WHAT THE HELL'S THIS?
HIS NAME'S LEO.
"HE CAN'T TALK. I BROUGHT HIM BACK FROM THE DEAD. WELL, SORT OF. HE USED TO BE GIÒ SABATINI, BUT HE ISN'T ANYMORE.
"IN THE AMBUSH THERE WERE JUST...BULLETS EVERYWHERE. GIÒ CAUGHT A COUPLE IN THE HEAD. HIS BRAIN WAS TOO DAMAGED TO BE PRESERVED.
"I WASN'T ABLE TO TRULY RESURRECT HIM.

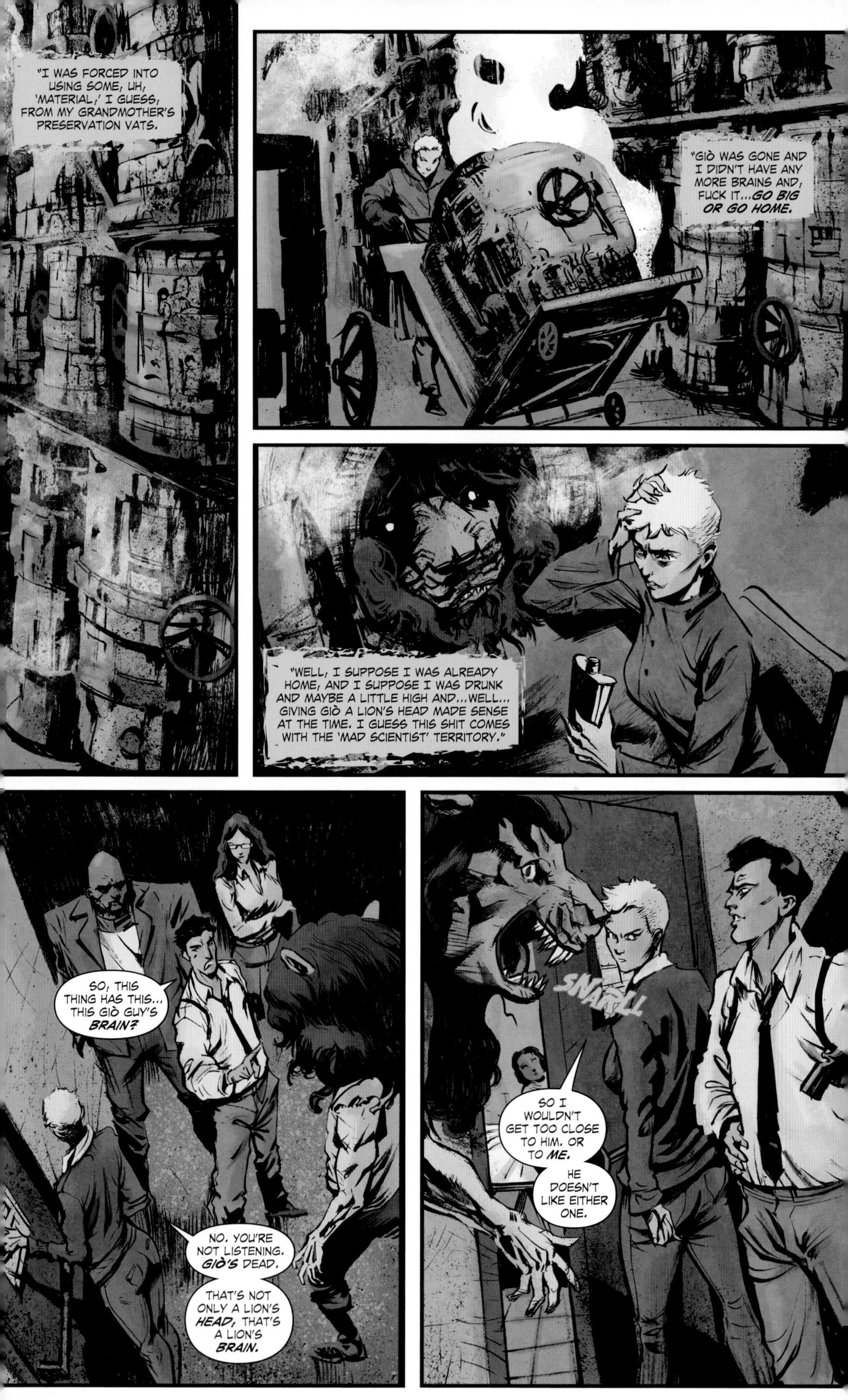
"I WAS FORCED INTO USING SOME, UH, 'MATERIAL,' I GUESS, FROM MY GRANDMOTHER'S PRESERVATION VATS.
"GIÒ WAS GONE AND I DIDN'T HAVE ANY MORE BRAINS AND, FUCK IT...GO BIG OR GO HOME.
"WELL, I SUPPOSE I WAS ALREADY HOME, AND I SUPPOSE I WAS DRUNK AND MAYBE A LITTLE HIGH AND...WELL... GIVING GIÒ A LION'S HEAD MADE SENSE AT THE TIME. I GUESS THIS SHIT COMES WITH THE 'MAD SCIENTIST' TERRITORY."
SO, THIS THING HAS THIS... THIS GIÒ GUY'S BRAIN?
NO. YOU'RE NOT LISTENING. GIÒ'S DEAD.
THAT'S NOT ONLY A LION'S HEAD, THAT'S A LION'S BRAIN.
SNARLL
SO I WOULDN'T GET TOO CLOSE TO HIM. OR TO ME.
HE DOESN'T LIKE EITHER ONE.

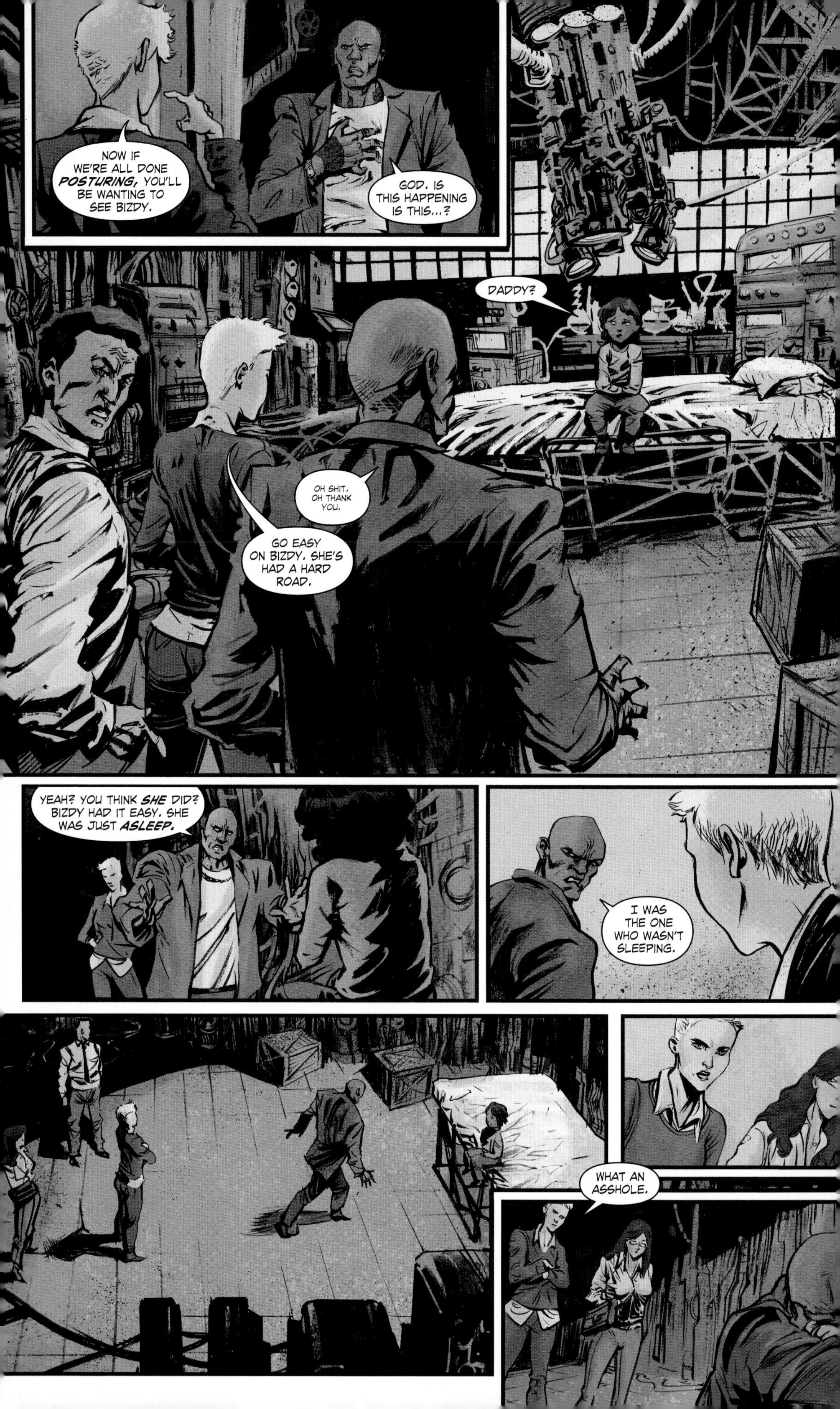

NOW IF WE'RE ALL DONE POSTURING, YOU'LL BE WANTING TO SEE BIZDY.
GOD. IS THIS HAPPENING IS THIS...?
DADDY?
OH SHIT. OH THANK YOU.
GO EASY ON BIZDY. SHE'S HAD A HARD ROAD.
YEAH? YOU THINK SHE DID? BIZDY HAD IT EASY. SHE WAS JUST ASLEEP.
I WAS THE ONE WHO WASN'T SLEEPING.
WHAT AN ASSHOLE.

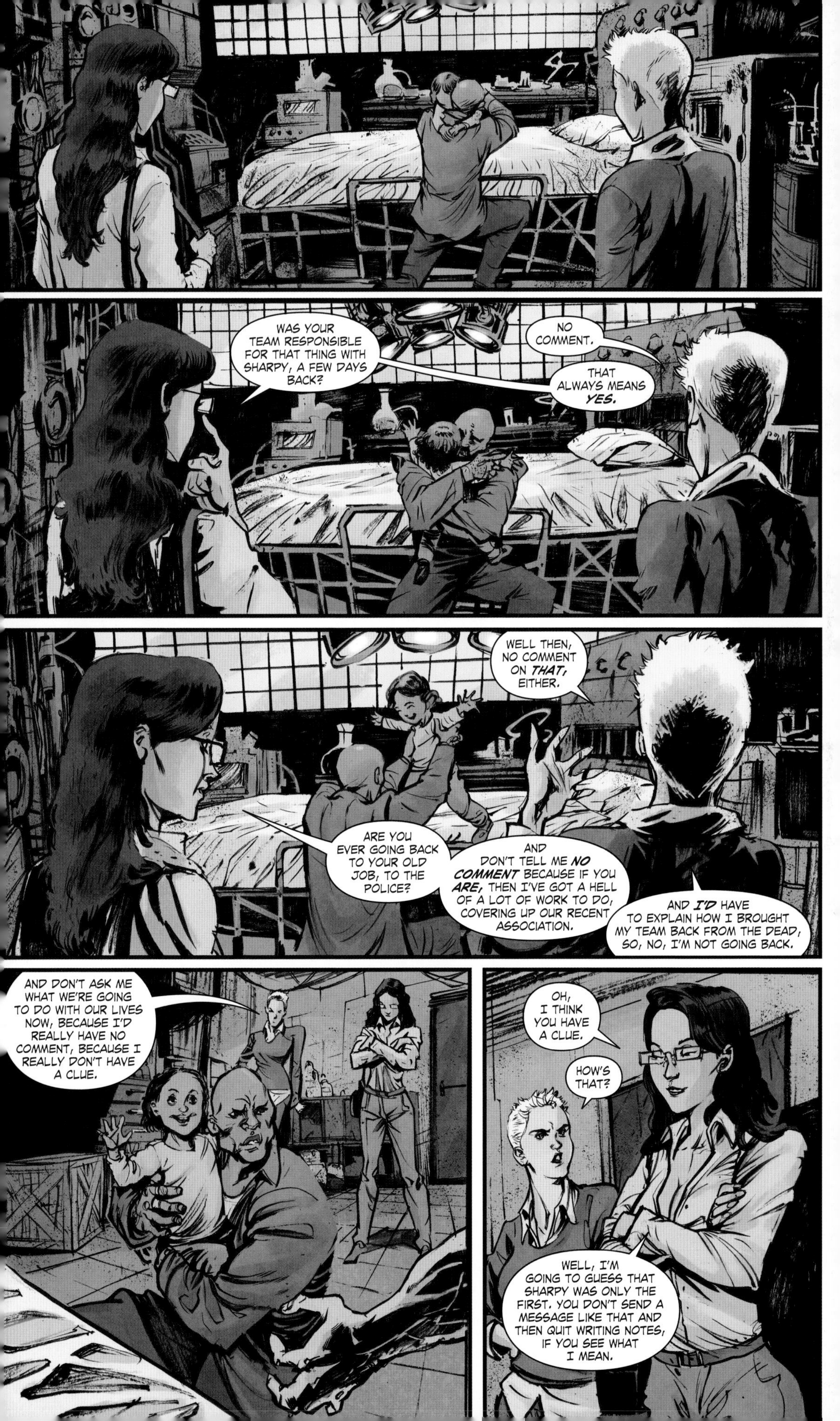
WAS YOUR TEAM RESPONSIBLE FOR THAT THING WITH SHARPY, A FEW DAYS BACK?
NO COMMENT.
THAT ALWAYS MEANS **YES.**
WELL THEN, NO COMMENT ON **THAT,** EITHER.
ARE YOU EVER GOING BACK TO YOUR OLD JOB, TO THE POLICE?
AND DON'T TELL ME **NO COMMENT** BECAUSE IF YOU **ARE,** THEN I'VE GOT A HELL OF A LOT OF WORK TO DO, COVERING UP OUR RECENT ASSOCIATION.
AND **I'D** HAVE TO EXPLAIN HOW I BROUGHT MY TEAM BACK FROM THE DEAD, SO, NO, I'M NOT GOING BACK.
AND DON'T ASK ME WHAT WE'RE GOING TO DO WITH OUR LIVES NOW, BECAUSE I'D REALLY HAVE NO COMMENT, BECAUSE I REALLY DON'T HAVE A CLUE.
OH, I THINK YOU HAVE A CLUE.
HOW'S THAT?
WELL, I'M GOING TO GUESS THAT SHARPY WAS ONLY THE FIRST. YOU DON'T SEND A MESSAGE LIKE THAT AND THEN QUIT WRITING NOTES, IF YOU SEE WHAT I MEAN.

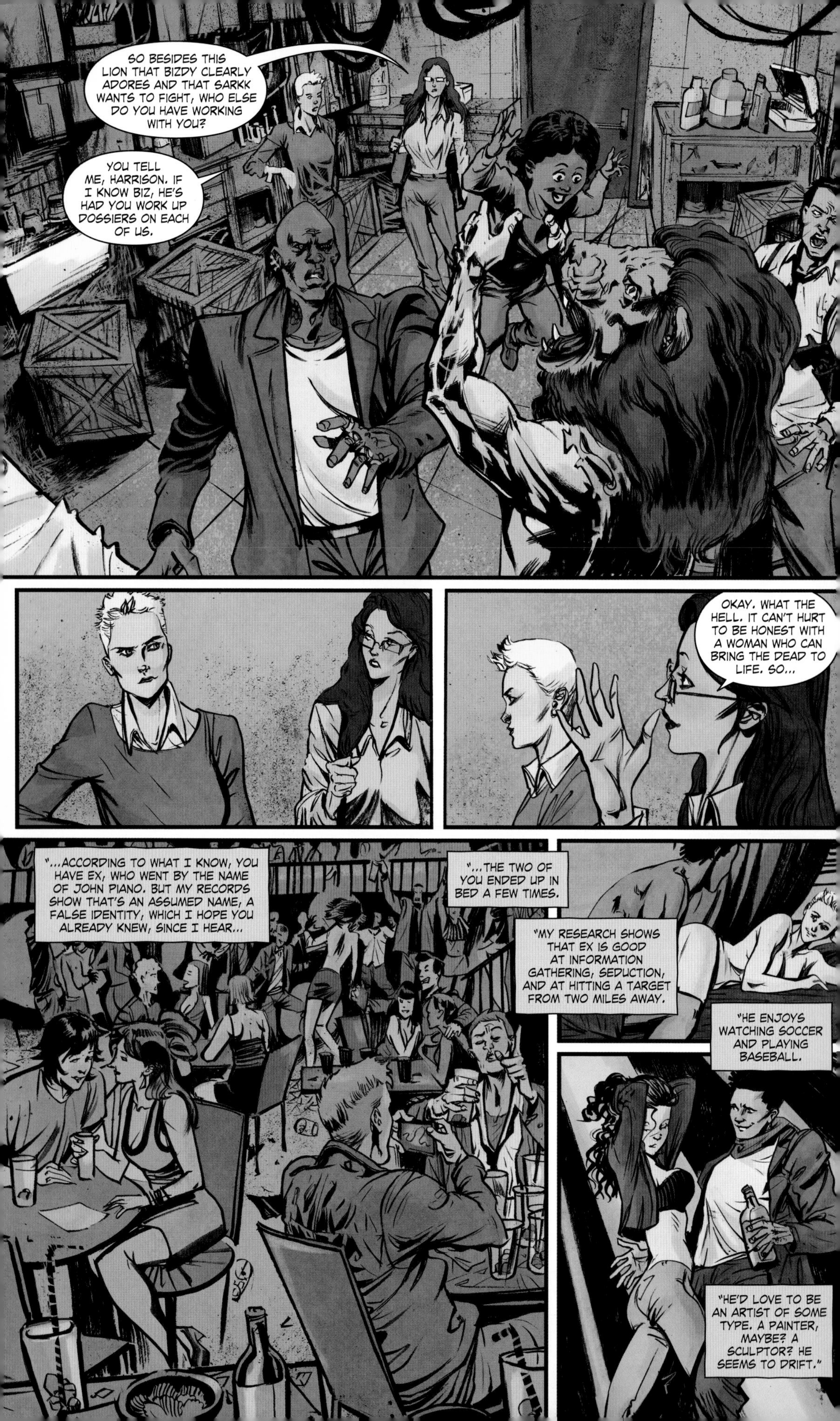
SO BESIDES THIS LION THAT BIZDY CLEARLY ADORES AND THAT SARKK WANTS TO FIGHT, WHO ELSE DO YOU HAVE WORKING WITH YOU?
YOU TELL ME, HARRISON. IF I KNOW BIZ, HE'S HAD YOU WORK UP DOSSIERS ON EACH OF US.
OKAY. WHAT THE HELL. IT CAN'T HURT TO BE HONEST WITH A WOMAN WHO CAN BRING THE DEAD TO LIFE. SO...
"...ACCORDING TO WHAT I KNOW, YOU HAVE EX, WHO WENT BY THE NAME OF JOHN PIANO. BUT MY RECORDS SHOW THAT'S AN ASSUMED NAME, A FALSE IDENTITY, WHICH I HOPE YOU ALREADY KNEW, SINCE I HEAR...
"...THE TWO OF YOU ENDED UP IN BED A FEW TIMES.
"MY RESEARCH SHOWS THAT EX IS GOOD AT INFORMATION GATHERING, SEDUCTION, AND AT HITTING A TARGET FROM TWO MILES AWAY.
"HE ENJOYS WATCHING SOCCER AND PLAYING BASEBALL.
"HE'D LOVE TO BE AN ARTIST OF SOME TYPE. A PAINTER, MAYBE? A SCULPTOR? HE SEEMS TO DRIFT."

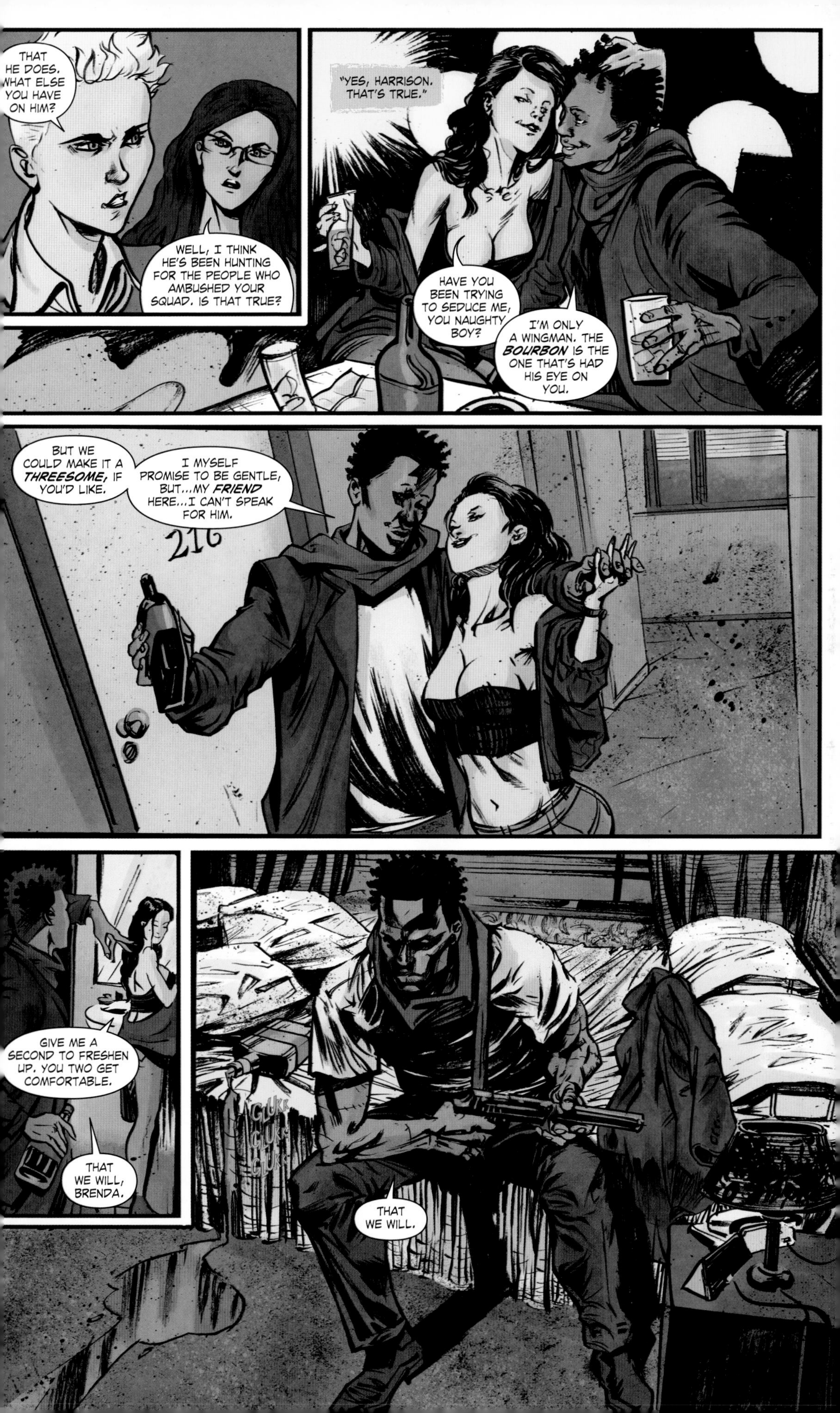
THAT HE DOES. WHAT ELSE YOU HAVE ON HIM?
WELL, I THINK HE'S BEEN HUNTING FOR THE PEOPLE WHO AMBUSHED YOUR SQUAD. IS THAT TRUE?
"YES, HARRISON. THAT'S TRUE."
HAVE YOU BEEN TRYING TO SEDUCE ME, YOU NAUGHTY BOY?
I'M ONLY A WINGMAN. THE BOURBON IS THE ONE THAT'S HAD HIS EYE ON YOU.
BUT WE COULD MAKE IT A THREESOME, IF YOU'D LIKE.
I MYSELF PROMISE TO BE GENTLE, BUT...MY FRIEND HERE...I CAN'T SPEAK FOR HIM.
216
GIVE ME A SECOND TO FRESHEN UP. YOU TWO GET COMFORTABLE.
THAT WE WILL, BRENDA.
GLUKK GLUKK GLUKK
THAT WE WILL.

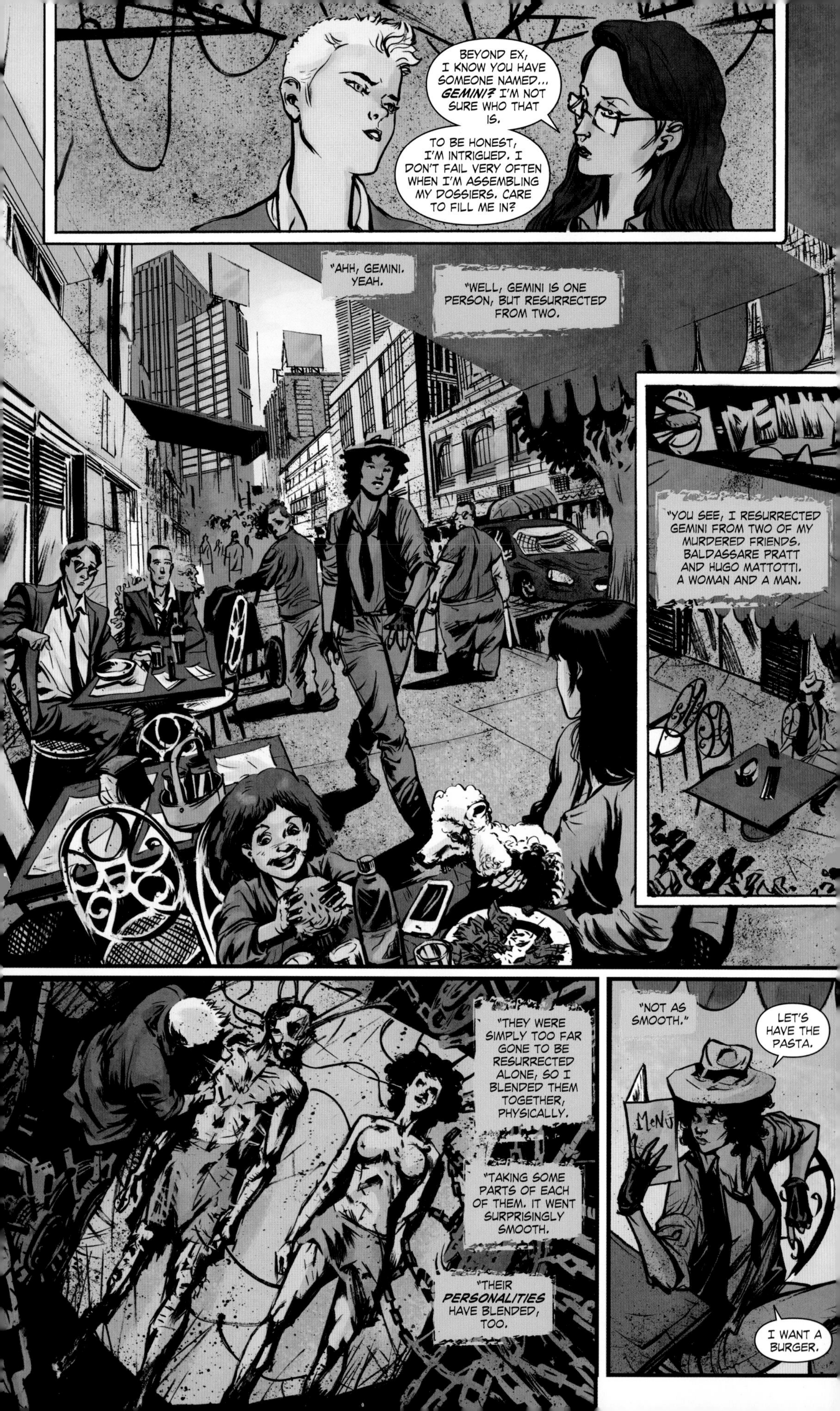

BEYOND EX, I KNOW YOU HAVE SOMEONE NAMED... *GEMINI?* I'M NOT SURE WHO THAT IS.
TO BE HONEST, I'M INTRIGUED. I DON'T FAIL VERY OFTEN WHEN I'M ASSEMBLING MY DOSSIERS. CARE TO FILL ME IN?
"AHH, GEMINI. YEAH.
"WELL, GEMINI IS ONE PERSON, BUT RESURRECTED FROM TWO.
"YOU SEE, I RESURRECTED GEMINI FROM TWO OF MY MURDERED FRIENDS. BALDASSARE PRATT AND HUGO MATTOTTI. A WOMAN AND A MAN.
"THEY WERE SIMPLY TOO FAR GONE TO BE RESURRECTED ALONE, SO I BLENDED THEM TOGETHER, PHYSICALLY.
"TAKING SOME PARTS OF EACH OF THEM. IT WENT SURPRISINGLY SMOOTH.
"THEIR *PERSONALITIES* HAVE BLENDED, TOO.
"NOT AS SMOOTH."
LET'S HAVE THE PASTA.
MENU
I WANT A BURGER.

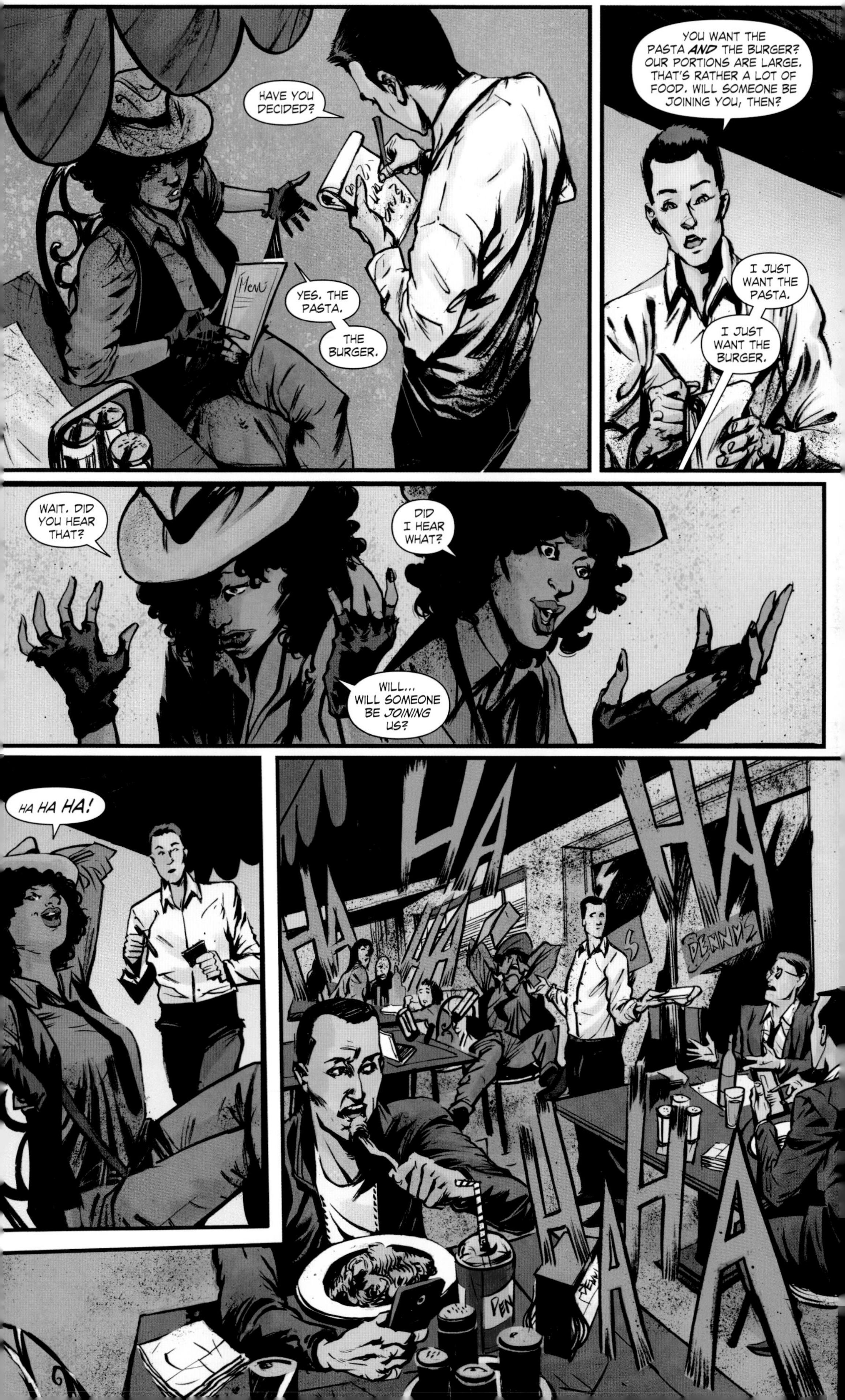
HAVE YOU DECIDED?
YES. THE PASTA.
THE BURGER.
YOU WANT THE PASTA AND THE BURGER? OUR PORTIONS ARE LARGE. THAT'S RATHER A LOT OF FOOD. WILL SOMEONE BE JOINING YOU, THEN?
I JUST WANT THE PASTA.
I JUST WANT THE BURGER.
WAIT. DID YOU HEAR THAT?
DID I HEAR WHAT?
WILL... WILL SOMEONE BE JOINING US?
HA HA HA!
HA HA HA HA HA HA
DENNY'S

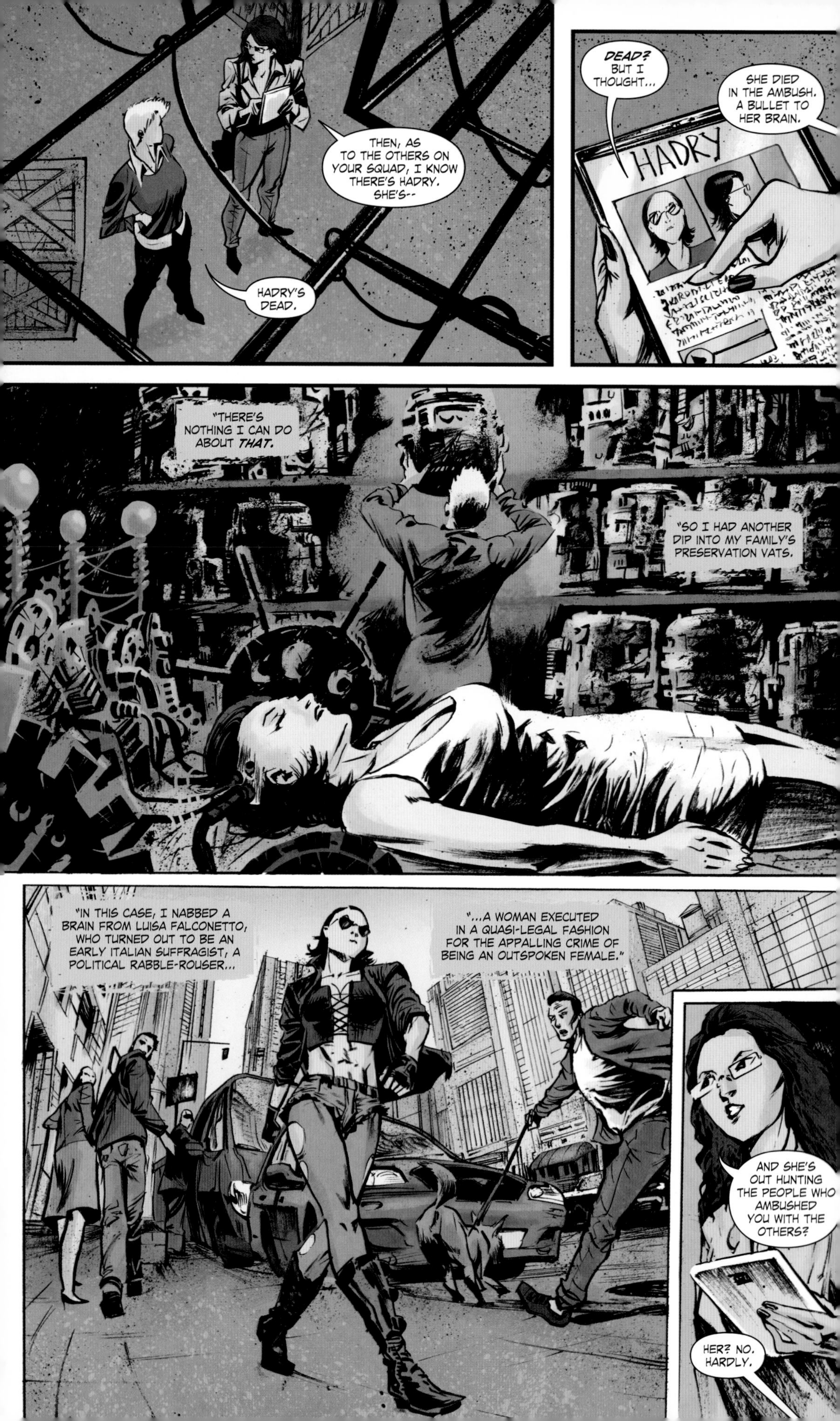
THEN, AS TO THE OTHERS ON YOUR SQUAD, I KNOW THERE'S HADRY. SHE'S--
HADRY'S DEAD.
DEAD? BUT I THOUGHT...
SHE DIED IN THE AMBUSH. A BULLET TO HER BRAIN.
HADRY
"THERE'S NOTHING I CAN DO ABOUT THAT.
"SO I HAD ANOTHER DIP INTO MY FAMILY'S PRESERVATION VATS.
"IN THIS CASE, I NABBED A BRAIN FROM LUISA FALCONETTO, WHO TURNED OUT TO BE AN EARLY ITALIAN SUFFRAGIST, A POLITICAL RABBLE-ROUSER...
"...A WOMAN EXECUTED IN A QUASI-LEGAL FASHION FOR THE APPALLING CRIME OF BEING AN OUTSPOKEN FEMALE."
AND SHE'S OUT HUNTING THE PEOPLE WHO AMBUSHED YOU WITH THE OTHERS?
HER? NO. HARDLY.

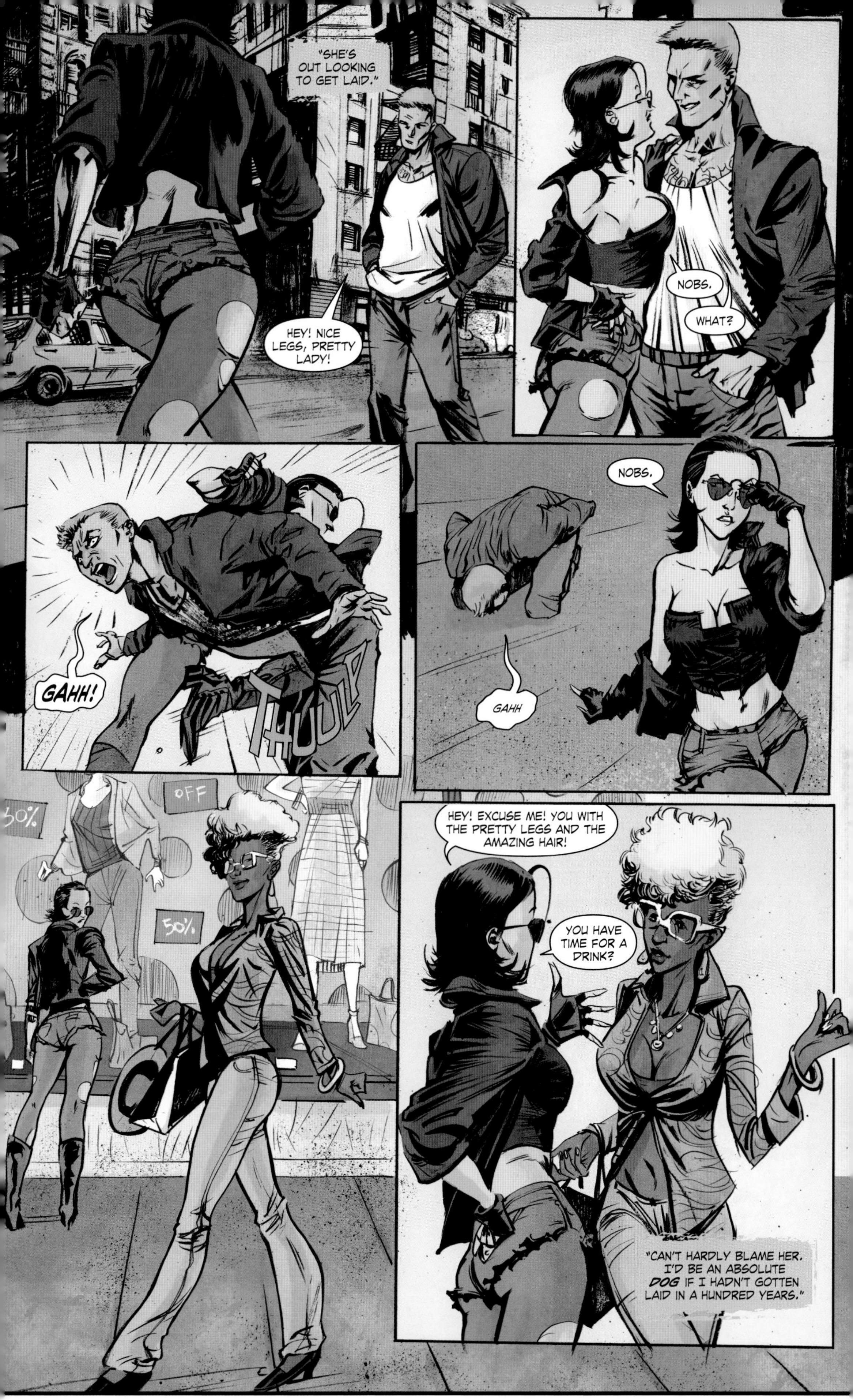
"SHE'S OUT LOOKING TO GET LAID."
HEY! NICE LEGS, PRETTY LADY!
NOBS.
WHAT?
GAHH!
THUUD
NOBS.
GAHH
OFF
30%
50%
HEY! EXCUSE ME! YOU WITH THE PRETTY LEGS AND THE AMAZING HAIR!
YOU HAVE TIME FOR A DRINK?
"CAN'T HARDLY BLAME HER. I'D BE AN ABSOLUTE DOG IF I HADN'T GOTTEN LAID IN A HUNDRED YEARS."

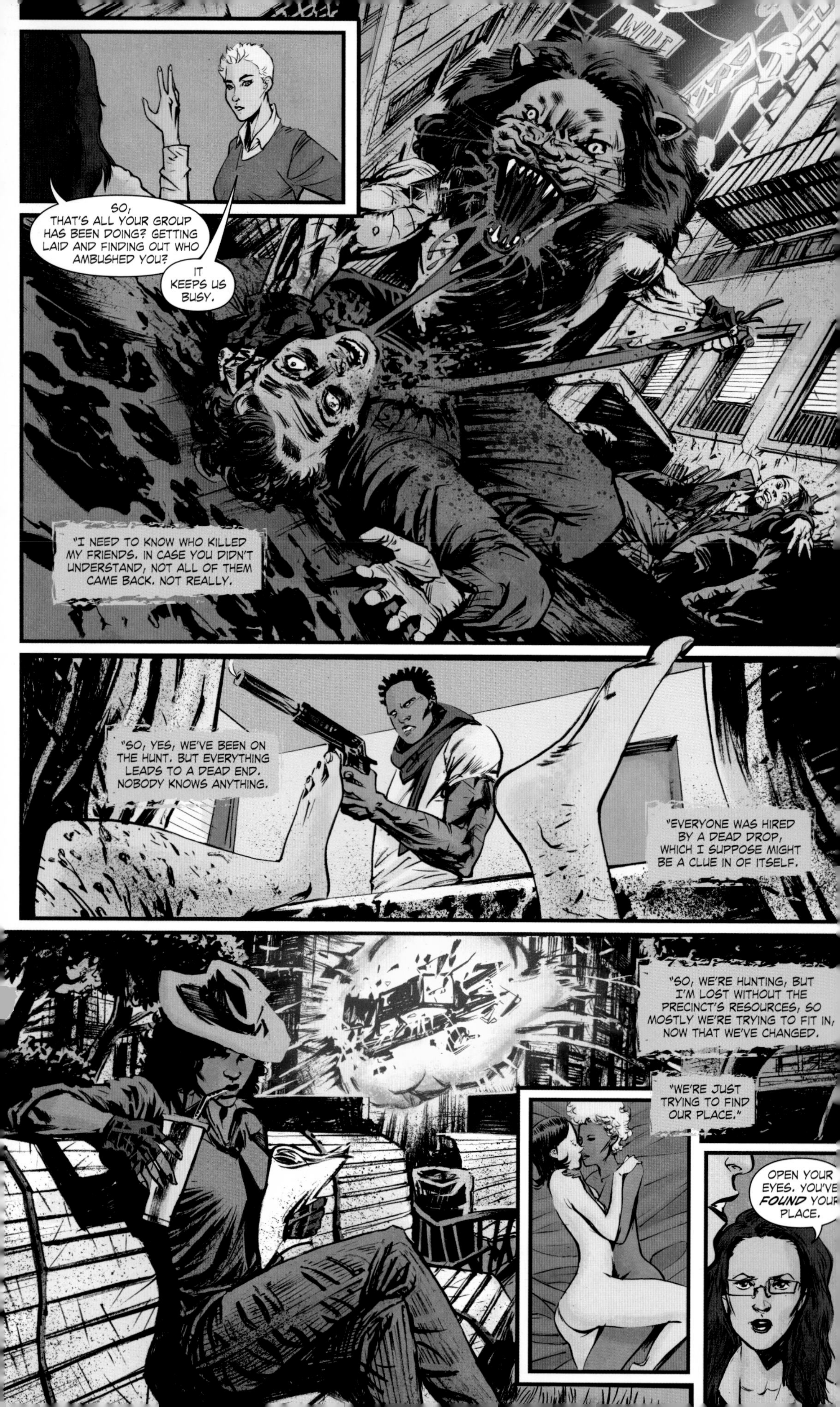
SO, THAT'S ALL YOUR GROUP HAS BEEN DOING? GETTING LAID AND FINDING OUT WHO AMBUSHED YOU?
IT KEEPS US BUSY.
"I NEED TO KNOW WHO KILLED MY FRIENDS. IN CASE YOU DIDN'T UNDERSTAND, NOT ALL OF THEM CAME BACK. NOT REALLY.
"SO, YES, WE'VE BEEN ON THE HUNT. BUT EVERYTHING LEADS TO A DEAD END. NOBODY KNOWS ANYTHING.
"EVERYONE WAS HIRED BY A DEAD DROP, WHICH I SUPPOSE MIGHT BE A CLUE IN OF ITSELF.
"SO, WE'RE HUNTING, BUT I'M LOST WITHOUT THE PRECINCT'S RESOURCES, SO MOSTLY WE'RE TRYING TO FIT IN, NOW THAT WE'VE CHANGED.
"WE'RE JUST TRYING TO FIND OUR PLACE."
OPEN YOUR EYES. YOU'VE *FOUND* YOUR PLACE.

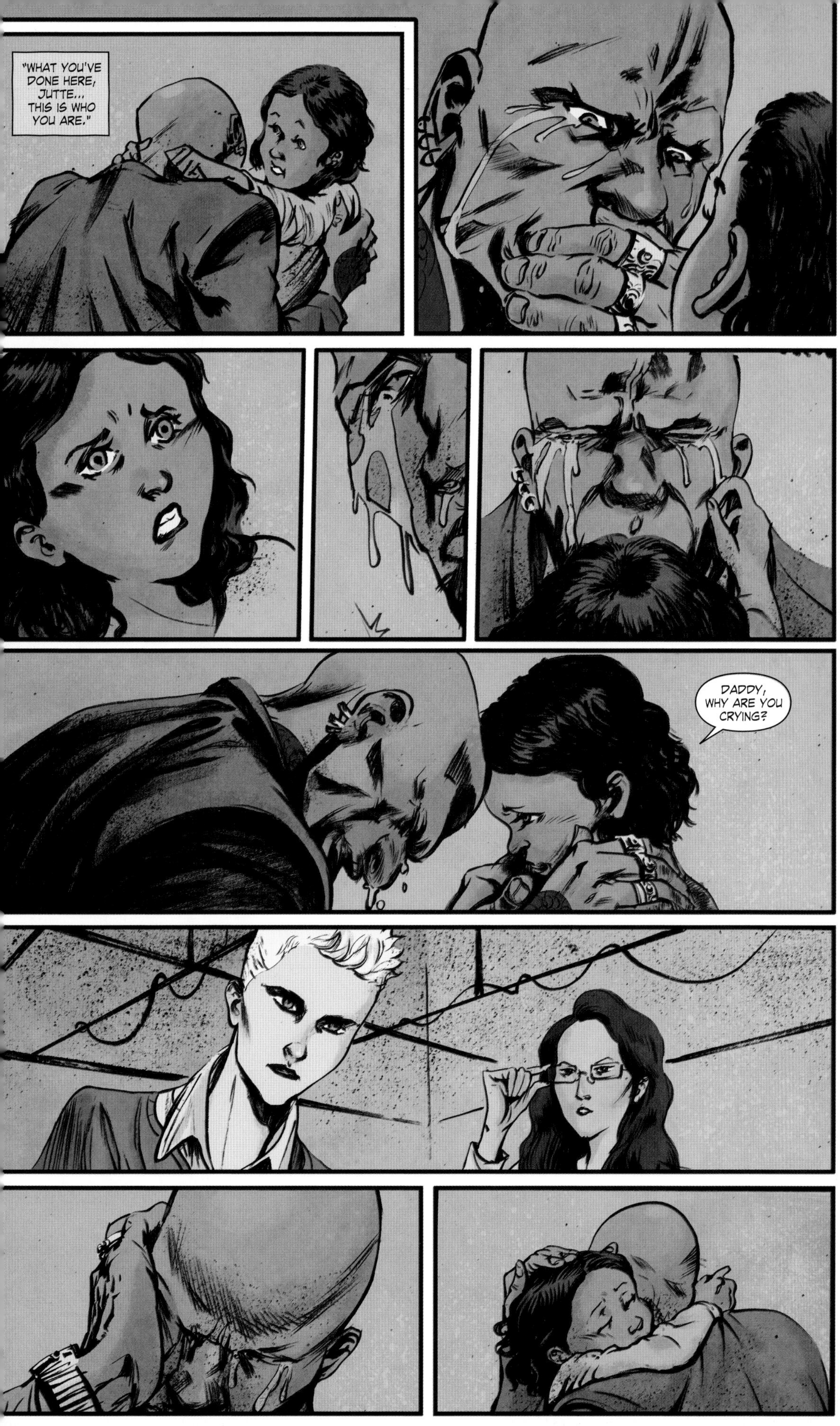
"WHAT YOU'VE DONE HERE, JUTTE... THIS IS WHO YOU ARE."
DADDY, WHY ARE YOU CRYING?

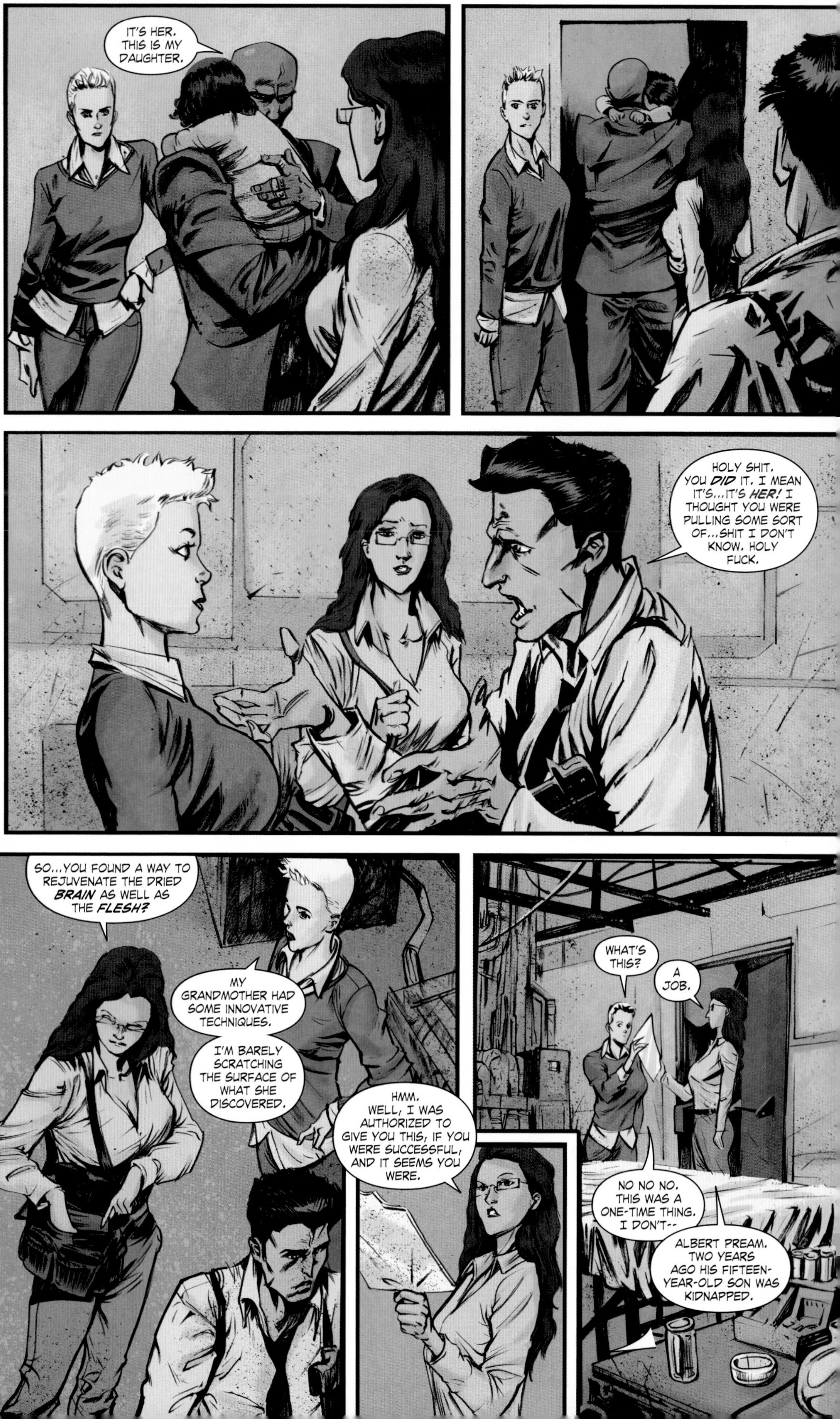
IT'S HER. THIS IS MY DAUGHTER.
HOLY SHIT. YOU DID IT. I MEAN IT'S...IT'S HER! I THOUGHT YOU WERE PULLING SOME SORT OF...SHIT I DON'T KNOW. HOLY FUCK.
SO...YOU FOUND A WAY TO REJUVENATE THE DRIED BRAIN AS WELL AS THE FLESH?
MY GRANDMOTHER HAD SOME INNOVATIVE TECHNIQUES.
I'M BARELY SCRATCHING THE SURFACE OF WHAT SHE DISCOVERED.
HMM. WELL, I WAS AUTHORIZED TO GIVE YOU THIS, IF YOU WERE SUCCESSFUL, AND IT SEEMS YOU WERE.
WHAT'S THIS?
A JOB.
NO NO NO. THIS WAS A ONE-TIME THING. I DON'T--
ALBERT PREAM. TWO YEARS AGO HIS FIFTEEN-YEAR-OLD SON WAS KIDNAPPED.

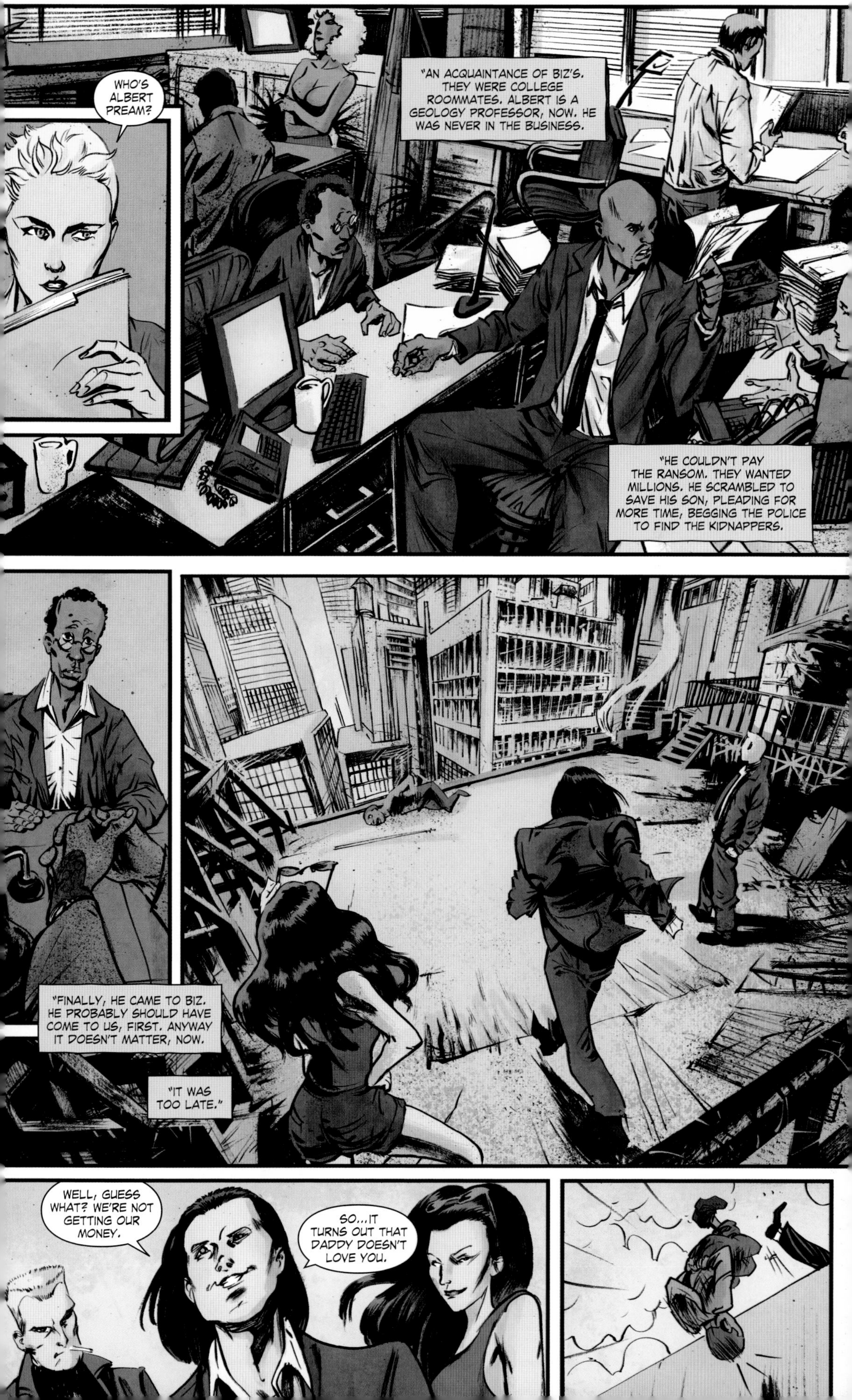

WHO'S ALBERT PREAM?
"AN ACQUAINTANCE OF BIZ'S. THEY WERE COLLEGE ROOMMATES. ALBERT IS A GEOLOGY PROFESSOR, NOW. HE WAS NEVER IN THE BUSINESS.
"HE COULDN'T PAY THE RANSOM. THEY WANTED MILLIONS. HE SCRAMBLED TO SAVE HIS SON, PLEADING FOR MORE TIME, BEGGING THE POLICE TO FIND THE KIDNAPPERS.
"FINALLY, HE CAME TO BIZ. HE PROBABLY SHOULD HAVE COME TO US, FIRST. ANYWAY IT DOESN'T MATTER, NOW.
"IT WAS TOO LATE."
WELL, GUESS WHAT? WE'RE NOT GETTING OUR MONEY.
SO...IT TURNS OUT THAT DADDY DOESN'T LOVE YOU.

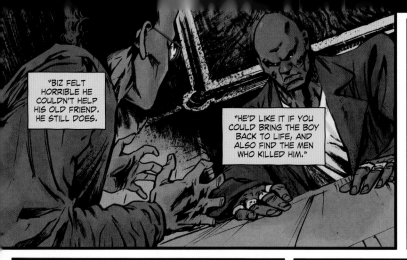

"BIZ FELT HORRIBLE HE COULDN'T HELP HIS OLD FRIEND. HE STILL DOES.

"HE'D LIKE IT IF YOU COULD BRING THE BOY BACK TO LIFE, AND ALSO FIND THE MEN WHO KILLED HIM."

WHY SHOULD I TAKE A DEAL LIKE THIS? WHAT'S IN IT FOR ME?

BUSINESS, THAT'S WHAT.

ALL THE RESOURCES YOU NEED. AND ONE MILLION DOLLARS.

AND BEFORE YOU ANSWER...

...LET ME TELL YOU THAT THERE WAS A SUSPECT IN THE KIDNAPPING...A SCHOOL CROSSING GUARD.

OKAY; SO WHAT?

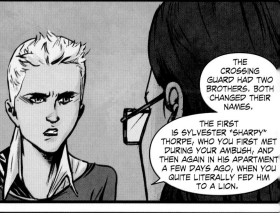

THE CROSSING GUARD HAD TWO BROTHERS. BOTH CHANGED THEIR NAMES.

THE FIRST IS SYLVESTER "SHARPY" THORPE, WHO YOU FIRST MET DURING YOUR AMBUSH, AND THEN AGAIN IN HIS APARTMENT A FEW DAYS AGO, WHEN YOU QUITE LITERALLY FED HIM TO A LION.

"AND THE OTHER BROTHER IS HUBERT GRANGE, CAPTAIN OF THE ELEVENTH PRECINCT, AND THE TIP OF THE ICEBERG ON WHAT HAS THE MAKINGS OF A RATHER INTERESTING CONSPIRACY."

SO HAVE FUN, FRANKENSTEIN.

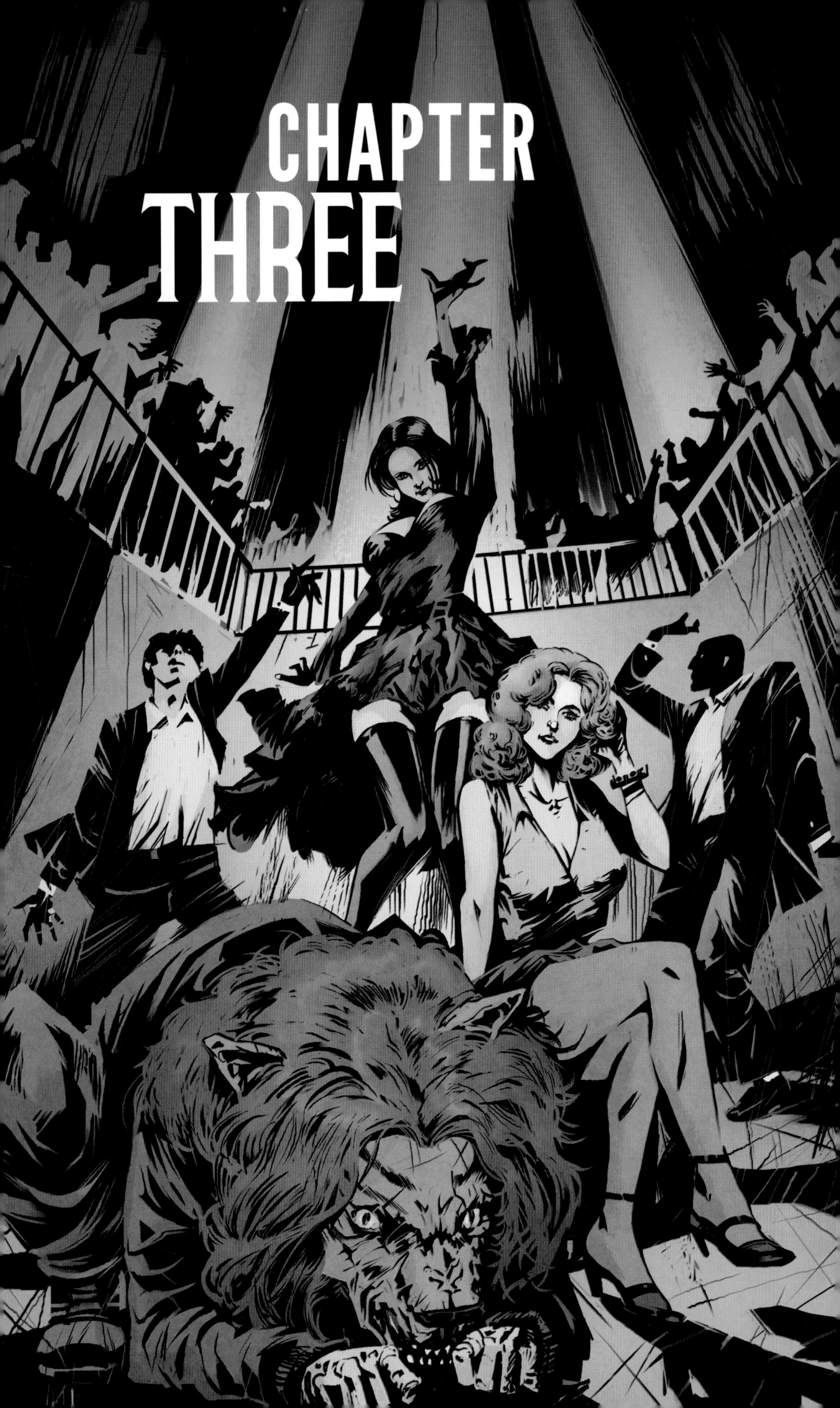
CHAPTER
THREE

1
2
3
4

a
n
d
h
i
k
m

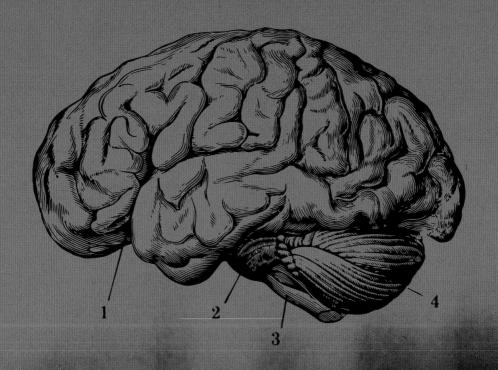

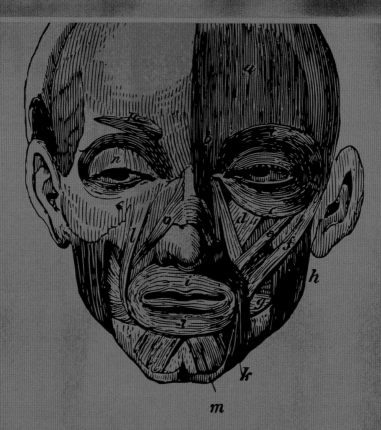

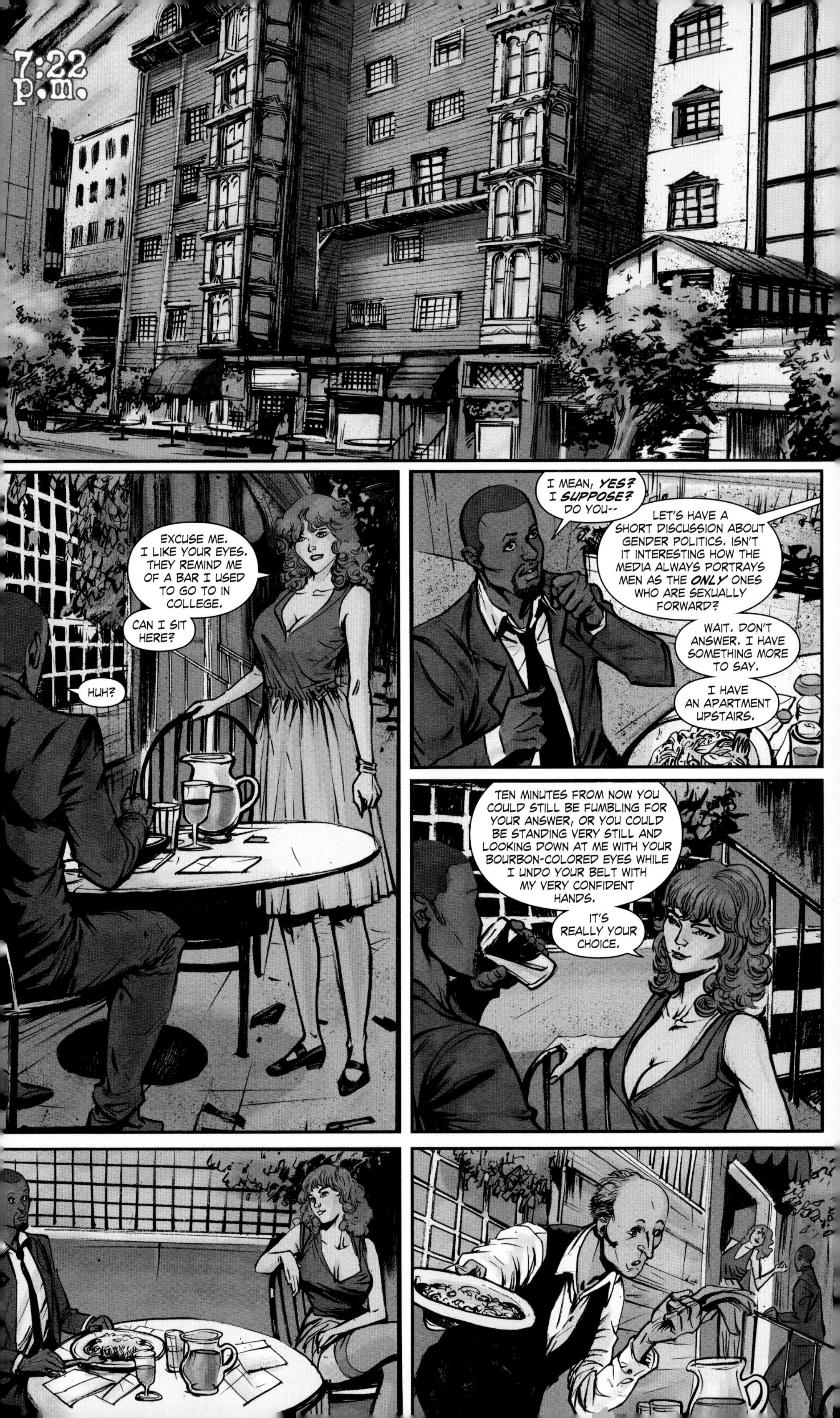
7:22 p.m.
EXCUSE ME. I LIKE YOUR EYES. THEY REMIND ME OF A BAR I USED TO GO TO IN COLLEGE.
CAN I SIT HERE?
HUH?
I MEAN, YES? I SUPPOSE? DO YOU--
LET'S HAVE A SHORT DISCUSSION ABOUT GENDER POLITICS. ISN'T IT INTERESTING HOW THE MEDIA ALWAYS PORTRAYS MEN AS THE ONLY ONES WHO ARE SEXUALLY FORWARD?
WAIT. DON'T ANSWER. I HAVE SOMETHING MORE TO SAY.
I HAVE AN APARTMENT UPSTAIRS.
TEN MINUTES FROM NOW YOU COULD STILL BE FUMBLING FOR YOUR ANSWER, OR YOU COULD BE STANDING VERY STILL AND LOOKING DOWN AT ME WITH YOUR BOURBON-COLORED EYES WHILE I UNDO YOUR BELT WITH MY VERY CONFIDENT HANDS.
IT'S REALLY YOUR CHOICE.

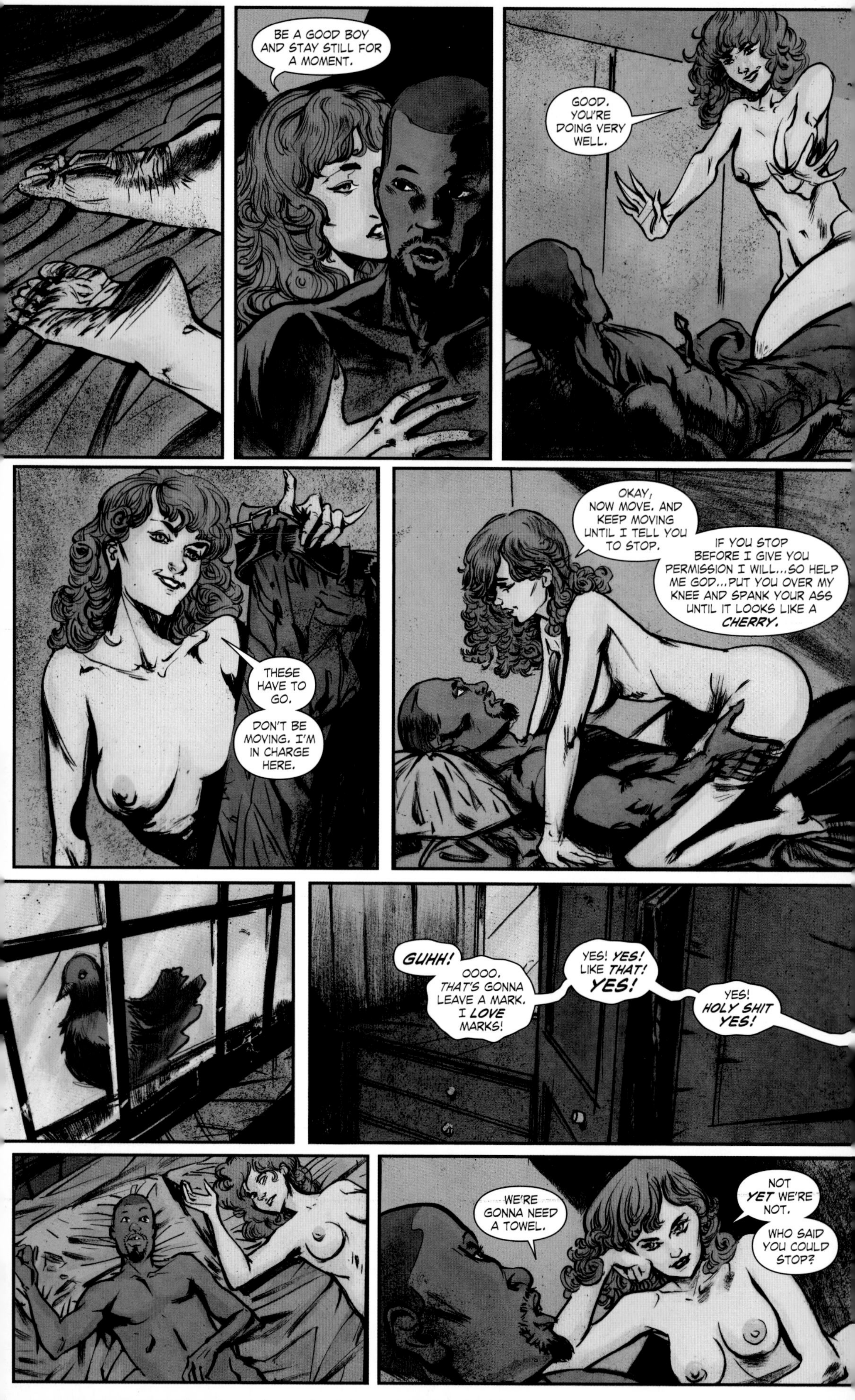
BE A GOOD BOY AND STAY STILL FOR A MOMENT.
GOOD. YOU'RE DOING VERY WELL.
THESE HAVE TO GO.
DON'T BE MOVING. I'M IN CHARGE HERE.
OKAY, NOW MOVE. AND KEEP MOVING UNTIL I TELL YOU TO STOP.
IF YOU STOP BEFORE I GIVE YOU PERMISSION I WILL...SO HELP ME GOD...PUT YOU OVER MY KNEE AND SPANK YOUR ASS UNTIL IT LOOKS LIKE A CHERRY.
GUHH!
OOOO. THAT'S GONNA LEAVE A MARK. I LOVE MARKS!
YES! YES! LIKE THAT! YES!
YES! HOLY SHIT YES!
WE'RE GONNA NEED A TOWEL.
NOT YET WE'RE NOT.
WHO SAID YOU COULD STOP?

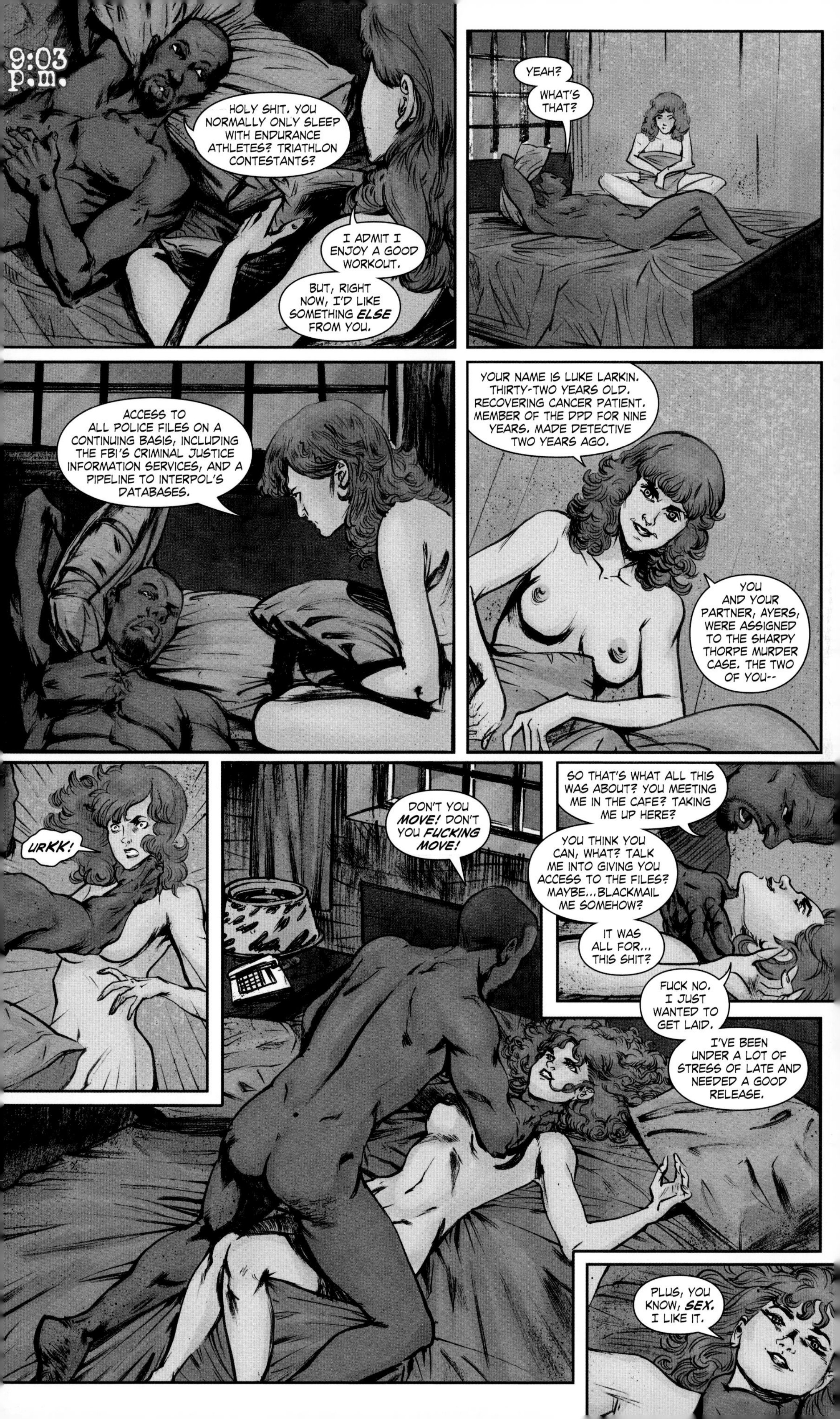
9:03 p.m.
HOLY SHIT. YOU NORMALLY ONLY SLEEP WITH ENDURANCE ATHLETES? TRIATHLON CONTESTANTS?
I ADMIT I ENJOY A GOOD WORKOUT.
BUT, RIGHT NOW, I'D LIKE SOMETHING ELSE FROM YOU.
YEAH?
WHAT'S THAT?
ACCESS TO ALL POLICE FILES ON A CONTINUING BASIS, INCLUDING THE FBI'S CRIMINAL JUSTICE INFORMATION SERVICES, AND A PIPELINE TO INTERPOL'S DATABASES.
YOUR NAME IS LUKE LARKIN. THIRTY-TWO YEARS OLD. RECOVERING CANCER PATIENT. MEMBER OF THE DPD FOR NINE YEARS. MADE DETECTIVE TWO YEARS AGO.
YOU AND YOUR PARTNER, AYERS, WERE ASSIGNED TO THE SHARPY THORPE MURDER CASE. THE TWO OF YOU--
URKK!
DON'T YOU MOVE! DON'T YOU FUCKING MOVE!
SO THAT'S WHAT ALL THIS WAS ABOUT? YOU MEETING ME IN THE CAFE? TAKING ME UP HERE?
YOU THINK YOU CAN, WHAT? TALK ME INTO GIVING YOU ACCESS TO THE FILES? MAYBE...BLACKMAIL ME SOMEHOW?
IT WAS ALL FOR... THIS SHIT?
FUCK NO. I JUST WANTED TO GET LAID.
I'VE BEEN UNDER A LOT OF STRESS OF LATE AND NEEDED A GOOD RELEASE.
PLUS, YOU KNOW, SEX. I LIKE IT.

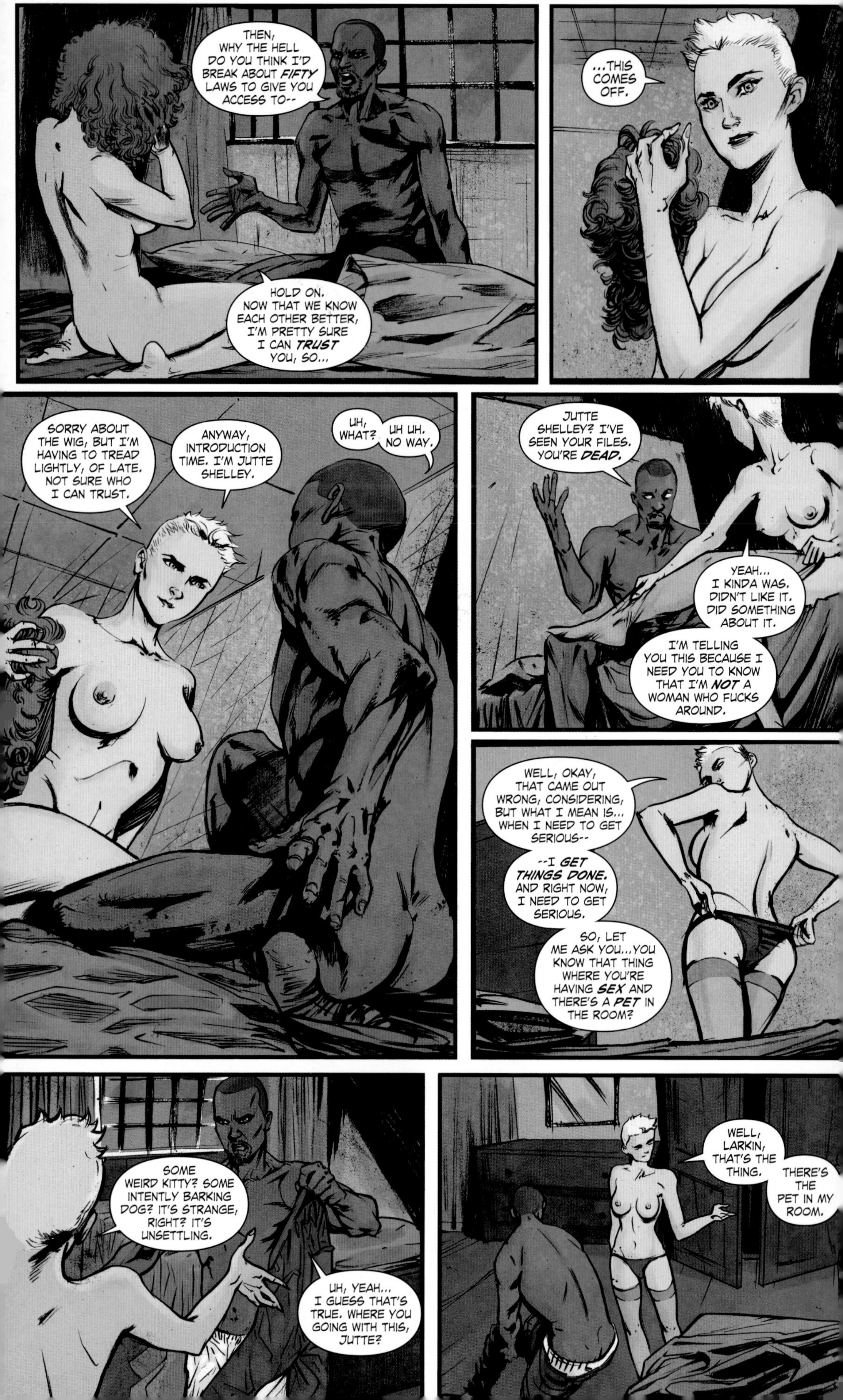
THEN, WHY THE HELL DO YOU THINK I'D BREAK ABOUT FIFTY LAWS TO GIVE YOU ACCESS TO--
HOLD ON. NOW THAT WE KNOW EACH OTHER BETTER, I'M PRETTY SURE I CAN TRUST YOU, SO...
...THIS COMES OFF.
SORRY ABOUT THE WIG, BUT I'M HAVING TO TREAD LIGHTLY, OF LATE. NOT SURE WHO I CAN TRUST.
ANYWAY, INTRODUCTION TIME. I'M JUTTE SHELLEY.
UH, WHAT?
UH UH. NO WAY.
JUTTE SHELLEY? I'VE SEEN YOUR FILES. YOU'RE DEAD.
YEAH... I KINDA WAS. DIDN'T LIKE IT. DID SOMETHING ABOUT IT.
I'M TELLING YOU THIS BECAUSE I NEED YOU TO KNOW THAT I'M NOT A WOMAN WHO FUCKS AROUND.
WELL, OKAY, THAT CAME OUT WRONG, CONSIDERING, BUT WHAT I MEAN IS... WHEN I NEED TO GET SERIOUS--
--I GET THINGS DONE. AND RIGHT NOW, I NEED TO GET SERIOUS.
SO, LET ME ASK YOU...YOU KNOW THAT THING WHERE YOU'RE HAVING SEX AND THERE'S A PET IN THE ROOM?
SOME WEIRD KITTY? SOME INTENTLY BARKING DOG? IT'S STRANGE, RIGHT? IT'S UNSETTLING.
UH, YEAH... I GUESS THAT'S TRUE. WHERE YOU GOING WITH THIS, JUTTE?
WELL, LARKIN, THAT'S THE THING.
THERE'S THE PET IN MY ROOM.

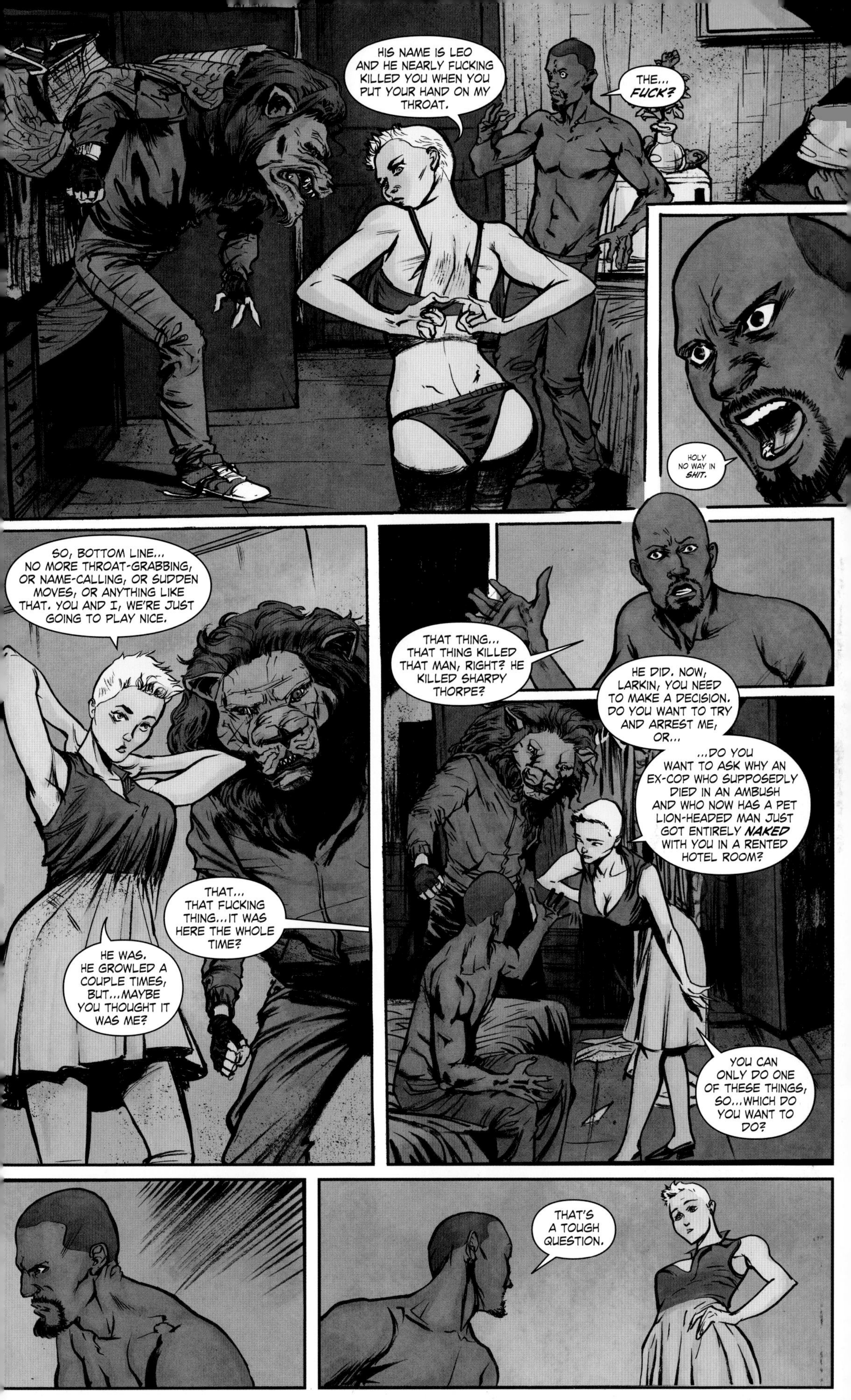
HIS NAME IS LEO AND HE NEARLY FUCKING KILLED YOU WHEN YOU PUT YOUR HAND ON MY THROAT.
THE... FUCK?
HOLY NO WAY IN SHIT.
SO, BOTTOM LINE... NO MORE THROAT-GRABBING, OR NAME-CALLING, OR SUDDEN MOVES, OR ANYTHING LIKE THAT. YOU AND I, WE'RE JUST GOING TO PLAY NICE.
THAT... THAT FUCKING THING...IT WAS HERE THE WHOLE TIME?
HE WAS. HE GROWLED A COUPLE TIMES, BUT...MAYBE YOU THOUGHT IT WAS ME?
THAT THING... THAT THING KILLED THAT MAN, RIGHT? HE KILLED SHARPY THORPE?
HE DID. NOW, LARKIN, YOU NEED TO MAKE A DECISION. DO YOU WANT TO TRY AND ARREST ME, OR...
...DO YOU WANT TO ASK WHY AN EX-COP WHO SUPPOSEDLY DIED IN AN AMBUSH AND WHO NOW HAS A PET LION-HEADED MAN JUST GOT ENTIRELY NAKED WITH YOU IN A RENTED HOTEL ROOM?
YOU CAN ONLY DO ONE OF THESE THINGS, SO...WHICH DO YOU WANT TO DO?
THAT'S A TOUGH QUESTION.

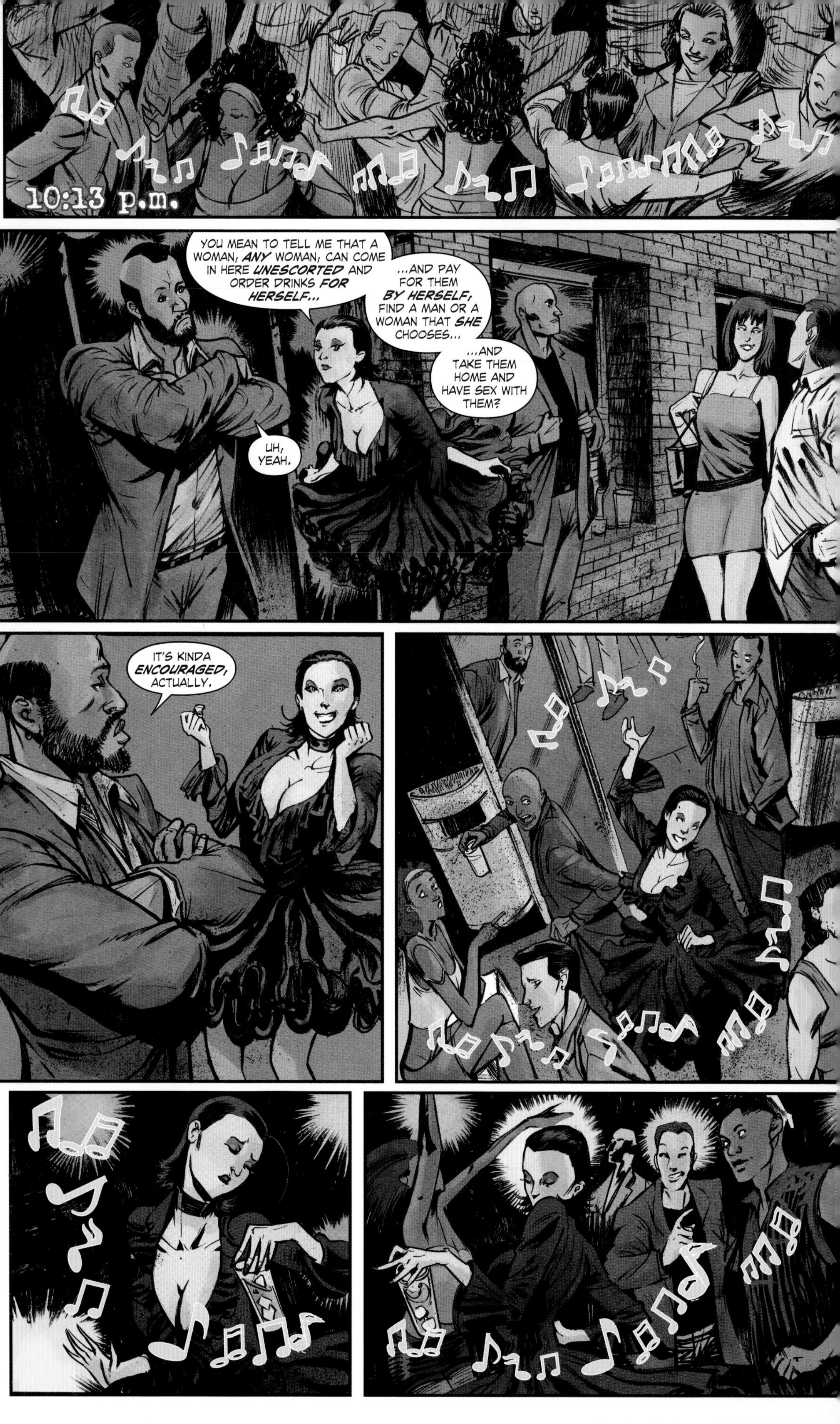
10:13 p.m.
YOU MEAN TO TELL ME THAT A WOMAN, ANY WOMAN, CAN COME IN HERE UNESCORTED AND ORDER DRINKS FOR HERSELF...
...AND PAY FOR THEM BY HERSELF, FIND A MAN OR A WOMAN THAT SHE CHOOSES...
...AND TAKE THEM HOME AND HAVE SEX WITH THEM?
UH, YEAH.
IT'S KINDA ENCOURAGED, ACTUALLY.

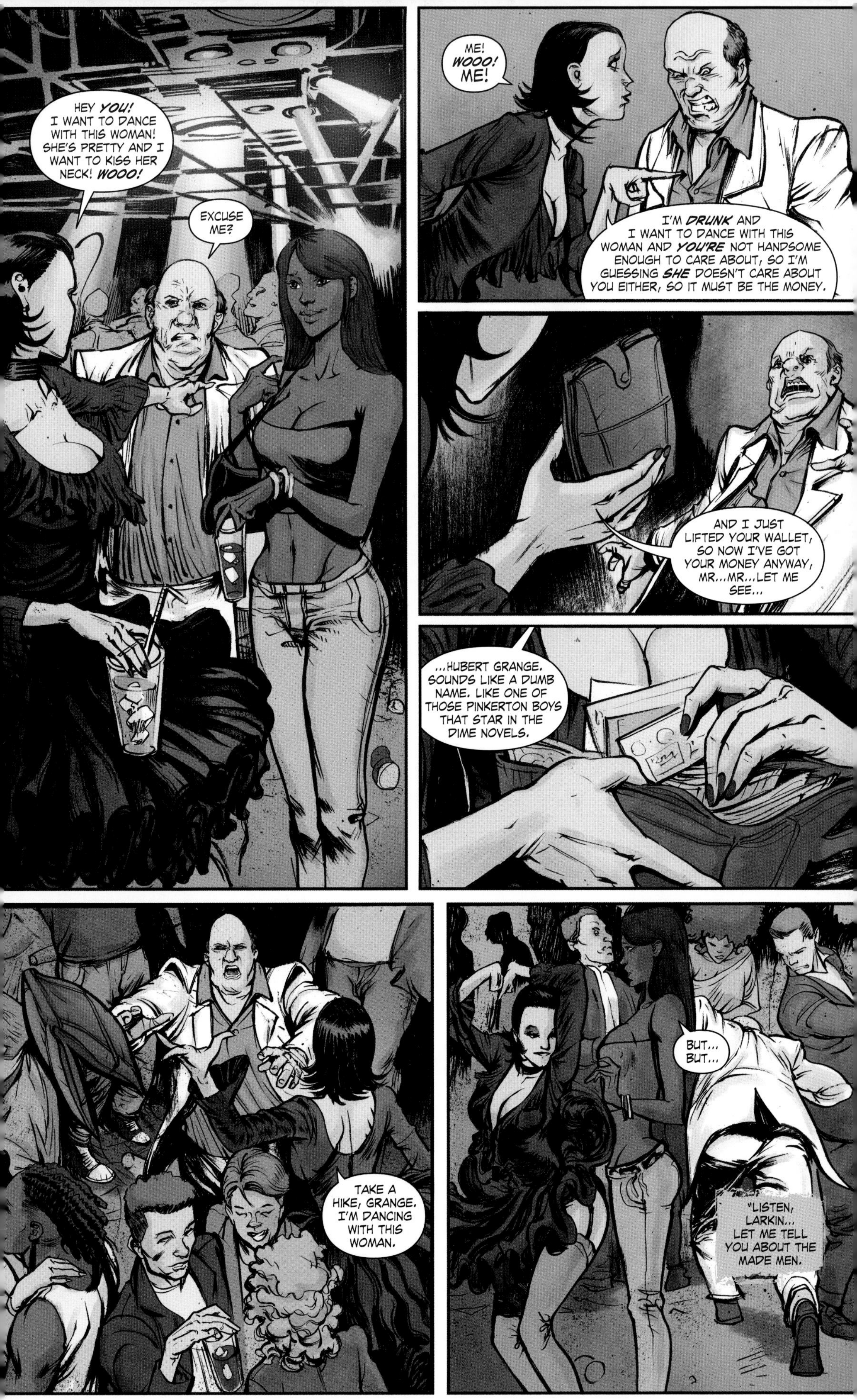

HEY YOU! I WANT TO DANCE WITH THIS WOMAN! SHE'S PRETTY AND I WANT TO KISS HER NECK! WOOO!
EXCUSE ME?
ME! WOOO! ME!
I'M DRUNK AND I WANT TO DANCE WITH THIS WOMAN AND YOU'RE NOT HANDSOME ENOUGH TO CARE ABOUT, SO I'M GUESSING SHE DOESN'T CARE ABOUT YOU EITHER, SO IT MUST BE THE MONEY.
AND I JUST LIFTED YOUR WALLET, SO NOW I'VE GOT YOUR MONEY ANYWAY, MR...MR...LET ME SEE...
...HUBERT GRANGE. SOUNDS LIKE A DUMB NAME. LIKE ONE OF THOSE PINKERTON BOYS THAT STAR IN THE DIME NOVELS.
TAKE A HIKE, GRANGE. I'M DANCING WITH THIS WOMAN.
BUT... BUT...
"LISTEN, LARKIN... LET ME TELL YOU ABOUT THE MADE MEN.

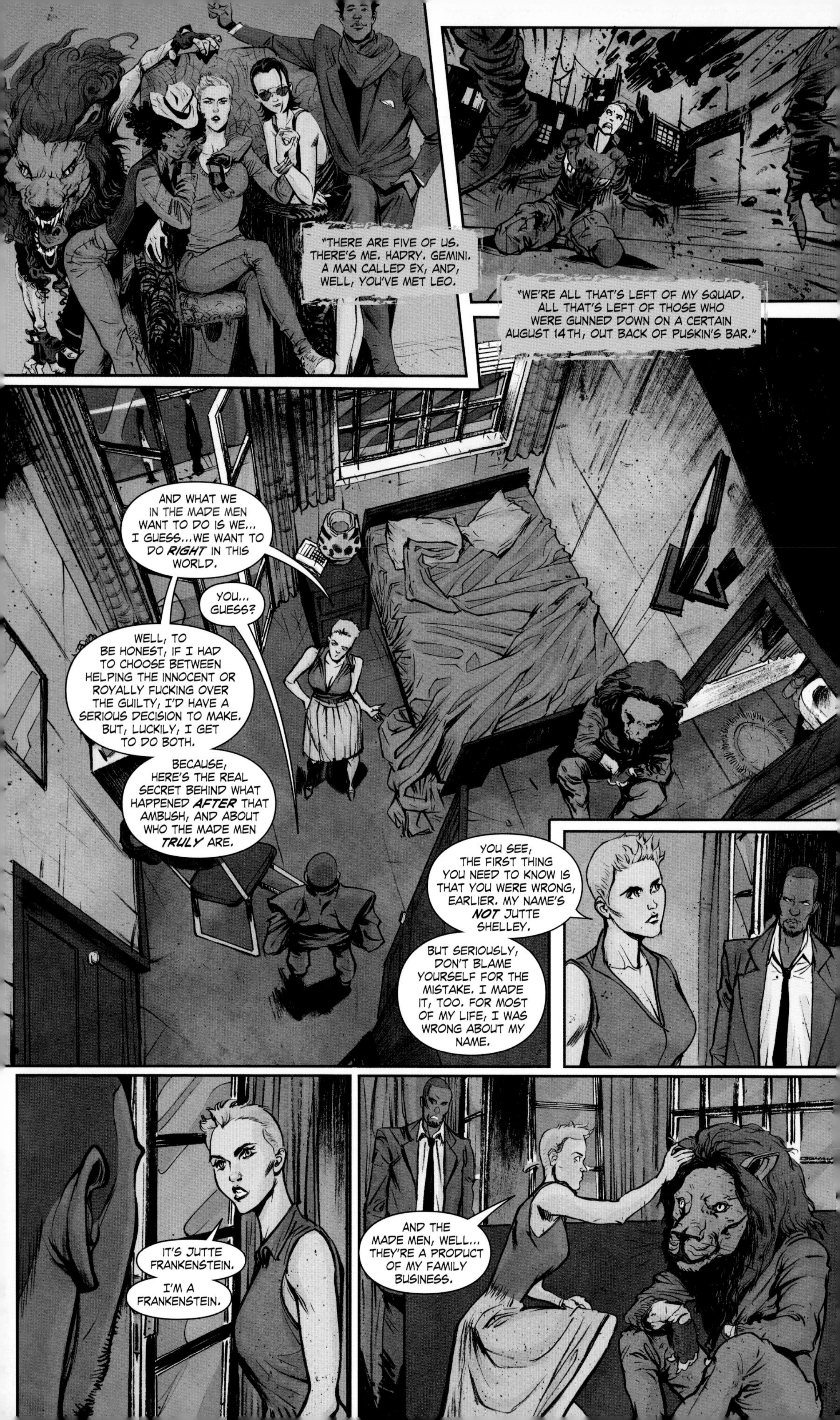

"THERE ARE FIVE OF US. THERE'S ME. HADRY. GEMINI. A MAN CALLED EX, AND, WELL, YOU'VE MET LEO.
"WE'RE ALL THAT'S LEFT OF MY SQUAD. ALL THAT'S LEFT OF THOSE WHO WERE GUNNED DOWN ON A CERTAIN AUGUST 14TH, OUT BACK OF PUSKIN'S BAR."
AND WHAT WE IN THE MADE MEN WANT TO DO IS WE... I GUESS...WE WANT TO DO RIGHT IN THIS WORLD.
YOU... GUESS?
WELL, TO BE HONEST, IF I HAD TO CHOOSE BETWEEN HELPING THE INNOCENT OR ROYALLY FUCKING OVER THE GUILTY, I'D HAVE A SERIOUS DECISION TO MAKE. BUT, LUCKILY, I GET TO DO BOTH.
BECAUSE, HERE'S THE REAL SECRET BEHIND WHAT HAPPENED AFTER THAT AMBUSH, AND ABOUT WHO THE MADE MEN TRULY ARE.
YOU SEE, THE FIRST THING YOU NEED TO KNOW IS THAT YOU WERE WRONG, EARLIER. MY NAME'S NOT JUTTE SHELLEY.
BUT SERIOUSLY, DON'T BLAME YOURSELF FOR THE MISTAKE. I MADE IT, TOO. FOR MOST OF MY LIFE, I WAS WRONG ABOUT MY NAME.
IT'S JUTTE FRANKENSTEIN.
I'M A FRANKENSTEIN.
AND THE MADE MEN, WELL... THEY'RE A PRODUCT OF MY FAMILY BUSINESS.

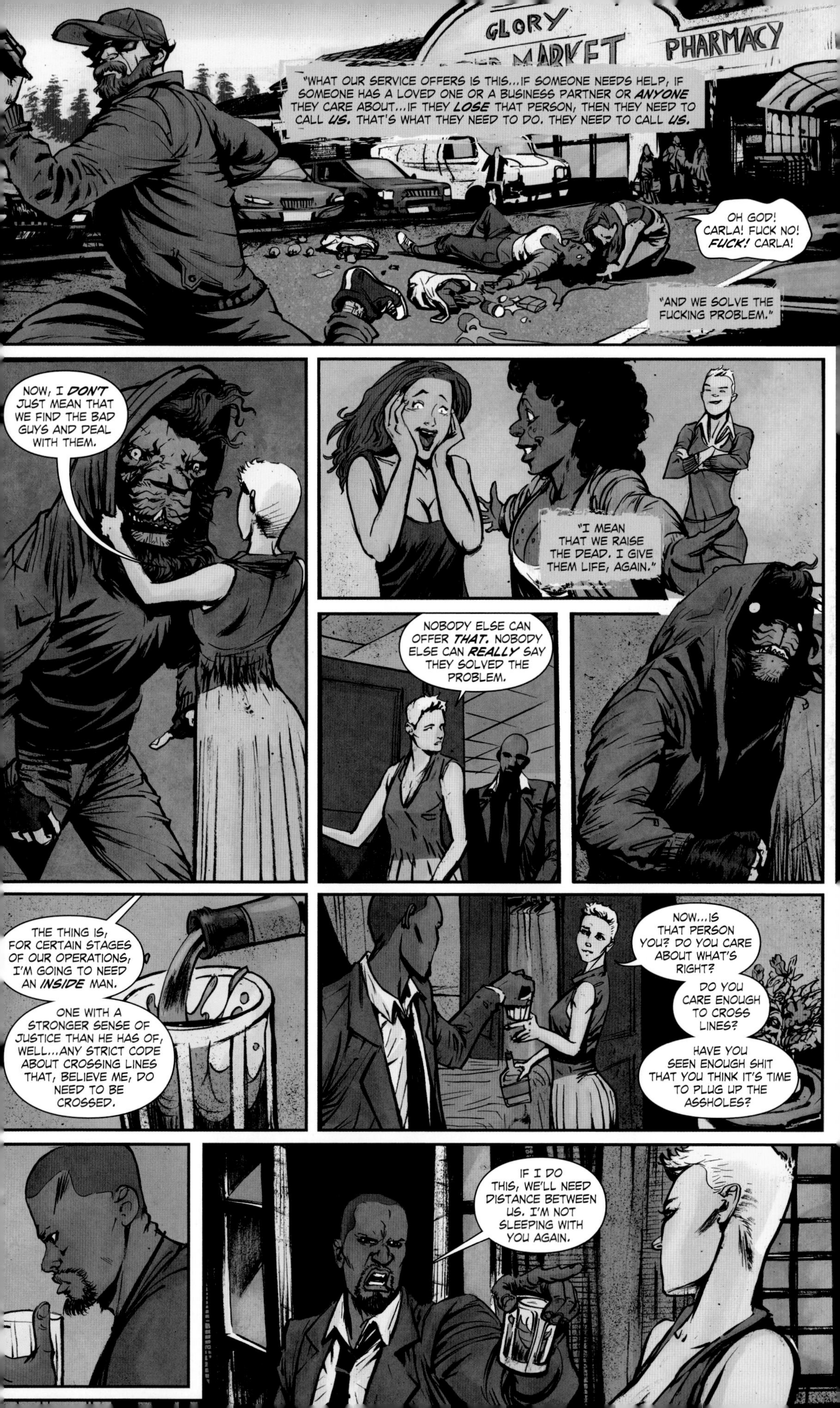
GLORY
MARKET
PHARMACY
"WHAT OUR SERVICE OFFERS IS THIS...IF SOMEONE NEEDS HELP, IF SOMEONE HAS A LOVED ONE OR A BUSINESS PARTNER OR ANYONE THEY CARE ABOUT...IF THEY LOSE THAT PERSON, THEN THEY NEED TO CALL US. THAT'S WHAT THEY NEED TO DO. THEY NEED TO CALL US.
OH GOD! CARLA! FUCK NO! FUCK! CARLA!
"AND WE SOLVE THE FUCKING PROBLEM."
NOW, I DON'T JUST MEAN THAT WE FIND THE BAD GUYS AND DEAL WITH THEM.
"I MEAN THAT WE RAISE THE DEAD. I GIVE THEM LIFE, AGAIN."
NOBODY ELSE CAN OFFER THAT. NOBODY ELSE CAN REALLY SAY THEY SOLVED THE PROBLEM.
THE THING IS, FOR CERTAIN STAGES OF OUR OPERATIONS, I'M GOING TO NEED AN INSIDE MAN.
ONE WITH A STRONGER SENSE OF JUSTICE THAN HE HAS OF, WELL...ANY STRICT CODE ABOUT CROSSING LINES THAT, BELIEVE ME, DO NEED TO BE CROSSED.
NOW...IS THAT PERSON YOU? DO YOU CARE ABOUT WHAT'S RIGHT?
DO YOU CARE ENOUGH TO CROSS LINES?
HAVE YOU SEEN ENOUGH SHIT THAT YOU THINK IT'S TIME TO PLUG UP THE ASSHOLES?
IF I DO THIS, WE'LL NEED DISTANCE BETWEEN US. I'M NOT SLEEPING WITH YOU AGAIN.

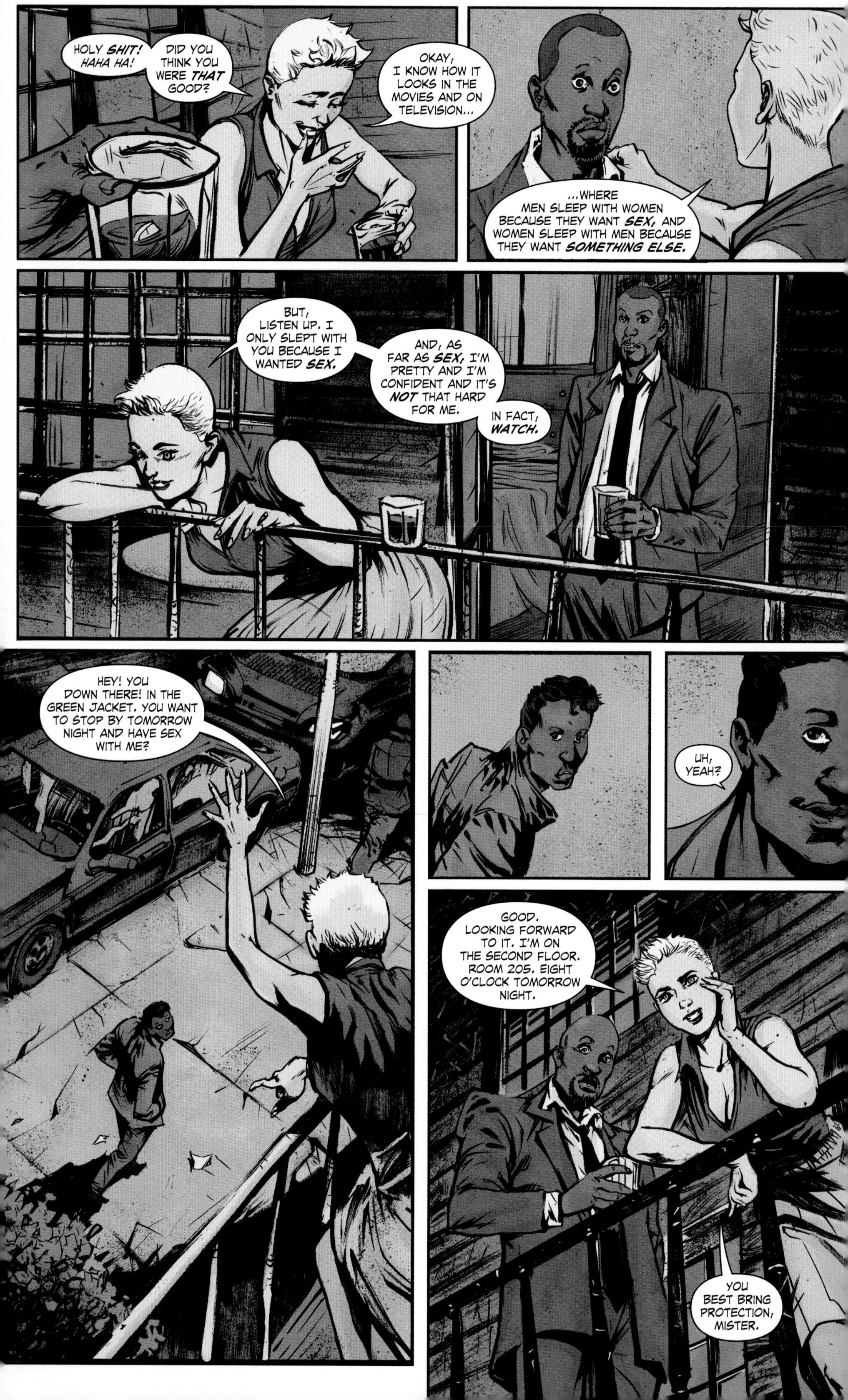
HOLY SHIT! HAHA HA!
DID YOU THINK YOU WERE THAT GOOD?
OKAY, I KNOW HOW IT LOOKS IN THE MOVIES AND ON TELEVISION...
...WHERE MEN SLEEP WITH WOMEN BECAUSE THEY WANT SEX, AND WOMEN SLEEP WITH MEN BECAUSE THEY WANT SOMETHING ELSE.
BUT, LISTEN UP. I ONLY SLEPT WITH YOU BECAUSE I WANTED SEX.
AND, AS FAR AS SEX, I'M PRETTY AND I'M CONFIDENT AND IT'S NOT THAT HARD FOR ME.
IN FACT, WATCH.
HEY! YOU DOWN THERE! IN THE GREEN JACKET. YOU WANT TO STOP BY TOMORROW NIGHT AND HAVE SEX WITH ME?
UH, YEAH?
GOOD. LOOKING FORWARD TO IT. I'M ON THE SECOND FLOOR. ROOM 205. EIGHT O'CLOCK TOMORROW NIGHT.
YOU BEST BRING PROTECTION, MISTER.

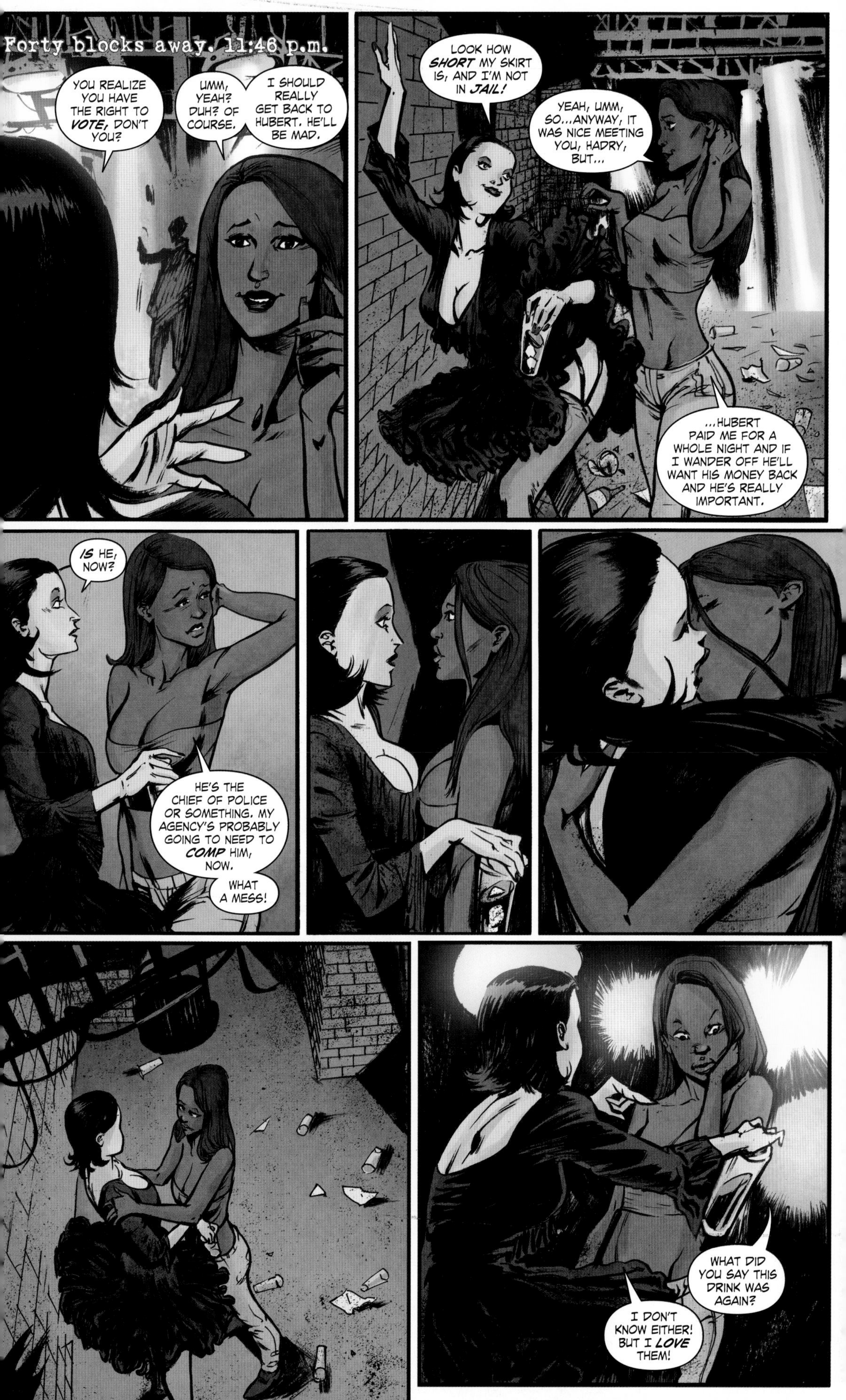

Forty blocks away. 11:46 p.m.
YOU REALIZE YOU HAVE THE RIGHT TO VOTE, DON'T YOU?
UMM, YEAH? DUH? OF COURSE.
I SHOULD REALLY GET BACK TO HUBERT. HE'LL BE MAD.
LOOK HOW SHORT MY SKIRT IS, AND I'M NOT IN JAIL!
YEAH, UMM, SO...ANYWAY, IT WAS NICE MEETING YOU, HADRY, BUT...
...HUBERT PAID ME FOR A WHOLE NIGHT AND IF I WANDER OFF HE'LL WANT HIS MONEY BACK AND HE'S REALLY IMPORTANT.
IS HE, NOW?
HE'S THE CHIEF OF POLICE OR SOMETHING. MY AGENCY'S PROBABLY GOING TO NEED TO COMP HIM, NOW.
WHAT A MESS!
WHAT DID YOU SAY THIS DRINK WAS AGAIN?
I DON'T KNOW EITHER! BUT I LOVE THEM!

Meanwhile.

PRETTY NICE PLACE FOR A POLICE CHIEF.

HONESTLY, I THINK POLICE CHIEFS OF MAJOR CITIES *SHOULD* HAVE MAJOR APARTMENTS TO MATCH.

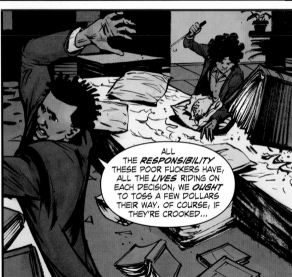

ALL THE *RESPONSIBILITY* THESE POOR FUCKERS HAVE, ALL THE *LIVES* RIDING ON EACH DECISION, WE *OUGHT* TO TOSS A FEW DOLLARS THEIR WAY. OF COURSE, IF THEY'RE CROOKED...

...WE SHOULD TOSS THEM TO THE LIONS.

12:07 a.m.

WHERE'S YOUR PET?

LEO'S BUSY ELSEWHERE. WE'RE ACTIVE PEOPLE. BUT IF YOU THINK YOU'RE ANY SAFER WITHOUT HIM KEEPING WATCH, YOU'RE IN FOR A DISAPPOINTMENT.

I'M A COP IN DETROIT. I'M *ALWAYS* IN FOR A DISAPPOINTMENT.

BUT, TO BUSINESS. *IF* I DO WHAT YOU'RE ASKING, IF I GIVE YOU ALL THIS INFORMATION YOU'RE ASKING FOR, AND ON A CONTINUING BASIS LIKE YOU'RE SAYING, WHAT'S IN IT FOR ME?

AND PLEASE DON'T SAY *MONEY*. AND DON'T SAY SEX.

WELL SHIT, WHAT *DO* YOU WANT ME TO SAY?

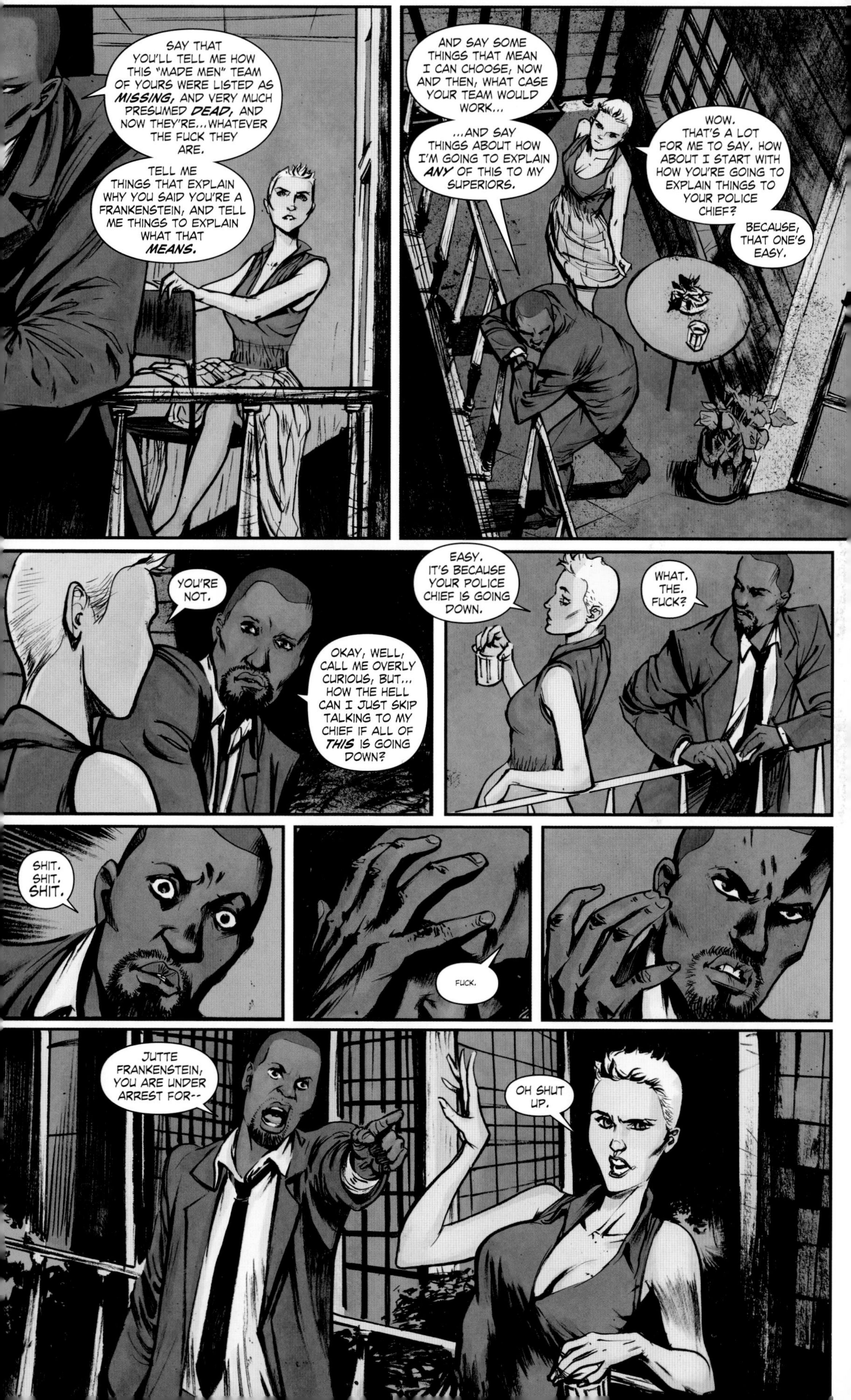
SAY THAT YOU'LL TELL ME HOW THIS "MADE MEN" TEAM OF YOURS WERE LISTED AS MISSING, AND VERY MUCH PRESUMED DEAD, AND NOW THEY'RE...WHATEVER THE FUCK THEY ARE.
TELL ME THINGS THAT EXPLAIN WHY YOU SAID YOU'RE A FRANKENSTEIN, AND TELL ME THINGS TO EXPLAIN WHAT THAT MEANS.
AND SAY SOME THINGS THAT MEAN I CAN CHOOSE, NOW AND THEN, WHAT CASE YOUR TEAM WOULD WORK...
...AND SAY THINGS ABOUT HOW I'M GOING TO EXPLAIN ANY OF THIS TO MY SUPERIORS.
WOW. THAT'S A LOT FOR ME TO SAY. HOW ABOUT I START WITH HOW YOU'RE GOING TO EXPLAIN THINGS TO YOUR POLICE CHIEF?
BECAUSE, THAT ONE'S EASY.
YOU'RE NOT.
OKAY, WELL, CALL ME OVERLY CURIOUS, BUT... HOW THE HELL CAN I JUST SKIP TALKING TO MY CHIEF IF ALL OF THIS IS GOING DOWN?
EASY. IT'S BECAUSE YOUR POLICE CHIEF IS GOING DOWN.
WHAT. THE. FUCK?
SHIT. SHIT. SHIT.
FUCK.
JUTTE FRANKENSTEIN, YOU ARE UNDER ARREST FOR--
OH SHUT UP.

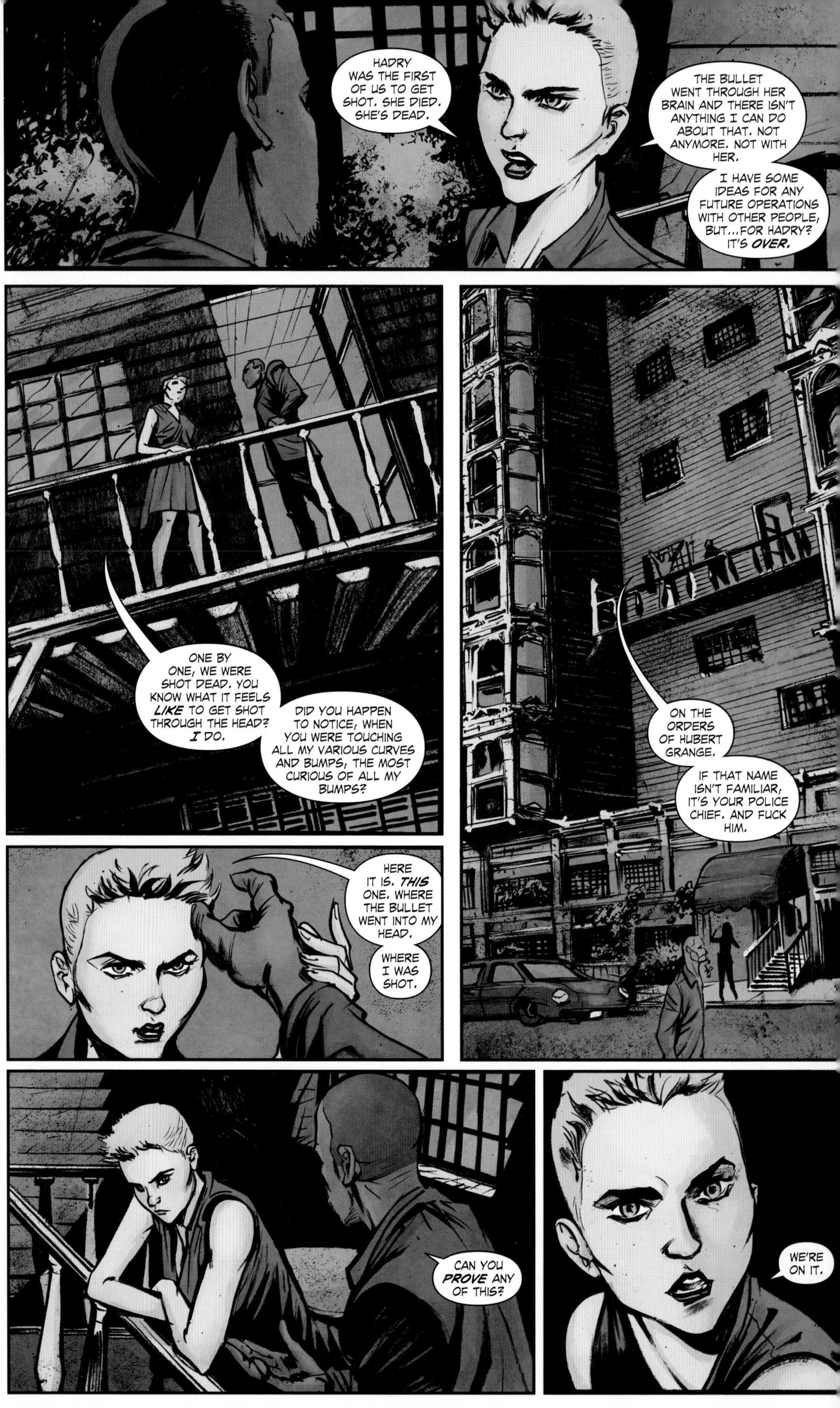
HADRY WAS THE FIRST OF US TO GET SHOT. SHE DIED. SHE'S DEAD.
THE BULLET WENT THROUGH HER BRAIN AND THERE ISN'T ANYTHING I CAN DO ABOUT THAT. NOT ANYMORE. NOT WITH HER.
I HAVE SOME IDEAS FOR ANY FUTURE OPERATIONS WITH OTHER PEOPLE, BUT...FOR HADRY? IT'S *OVER.*
ONE BY ONE, WE WERE SHOT DEAD. YOU KNOW WHAT IT FEELS *LIKE* TO GET SHOT THROUGH THE HEAD? *I* DO.
DID YOU HAPPEN TO NOTICE, WHEN YOU WERE TOUCHING ALL MY VARIOUS CURVES AND BUMPS, THE MOST CURIOUS OF ALL MY BUMPS?
HERE IT IS. *THIS* ONE. WHERE THE BULLET WENT INTO MY HEAD.
WHERE I WAS SHOT.
ON THE ORDERS OF HUBERT GRANGE.
IF THAT NAME ISN'T FAMILIAR, IT'S YOUR POLICE CHIEF. AND FUCK HIM.
CAN YOU *PROVE* ANY OF THIS?
WE'RE ON IT.

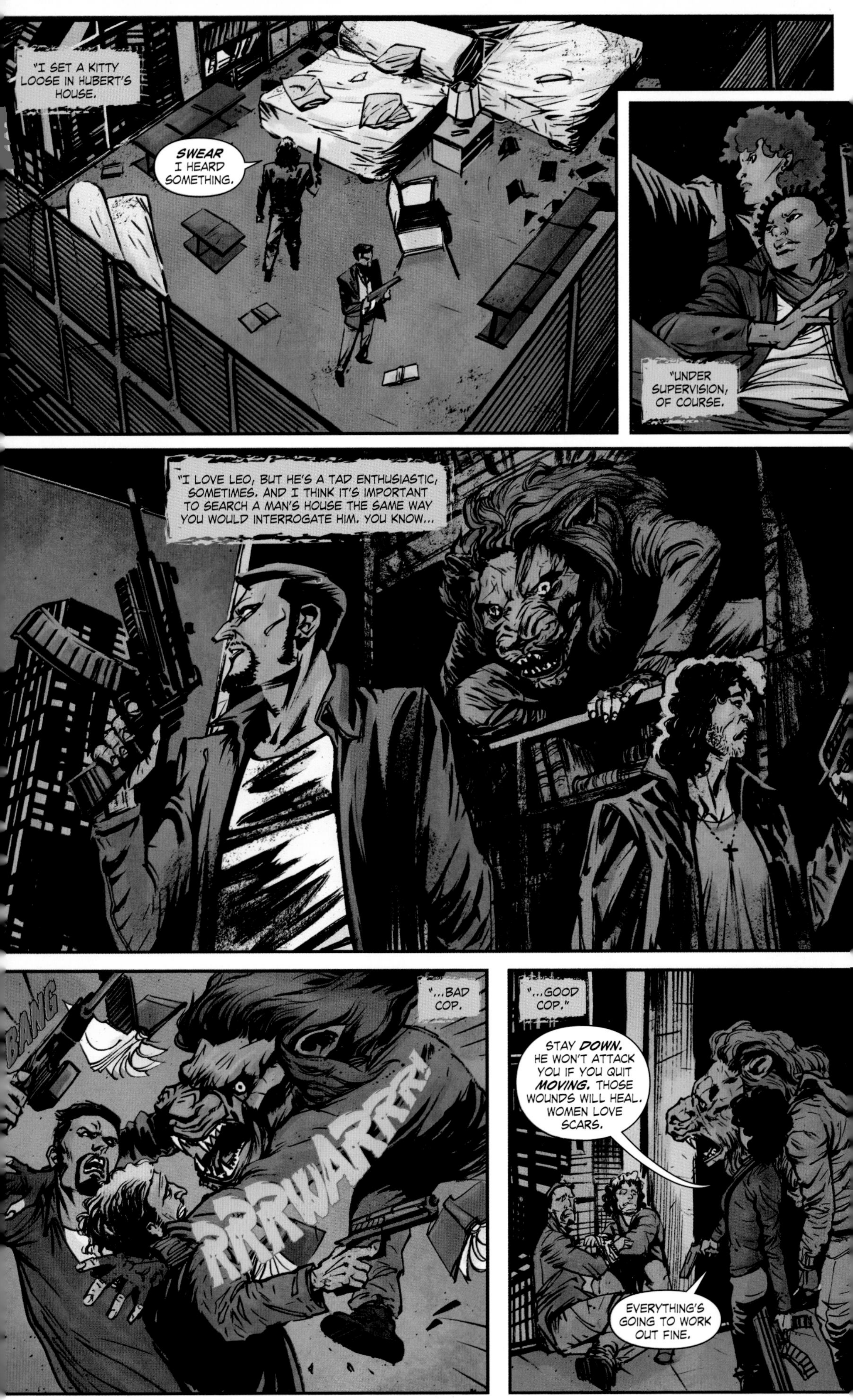
"I SET A KITTY LOOSE IN HUBERT'S HOUSE.
SWEAR I HEARD SOMETHING.
"UNDER SUPERVISION, OF COURSE.
"I LOVE LEO, BUT HE'S A TAD ENTHUSIASTIC, SOMETIMES. AND I THINK IT'S IMPORTANT TO SEARCH A MAN'S HOUSE THE SAME WAY YOU WOULD INTERROGATE HIM. YOU KNOW...
BANG
"...BAD COP.
RRRWARRR!
"...GOOD COP."
STAY DOWN. HE WON'T ATTACK YOU IF YOU QUIT MOVING. THOSE WOUNDS WILL HEAL. WOMEN LOVE SCARS.
EVERYTHING'S GOING TO WORK OUT FINE.

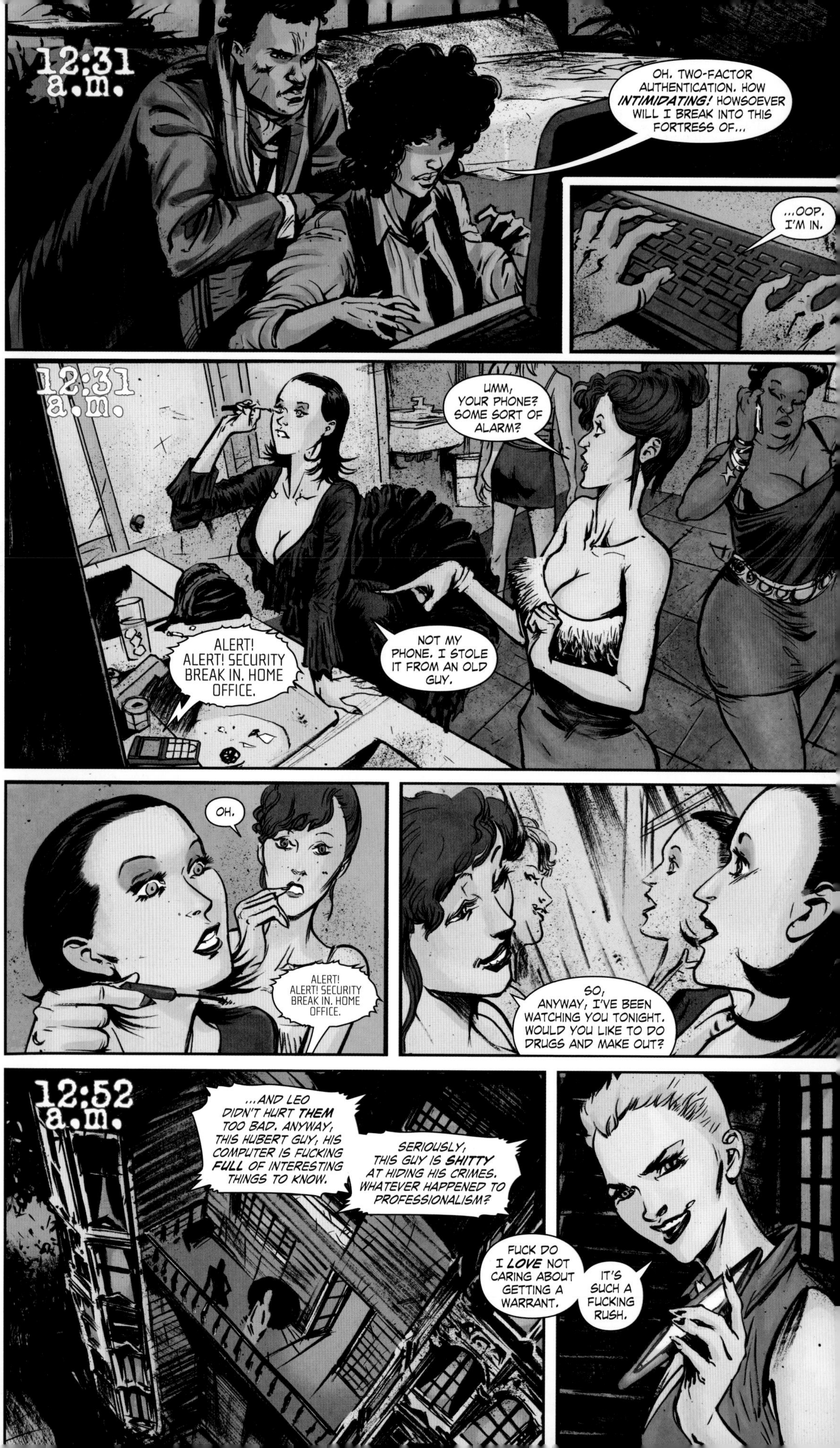
12:31 a.m.
OH. TWO-FACTOR AUTHENTICATION. HOW *INTIMIDATING!* HOWSOEVER WILL I BREAK INTO THIS FORTRESS OF...
...OOP. I'M IN.
12:31 a.m.
UMM, YOUR PHONE? SOME SORT OF ALARM?
ALERT! ALERT! SECURITY BREAK IN. HOME OFFICE.
NOT MY PHONE. I STOLE IT FROM AN OLD GUY.
OH.
ALERT! ALERT! SECURITY BREAK IN. HOME OFFICE.
SO, ANYWAY, I'VE BEEN WATCHING YOU TONIGHT. WOULD YOU LIKE TO DO DRUGS AND MAKE OUT?
12:52 a.m.
...AND LEO DIDN'T HURT **THEM** TOO BAD. ANYWAY, THIS HUBERT GUY, HIS COMPUTER IS FUCKING **FULL** OF INTERESTING THINGS TO KNOW.
SERIOUSLY, THIS GUY IS **SHITTY** AT HIDING HIS CRIMES. WHATEVER HAPPENED TO PROFESSIONALISM?
FUCK DO I **LOVE** NOT CARING ABOUT GETTING A WARRANT.
IT'S SUCH A FUCKING RUSH.

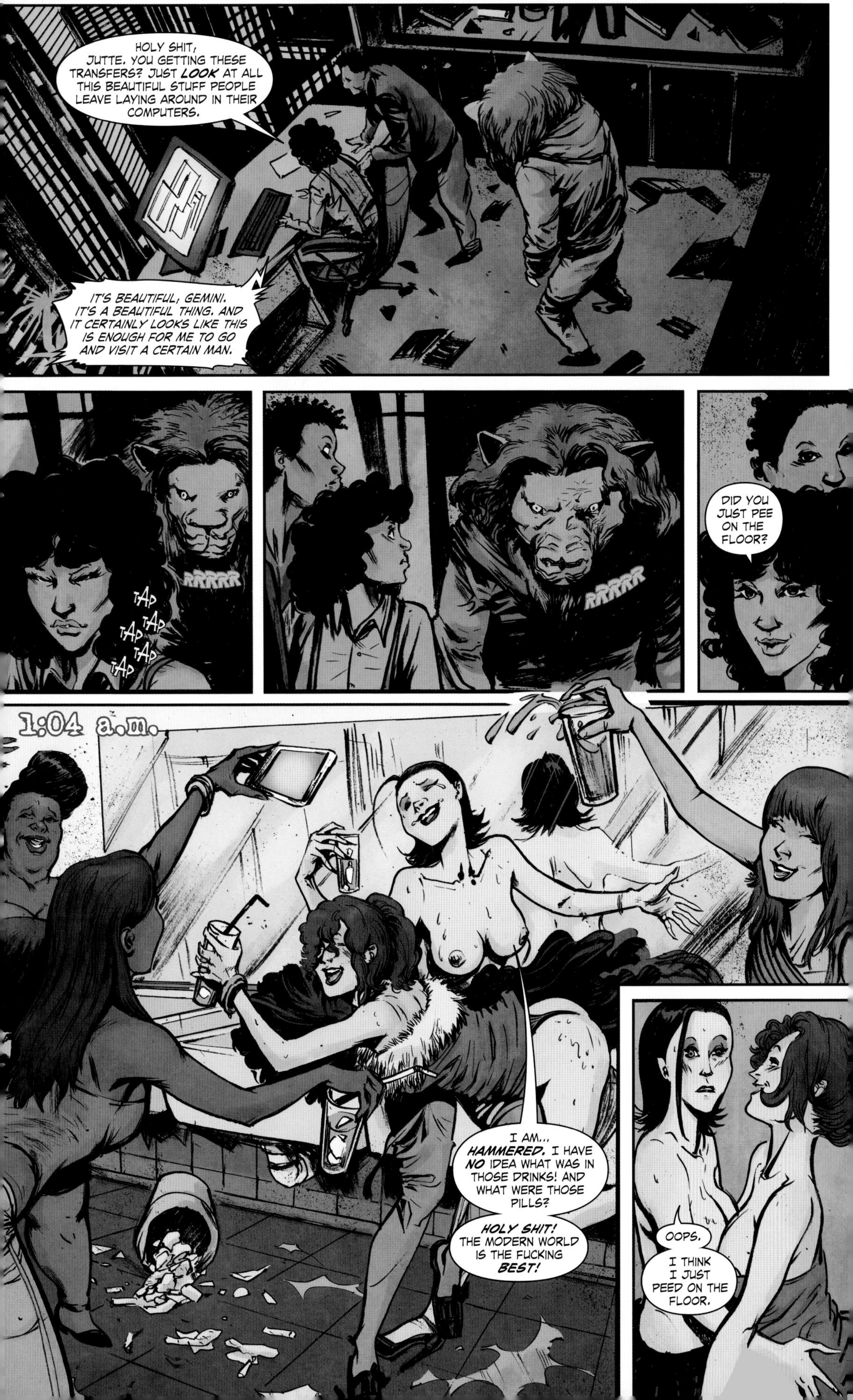
HOLY SHIT, JUTTE. YOU GETTING THESE TRANSFERS? JUST LOOK AT ALL THIS BEAUTIFUL STUFF PEOPLE LEAVE LAYING AROUND IN THEIR COMPUTERS.
IT'S BEAUTIFUL, GEMINI. IT'S A BEAUTIFUL THING. AND IT CERTAINLY LOOKS LIKE THIS IS ENOUGH FOR ME TO GO AND VISIT A CERTAIN MAN.
RRRRR
TAP TAP TAP TAP TAP
RRRRR
DID YOU JUST PEE ON THE FLOOR?
1:04 a.m.
I AM... HAMMERED. I HAVE NO IDEA WHAT WAS IN THOSE DRINKS! AND WHAT WERE THOSE PILLS?
HOLY SHIT! THE MODERN WORLD IS THE FUCKING BEST!
OOPS.
I THINK I JUST PEED ON THE FLOOR.

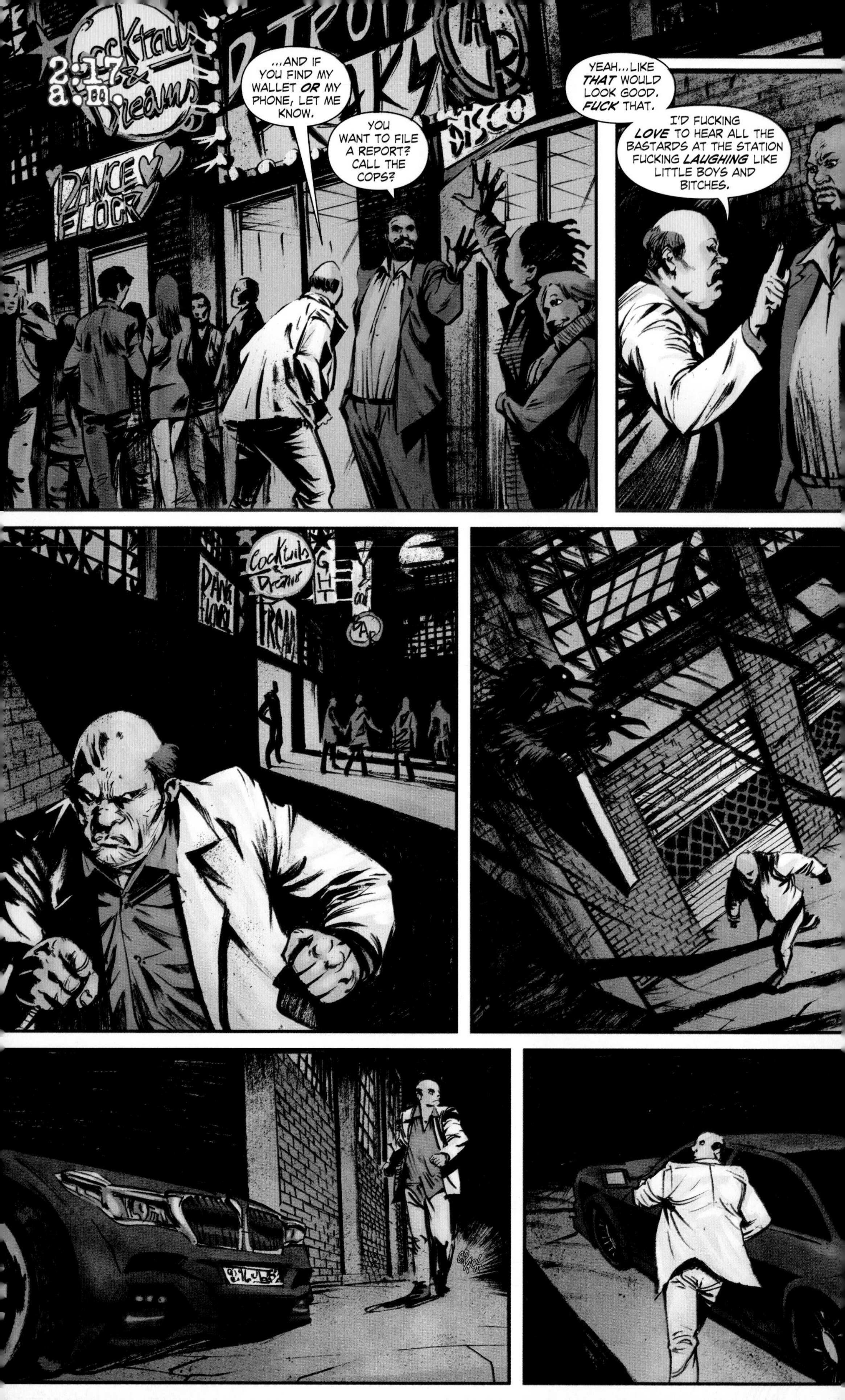
2:17 a.m.
Cocktails & Dreams
DANCE FLOOR
DISCO
...AND IF YOU FIND MY WALLET OR MY PHONE, LET ME KNOW.
YOU WANT TO FILE A REPORT? CALL THE COPS?
YEAH...LIKE THAT WOULD LOOK GOOD. FUCK THAT.
I'D FUCKING LOVE TO HEAR ALL THE BASTARDS AT THE STATION FUCKING LAUGHING LIKE LITTLE BOYS AND BITCHES.
CRACK

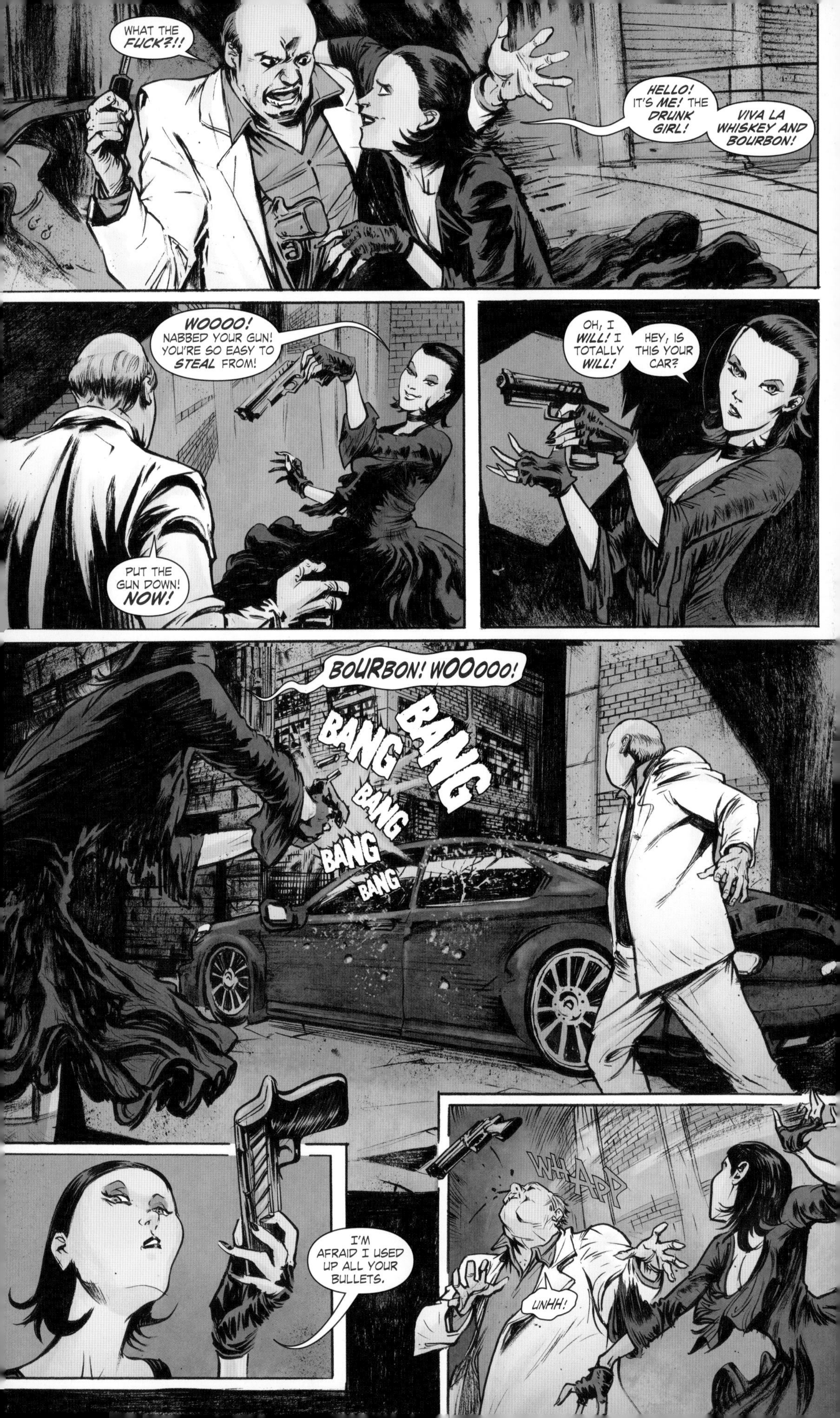
WHAT THE FUCK?!!
HELLO! IT'S ME! THE DRUNK GIRL!
VIVA LA WHISKEY AND BOURBON!
WOOOO! NABBED YOUR GUN! YOU'RE SO EASY TO STEAL FROM!
PUT THE GUN DOWN! NOW!
OH, I WILL! I TOTALLY WILL!
HEY, IS THIS YOUR CAR?
BOURBON! WOOOOO!
BANG
BANG
BANG
BANG
BANG
BANG
I'M AFRAID I USED UP ALL YOUR BULLETS.
WHAPP
UNHH!

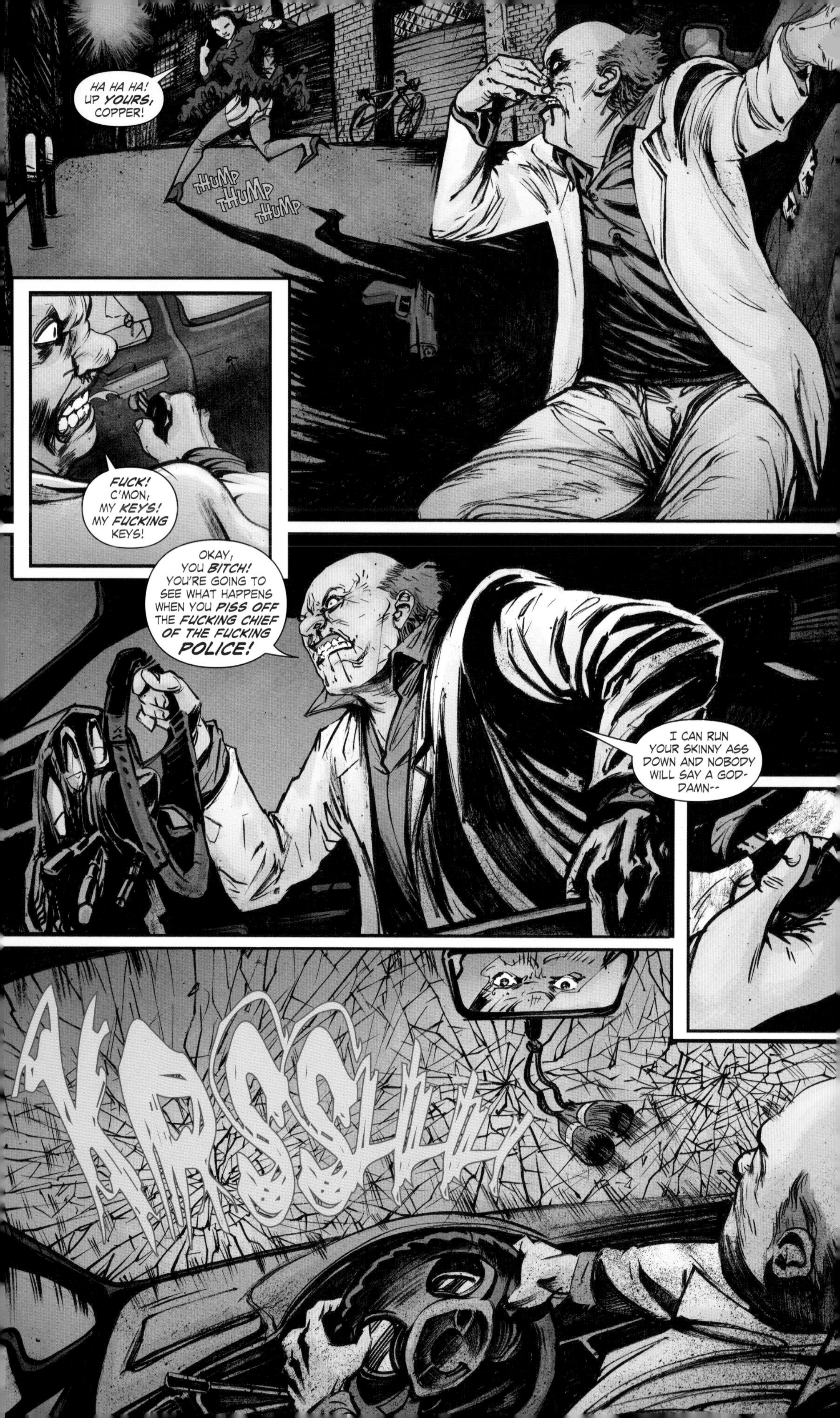
HA HA HA! UP YOURS, COPPER!
THUMP THUMP THUMP
FUCK! C'MON, MY KEYS! MY FUCKING KEYS!
OKAY, YOU BITCH! YOU'RE GOING TO SEE WHAT HAPPENS WHEN YOU PISS OFF THE FUCKING CHIEF OF THE FUCKING POLICE!
I CAN RUN YOUR SKINNY ASS DOWN AND NOBODY WILL SAY A GOD-DAMN--
KRSSHH

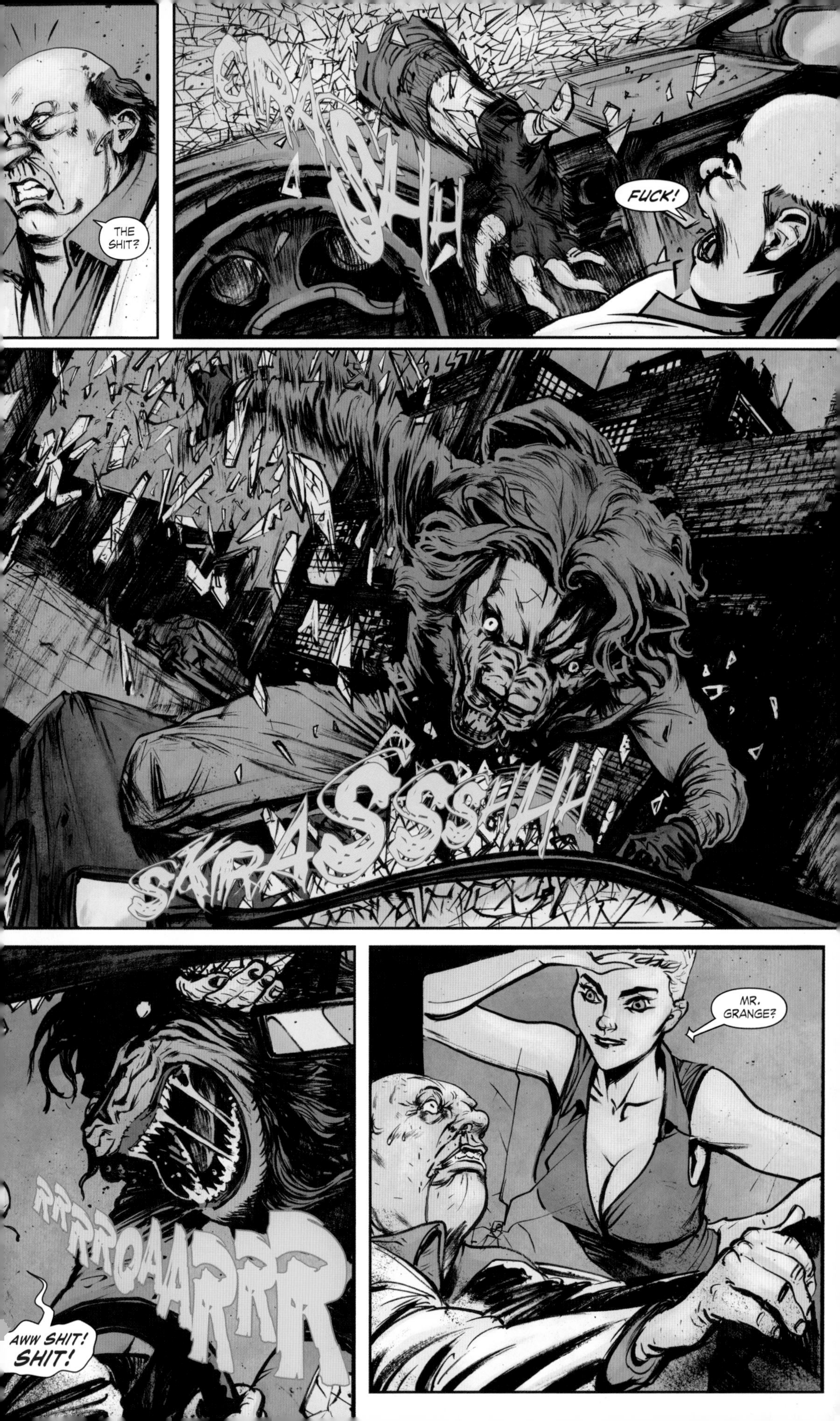
THE SHIT?
CRASHH
FUCK!
SKRASSSHHH
RRRROAARRR
AWW SHIT! SHIT!
MR. GRANGE?

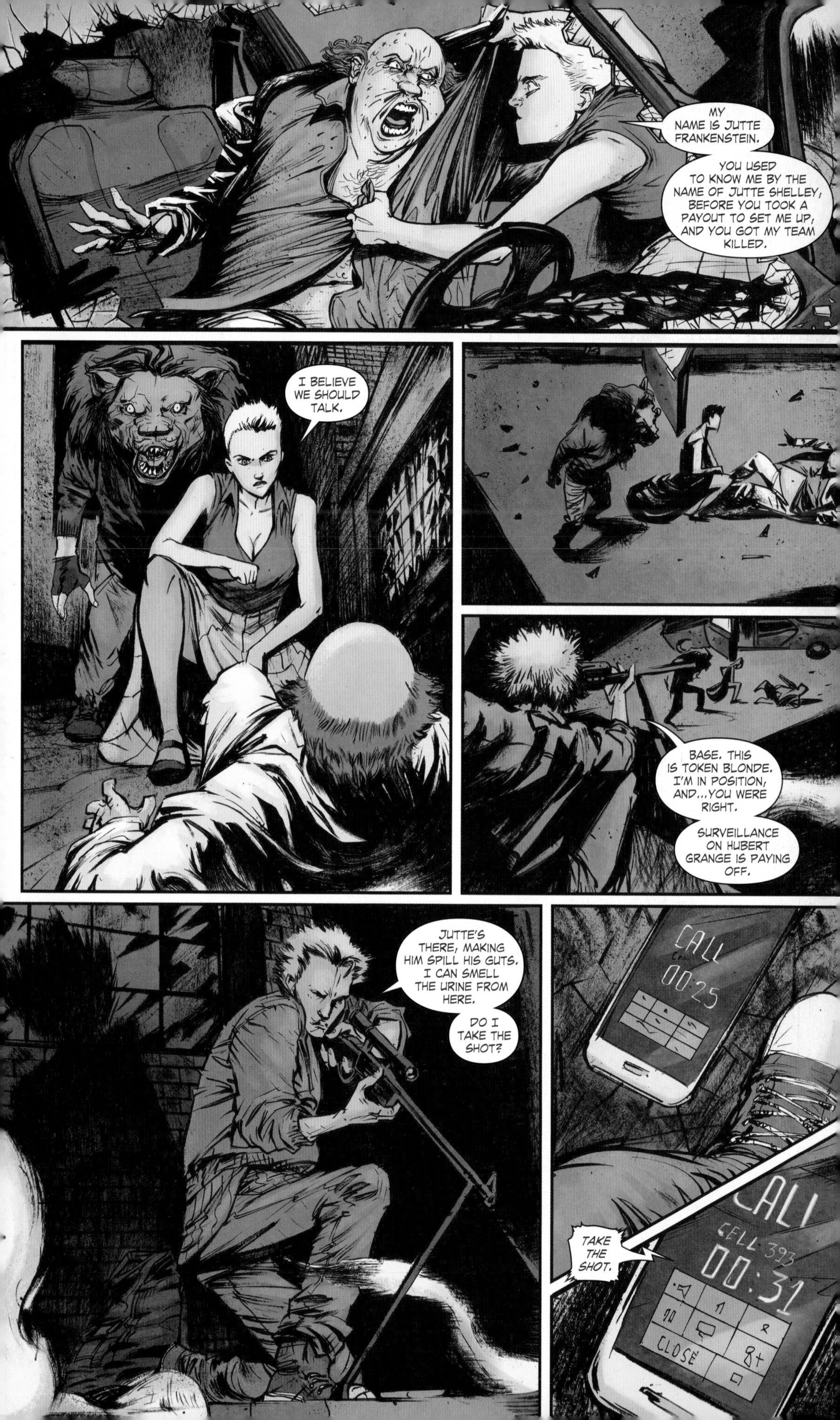

MY NAME IS JUTTE FRANKENSTEIN.
YOU USED TO KNOW ME BY THE NAME OF JUTTE SHELLEY, BEFORE YOU TOOK A PAYOUT TO SET ME UP, AND YOU GOT MY TEAM KILLED.
I BELIEVE WE SHOULD TALK.
BASE. THIS IS TOKEN BLONDE. I'M IN POSITION, AND...YOU WERE RIGHT.
SURVEILLANCE ON HUBERT GRANGE IS PAYING OFF.
JUTTE'S THERE, MAKING HIM SPILL HIS GUTS. I CAN SMELL THE URINE FROM HERE.
DO I TAKE THE SHOT?
CALL
00:25
CALL
CELL 393
00:31
CLOSE
TAKE THE SHOT.

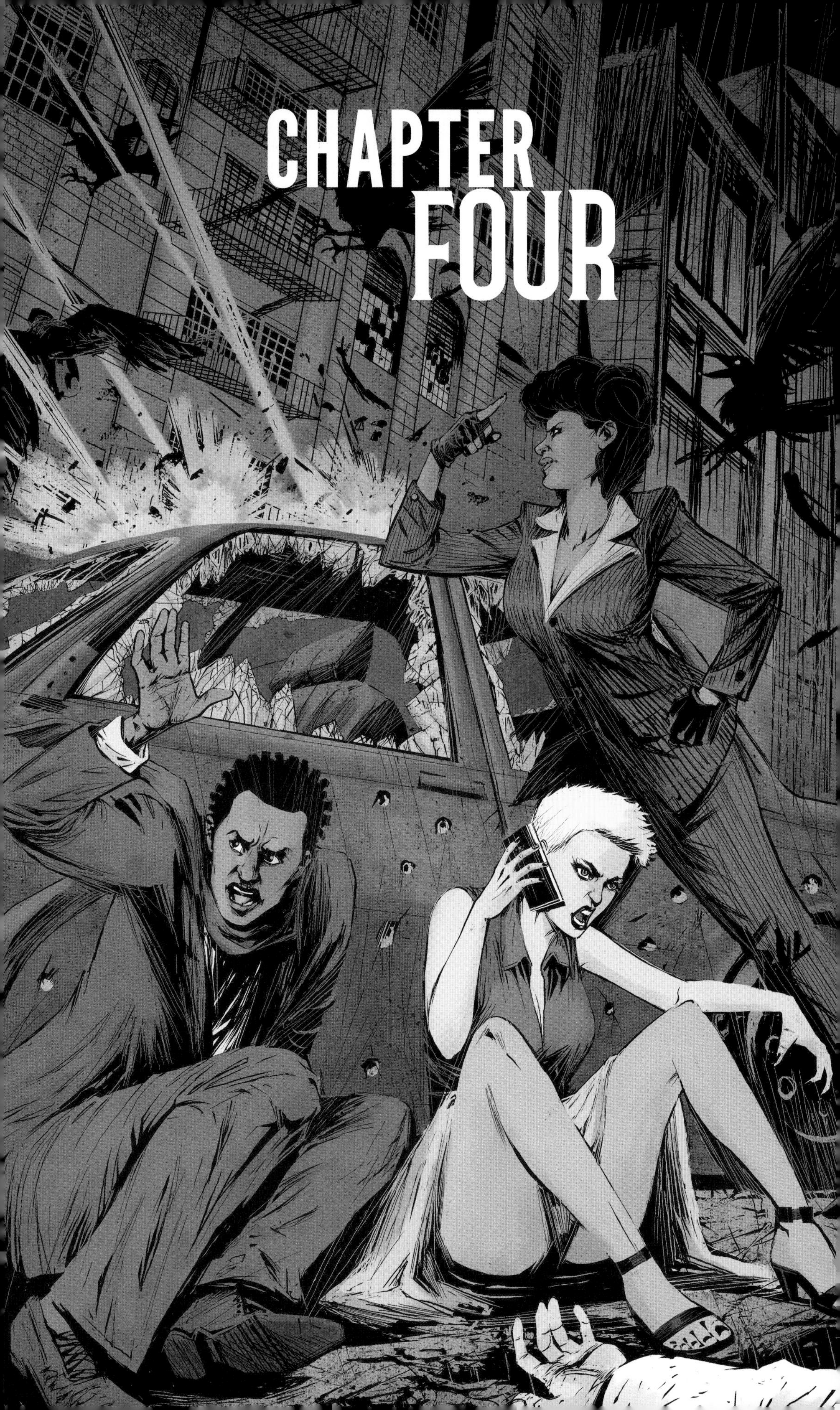
CHAPTER
FOUR

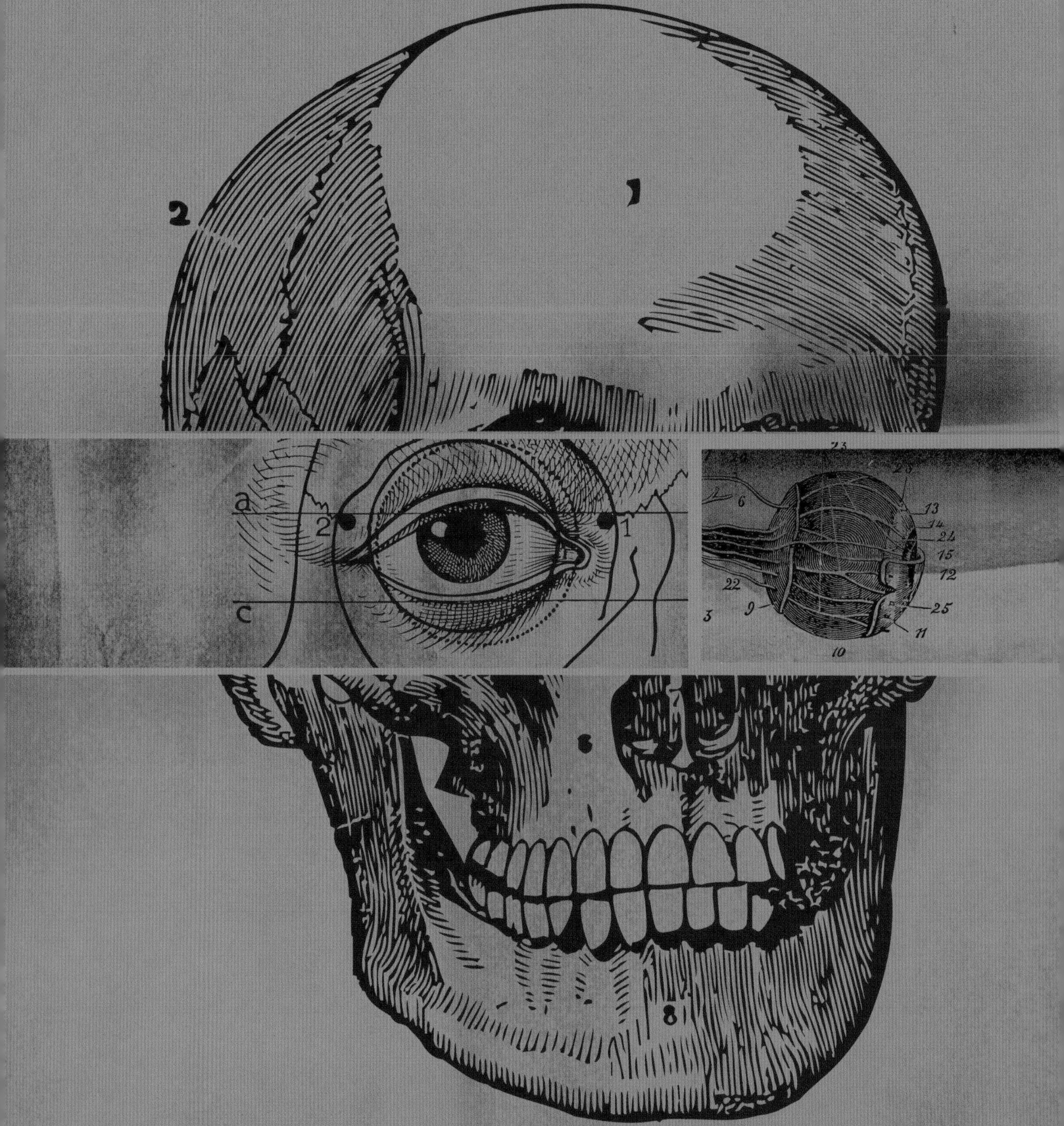
2
1
a
2
1
c
6
13
14
24
15
12
22
9
3
25
11
10
8

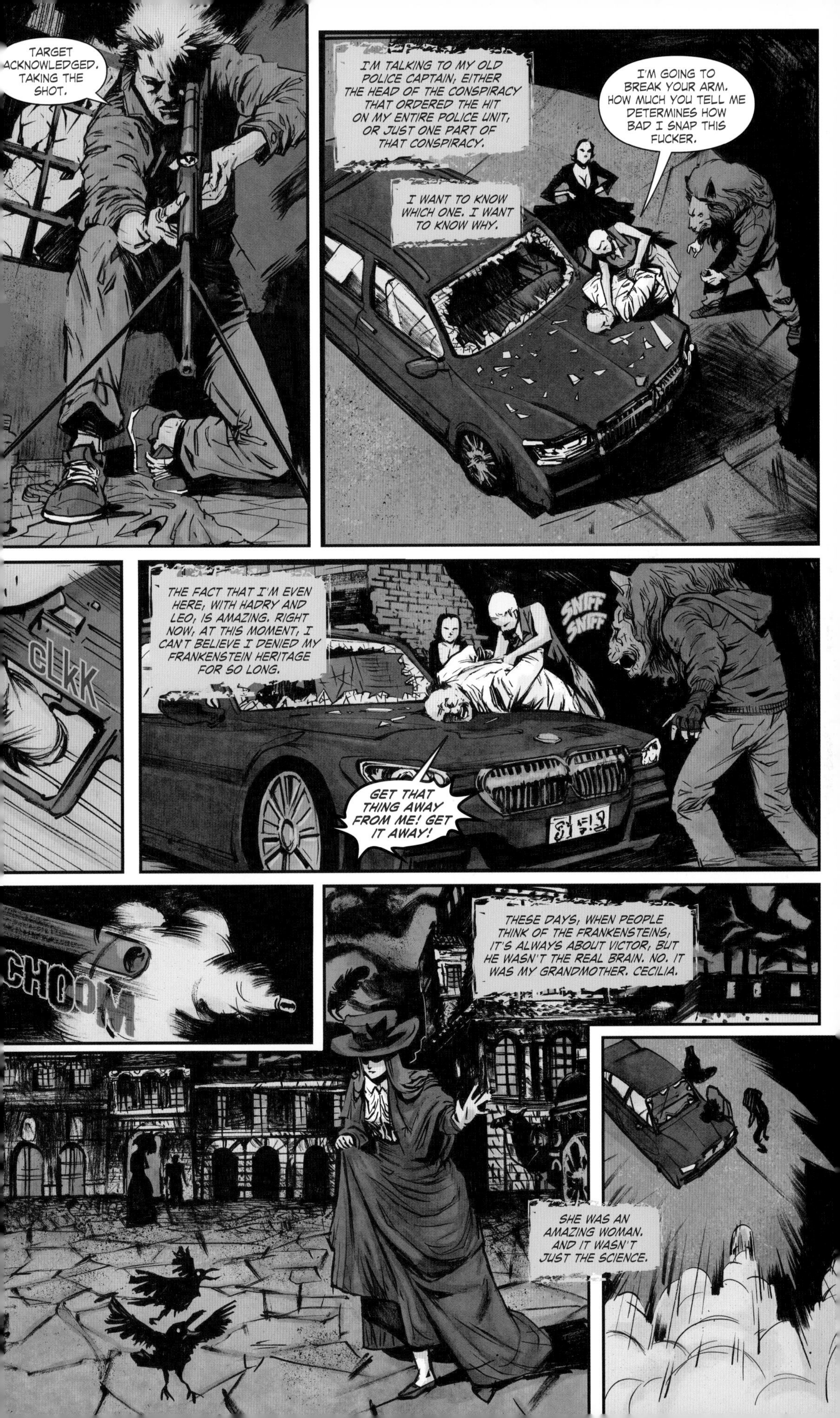
TARGET ACKNOWLEDGED. TAKING THE SHOT.
I'M TALKING TO MY OLD POLICE CAPTAIN; EITHER THE HEAD OF THE CONSPIRACY THAT ORDERED THE HIT ON MY ENTIRE POLICE UNIT, OR JUST ONE PART OF THAT CONSPIRACY.
I WANT TO KNOW WHICH ONE. I WANT TO KNOW WHY.
I'M GOING TO BREAK YOUR ARM. HOW MUCH YOU TELL ME DETERMINES HOW BAD I SNAP THIS FUCKER.
cLkK
THE FACT THAT I'M EVEN HERE; WITH HADRY AND LEO; IS AMAZING. RIGHT NOW, AT THIS MOMENT, I CAN'T BELIEVE I DENIED MY FRANKENSTEIN HERITAGE FOR SO LONG.
SNIFF SNIFF
GET THAT THING AWAY FROM ME! GET IT AWAY!
CHOOM
THESE DAYS, WHEN PEOPLE THINK OF THE FRANKENSTEINS, IT'S ALWAYS ABOUT VICTOR, BUT HE WASN'T THE REAL BRAIN. NO. IT WAS MY GRANDMOTHER. CECILIA.
SHE WAS AN AMAZING WOMAN. AND IT WASN'T JUST THE SCIENCE.

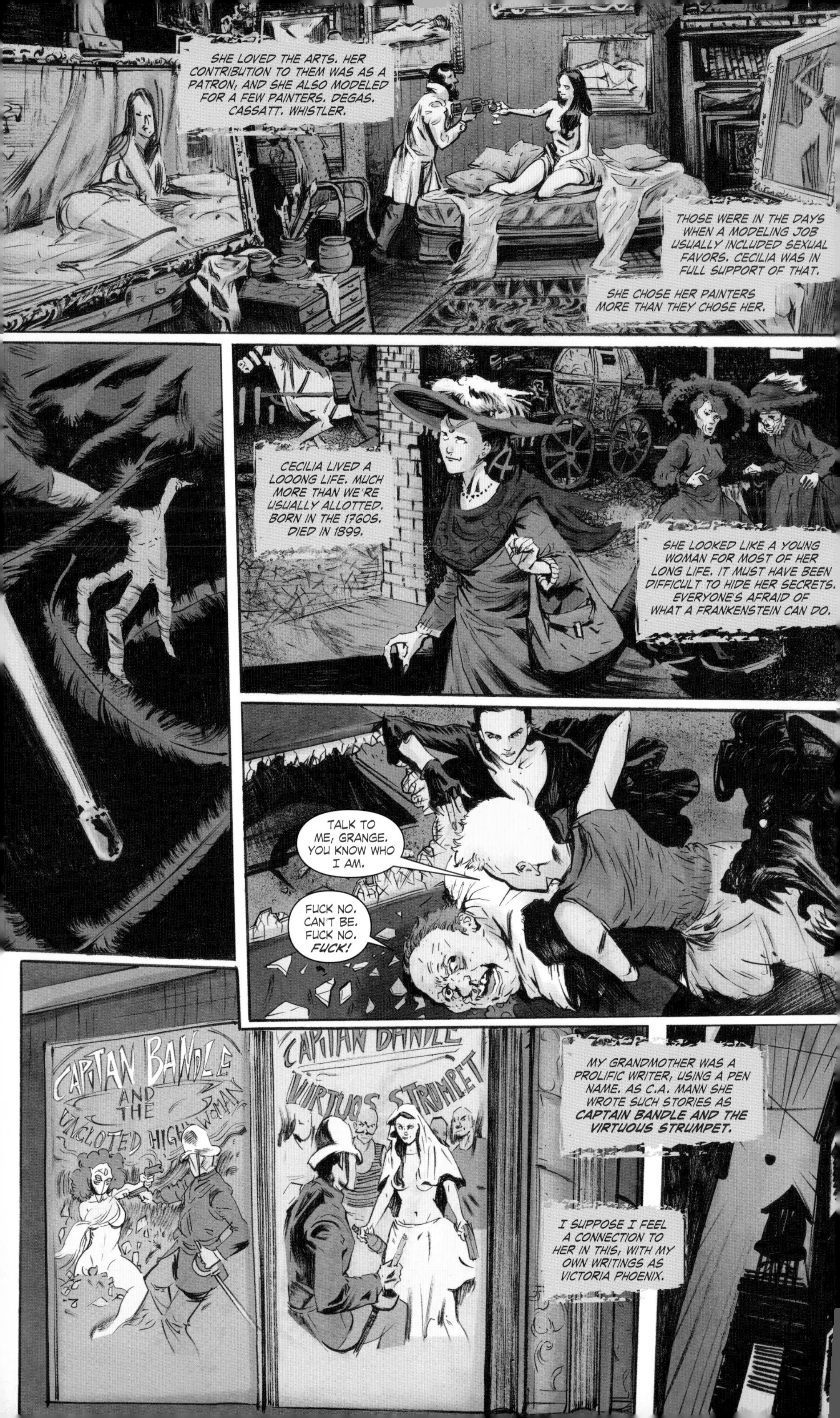
SHE LOVED THE ARTS. HER CONTRIBUTION TO THEM WAS AS A PATRON, AND SHE ALSO MODELED FOR A FEW PAINTERS. DEGAS. CASSATT. WHISTLER.
THOSE WERE IN THE DAYS WHEN A MODELING JOB USUALLY INCLUDED SEXUAL FAVORS. CECILIA WAS IN FULL SUPPORT OF THAT.
SHE CHOSE HER PAINTERS MORE THAN THEY CHOSE HER.
CECILIA LIVED A LOOONG LIFE. MUCH MORE THAN WE'RE USUALLY ALLOTTED. BORN IN THE 1760S. DIED IN 1899.
SHE LOOKED LIKE A YOUNG WOMAN FOR MOST OF HER LONG LIFE. IT MUST HAVE BEEN DIFFICULT TO HIDE HER SECRETS. EVERYONE'S AFRAID OF WHAT A FRANKENSTEIN CAN DO.
TALK TO ME, GRANGE. YOU KNOW WHO I AM.
FUCK NO. CAN'T BE. FUCK NO. FUCK!
CAPTAN BANDLE AND THE UNCLOTED HIGHWOMAN
CAPTAN BANDLE VIRTUOS STRUMPET
MY GRANDMOTHER WAS A PROLIFIC WRITER, USING A PEN NAME. AS C.A. MANN SHE WROTE SUCH STORIES AS CAPTAIN BANDLE AND THE VIRTUOUS STRUMPET.
I SUPPOSE I FEEL A CONNECTION TO HER IN THIS, WITH MY OWN WRITINGS AS VICTORIA PHOENIX.

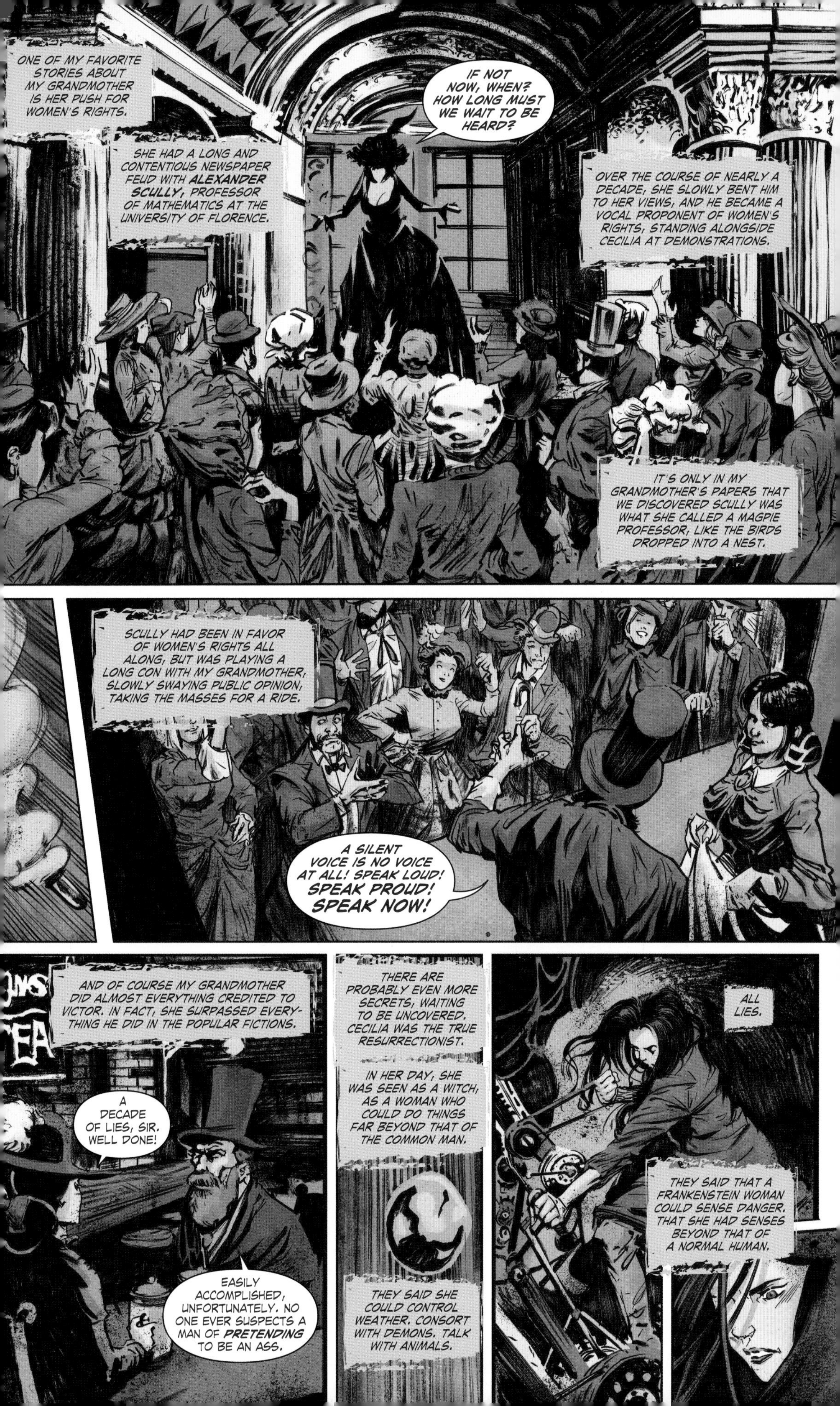
ONE OF MY FAVORITE STORIES ABOUT MY GRANDMOTHER IS HER PUSH FOR WOMEN'S RIGHTS.
SHE HAD A LONG AND CONTENTIOUS NEWSPAPER FEUD WITH ALEXANDER SCULLY, PROFESSOR OF MATHEMATICS AT THE UNIVERSITY OF FLORENCE.
IF NOT NOW, WHEN? HOW LONG MUST WE WAIT TO BE HEARD?
OVER THE COURSE OF NEARLY A DECADE, SHE SLOWLY BENT HIM TO HER VIEWS, AND HE BECAME A VOCAL PROPONENT OF WOMEN'S RIGHTS, STANDING ALONGSIDE CECILIA AT DEMONSTRATIONS.
IT'S ONLY IN MY GRANDMOTHER'S PAPERS THAT WE DISCOVERED SCULLY WAS WHAT SHE CALLED A MAGPIE PROFESSOR, LIKE THE BIRDS DROPPED INTO A NEST.
SCULLY HAD BEEN IN FAVOR OF WOMEN'S RIGHTS ALL ALONG, BUT WAS PLAYING A LONG CON WITH MY GRANDMOTHER, SLOWLY SWAYING PUBLIC OPINION, TAKING THE MASSES FOR A RIDE.
A SILENT VOICE IS NO VOICE AT ALL! SPEAK LOUD! SPEAK PROUD! SPEAK NOW!
AND OF COURSE MY GRANDMOTHER DID ALMOST EVERYTHING CREDITED TO VICTOR. IN FACT, SHE SURPASSED EVERY-THING HE DID IN THE POPULAR FICTIONS.
A DECADE OF LIES, SIR. WELL DONE!
EASILY ACCOMPLISHED, UNFORTUNATELY. NO ONE EVER SUSPECTS A MAN OF PRETENDING TO BE AN ASS.
THERE ARE PROBABLY EVEN MORE SECRETS, WAITING TO BE UNCOVERED. CECILIA WAS THE TRUE RESURRECTIONIST.
IN HER DAY, SHE WAS SEEN AS A WITCH, AS A WOMAN WHO COULD DO THINGS FAR BEYOND THAT OF THE COMMON MAN.
THEY SAID SHE COULD CONTROL WEATHER. CONSORT WITH DEMONS. TALK WITH ANIMALS.
ALL LIES.
THEY SAID THAT A FRANKENSTEIN WOMAN COULD SENSE DANGER. THAT SHE HAD SENSES BEYOND THAT OF A NORMAL HUMAN.

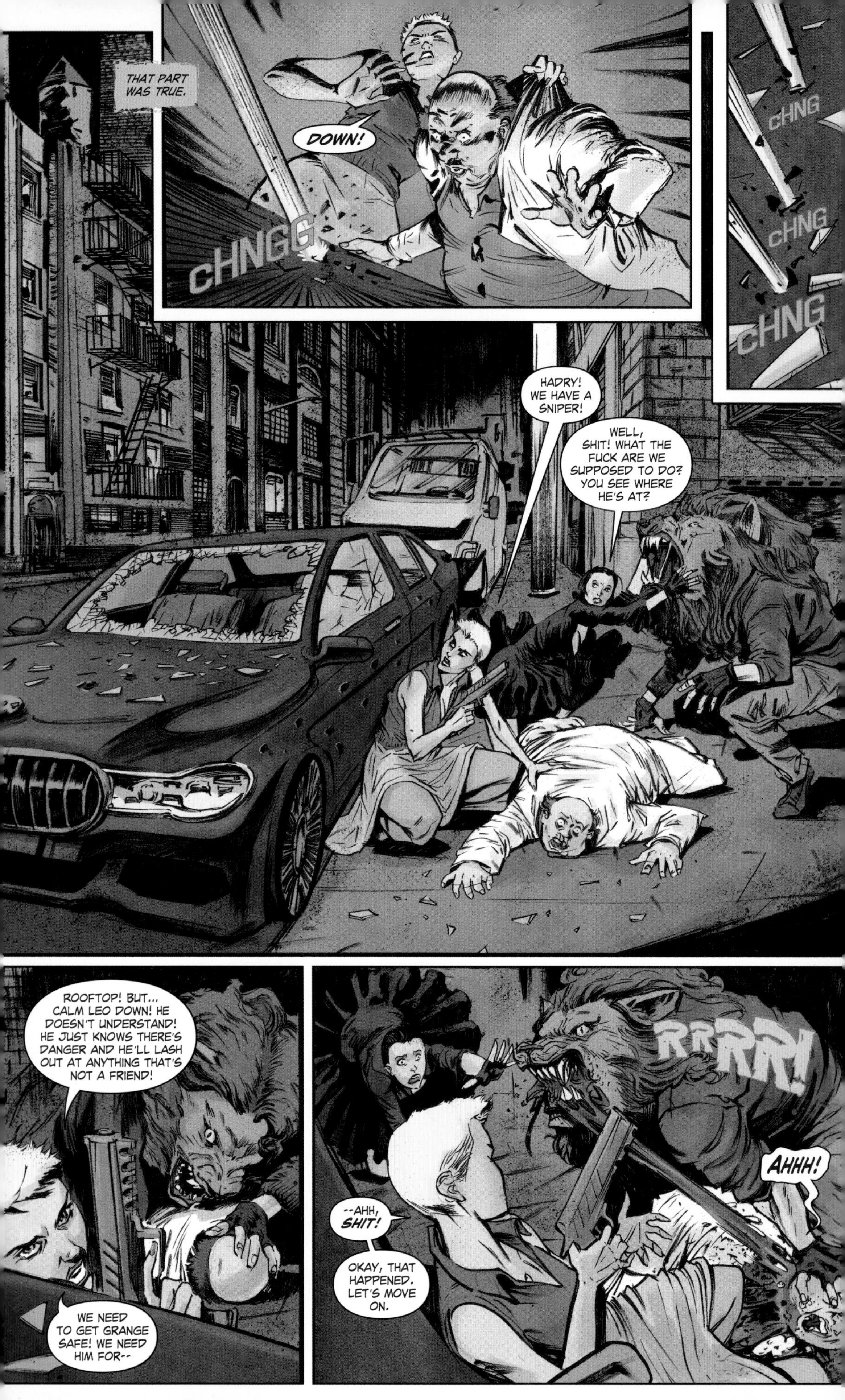
THAT PART WAS TRUE.
DOWN!
cHNGG
cHNG
cHNG
cHNG
HADRY! WE HAVE A SNIPER!
WELL, SHIT! WHAT THE FUCK ARE WE SUPPOSED TO DO? YOU SEE WHERE HE'S AT?
ROOFTOP! BUT... CALM LEO DOWN! HE DOESN'T UNDERSTAND! HE JUST KNOWS THERE'S DANGER AND HE'LL LASH OUT AT ANYTHING THAT'S NOT A FRIEND!
WE NEED TO GET GRANGE SAFE! WE NEED HIM FOR--
RRRR!
AHHH!
--AHH, SHIT!
OKAY, THAT HAPPENED. LET'S MOVE ON.

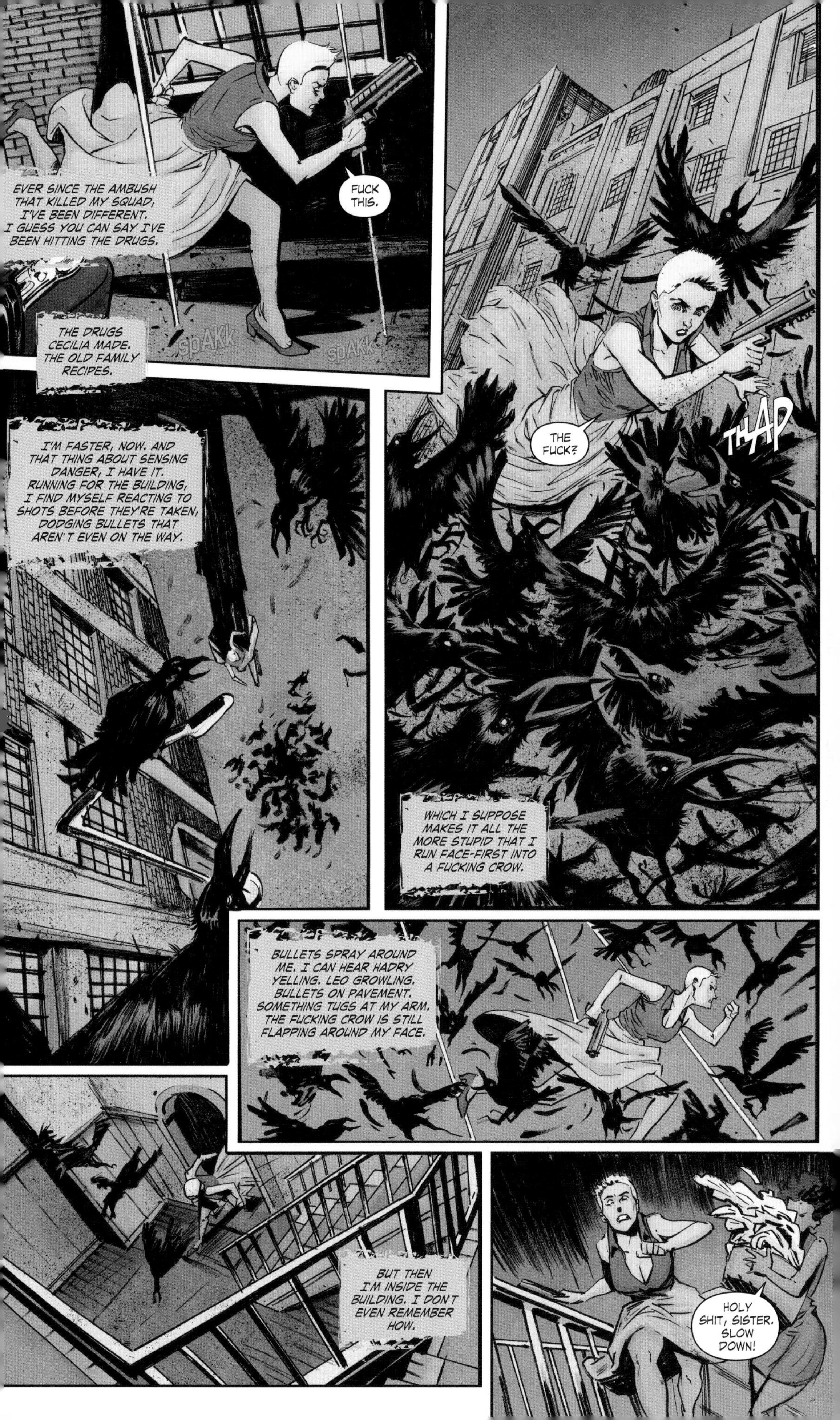
EVER SINCE THE AMBUSH THAT KILLED MY SQUAD, I'VE BEEN DIFFERENT. I GUESS YOU CAN SAY I'VE BEEN HITTING THE DRUGS.
FUCK THIS.
THE DRUGS CECILIA MADE. THE OLD FAMILY RECIPES.
spAKk
spAKk
THE FUCK?
THAP
I'M FASTER, NOW. AND THAT THING ABOUT SENSING DANGER, I HAVE IT. RUNNING FOR THE BUILDING, I FIND MYSELF REACTING TO SHOTS BEFORE THEY'RE TAKEN; DODGING BULLETS THAT AREN'T EVEN ON THE WAY.
WHICH I SUPPOSE MAKES IT ALL THE MORE STUPID THAT I RUN FACE-FIRST INTO A FUCKING CROW.
BULLETS SPRAY AROUND ME. I CAN HEAR HADRY YELLING. LEO GROWLING. BULLETS ON PAVEMENT. SOMETHING TUGS AT MY ARM. THE FUCKING CROW IS STILL FLAPPING AROUND MY FACE.
BUT THEN I'M INSIDE THE BUILDING. I DON'T EVEN REMEMBER HOW.
HOLY SHIT, SISTER. SLOW DOWN!

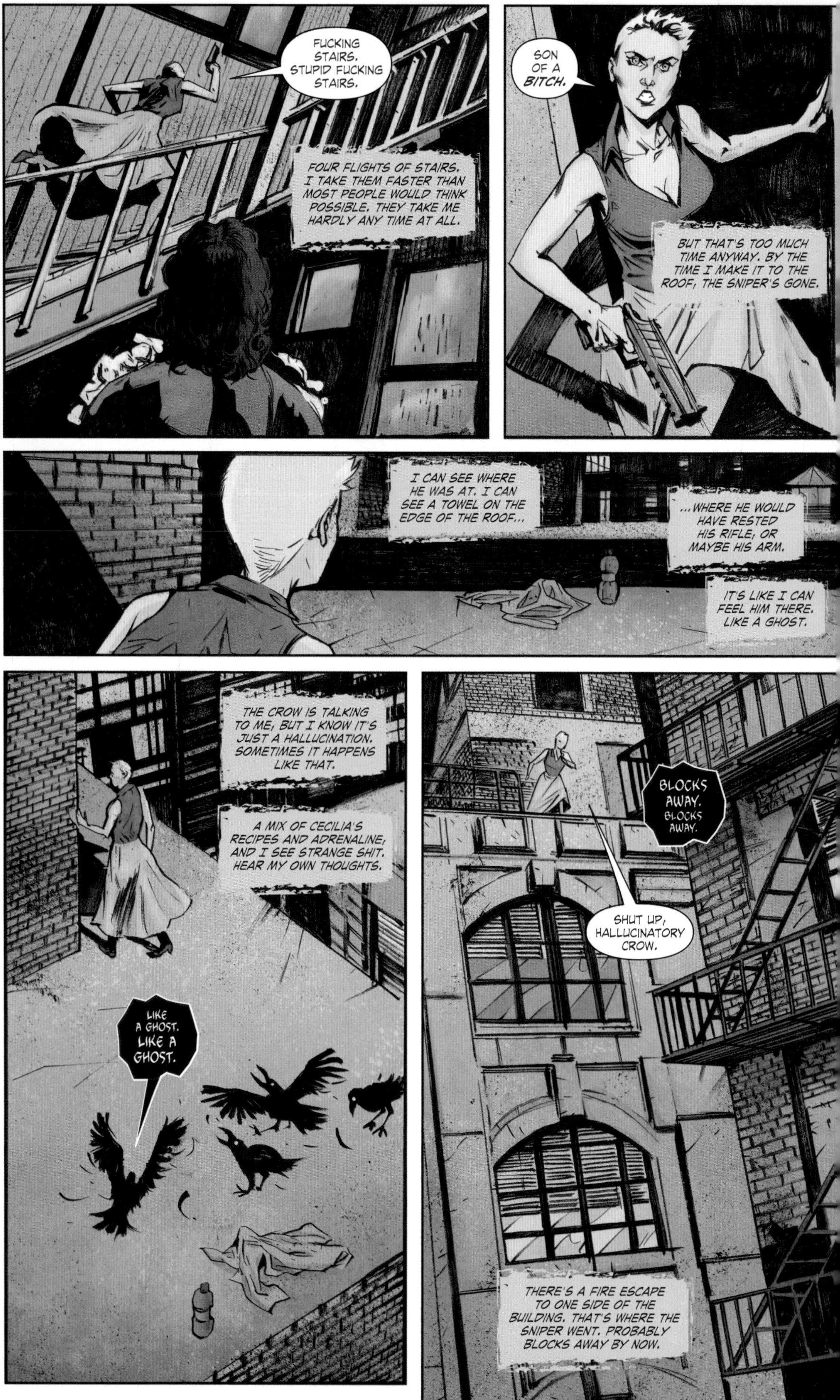

FUCKING STAIRS. STUPID FUCKING STAIRS.
FOUR FLIGHTS OF STAIRS. I TAKE THEM FASTER THAN MOST PEOPLE WOULD THINK POSSIBLE. THEY TAKE ME HARDLY ANY TIME AT ALL.
SON OF A BITCH.
BUT THAT'S TOO MUCH TIME ANYWAY. BY THE TIME I MAKE IT TO THE ROOF, THE SNIPER'S GONE.
I CAN SEE WHERE HE WAS AT. I CAN SEE A TOWEL ON THE EDGE OF THE ROOF...
...WHERE HE WOULD HAVE RESTED HIS RIFLE, OR MAYBE HIS ARM.
IT'S LIKE I CAN FEEL HIM THERE. LIKE A GHOST.
THE CROW IS TALKING TO ME, BUT I KNOW IT'S JUST A HALLUCINATION. SOMETIMES IT HAPPENS LIKE THAT.
A MIX OF CECILIA'S RECIPES AND ADRENALINE, AND I SEE STRANGE SHIT. HEAR MY OWN THOUGHTS.
LIKE A GHOST. LIKE A GHOST.
BLOCKS AWAY. BLOCKS AWAY.
SHUT UP, HALLUCINATORY CROW.
THERE'S A FIRE ESCAPE TO ONE SIDE OF THE BUILDING. THAT'S WHERE THE SNIPER WENT. PROBABLY BLOCKS AWAY BY NOW.

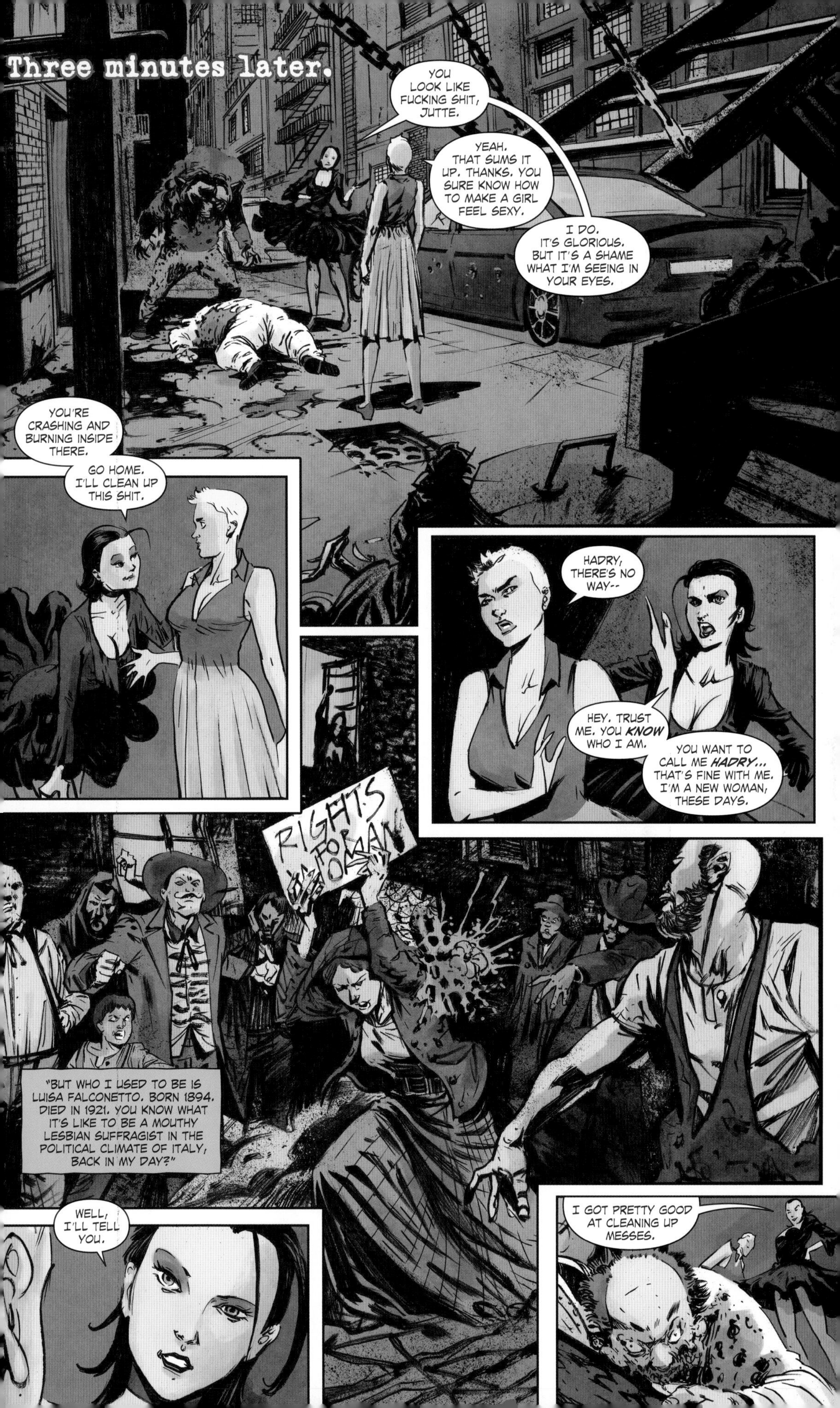
Three minutes later.
YOU LOOK LIKE FUCKING SHIT, JUTTE.
YEAH. THAT SUMS IT UP. THANKS. YOU SURE KNOW HOW TO MAKE A GIRL FEEL SEXY.
I DO. IT'S GLORIOUS. BUT IT'S A SHAME WHAT I'M SEEING IN YOUR EYES.
YOU'RE CRASHING AND BURNING INSIDE THERE.
GO HOME. I'LL CLEAN UP THIS SHIT.
HADRY, THERE'S NO WAY--
HEY. TRUST ME. YOU KNOW WHO I AM.
YOU WANT TO CALL ME HADRY... THAT'S FINE WITH ME. I'M A NEW WOMAN, THESE DAYS.
RIGHTS FOR WOMAN
"BUT WHO I USED TO BE IS LUISA FALCONETTO. BORN 1894. DIED IN 1921. YOU KNOW WHAT IT'S LIKE TO BE A MOUTHY LESBIAN SUFFRAGIST IN THE POLITICAL CLIMATE OF ITALY, BACK IN MY DAY?"
WELL, I'LL TELL YOU.
I GOT PRETTY GOOD AT CLEANING UP MESSES.

BEEP
BEEP
BEEP

HELLO, BOTTLE. I KNOW THAT I'M SUPPOSED TO FEEL BAD ABOUT WAKING UP WITH YOU, BUT SOCIETY IS WELCOME TO PUT A WEASEL UP ITS BUTT.

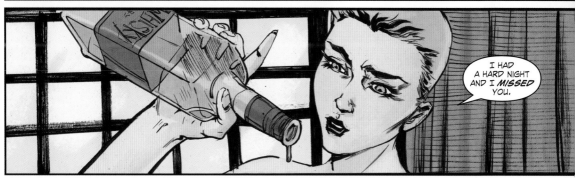

I HAD A HARD NIGHT AND I *MISSED* YOU.

EX? I WANT TO WORK ON THIS *PREAM* THING, TODAY. YEAH. GILBERT. THE MURDERED KID.

WHAT? *YEAH* I FUCKING *KNOW* THE GRANGE THING WENT TO HELL. WE'RE GOING TO NEED TO FIND ANOTHER LEAD.

I'LL TALK TO HARRISON AND BIZ. MAYBE LARKIN.

DID YOU SLEEP WITH LARKIN?

DID I? HMM, WHAT'S THAT JOKE AGAIN? OH, YEAH...NO, I *DIDN'T* SLEEP WITH THE COP. WE WERE TOO BUSY *FUCKING*.

AND DON'T GIVE ME SHIT ABOUT IT. *YOU* BROKE UP WITH ME. YOU'VE CEDED *ALL* RIGHTS.

I WANT YOU TO GO TALK TO THAT CROSSING GUARD, TODAY. THE SUSPECT. BILL CROGAN.

TAKE GEMINI. GEMINI'S UNNERVING AS HELL. THEY MAKE PEOPLE GET FLUMMOXED. AND TALKING.

CAN DO, FRANKENSTEIN.

DON'T CALL ME FRANKENSTEIN.

I HAVE A *TERRIBLE* HANGOVER.

I'M FRANKENSTEIN'S MONSTER.

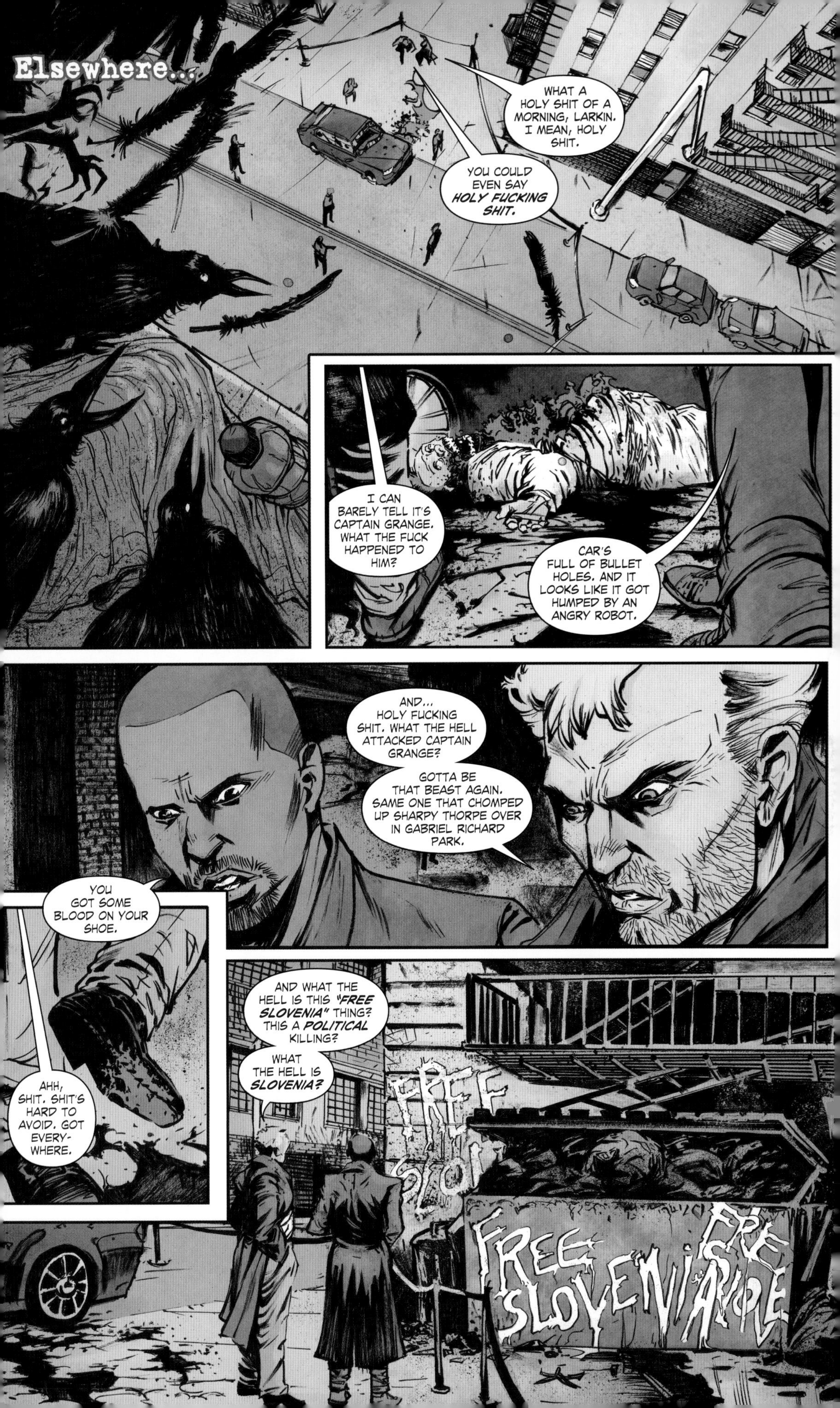
Elsewhere...
WHAT A HOLY SHIT OF A MORNING, LARKIN. I MEAN, HOLY SHIT.
YOU COULD EVEN SAY ***HOLY FUCKING SHIT.***
I CAN BARELY TELL IT'S CAPTAIN GRANGE. WHAT THE FUCK HAPPENED TO HIM?
CAR'S FULL OF BULLET HOLES. AND IT LOOKS LIKE IT GOT HUMPED BY AN ANGRY ROBOT.
AND... HOLY FUCKING SHIT. WHAT THE HELL ATTACKED CAPTAIN GRANGE?
GOTTA BE THAT BEAST AGAIN. SAME ONE THAT CHOMPED UP SHARPY THORPE OVER IN GABRIEL RICHARD PARK.
YOU GOT SOME BLOOD ON YOUR SHOE.
AHH, SHIT. SHIT'S HARD TO AVOID. GOT EVERY-WHERE.
AND WHAT THE HELL IS THIS ***"FREE SLOVENIA"*** THING? THIS A ***POLITICAL*** KILLING?
WHAT THE HELL IS ***SLOVENIA?***
FREE SLOVENIA

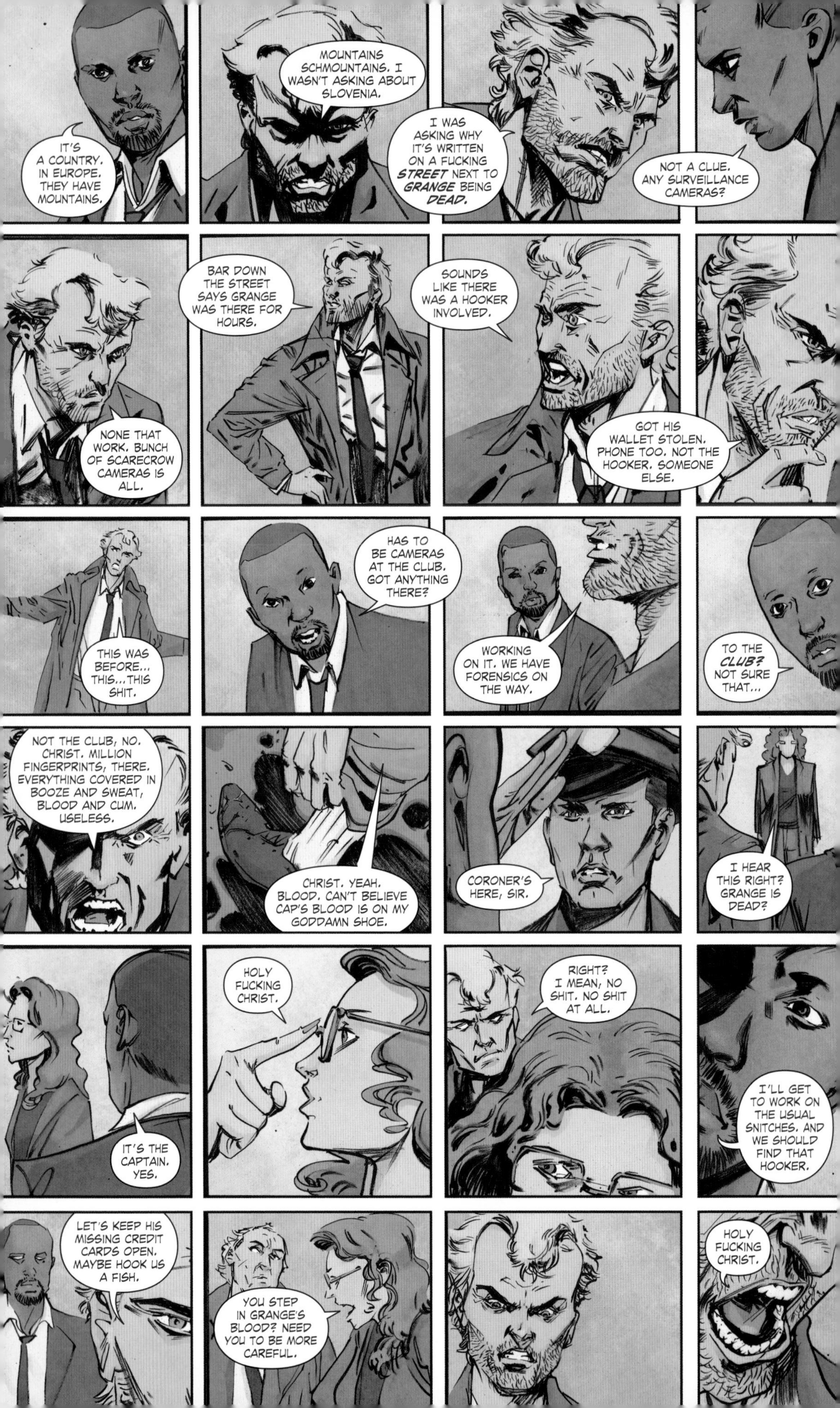
IT'S A COUNTRY. IN EUROPE. THEY HAVE MOUNTAINS.
MOUNTAINS SCHMOUNTAINS. I WASN'T ASKING ABOUT SLOVENIA.
I WAS ASKING WHY IT'S WRITTEN ON A FUCKING STREET NEXT TO GRANGE BEING DEAD.
NOT A CLUE. ANY SURVEILLANCE CAMERAS?
NONE THAT WORK. BUNCH OF SCARECROW CAMERAS IS ALL.
BAR DOWN THE STREET SAYS GRANGE WAS THERE FOR HOURS.
SOUNDS LIKE THERE WAS A HOOKER INVOLVED.
GOT HIS WALLET STOLEN. PHONE TOO. NOT THE HOOKER. SOMEONE ELSE.
THIS WAS BEFORE... THIS...THIS SHIT.
HAS TO BE CAMERAS AT THE CLUB. GOT ANYTHING THERE?
WORKING ON IT. WE HAVE FORENSICS ON THE WAY.
TO THE CLUB? NOT SURE THAT...
NOT THE CLUB, NO. CHRIST. MILLION FINGERPRINTS, THERE. EVERYTHING COVERED IN BOOZE AND SWEAT, BLOOD AND CUM. USELESS.
CHRIST. YEAH. BLOOD. CAN'T BELIEVE CAP'S BLOOD IS ON MY GODDAMN SHOE.
CORONER'S HERE, SIR.
I HEAR THIS RIGHT? GRANGE IS DEAD?
IT'S THE CAPTAIN. YES.
HOLY FUCKING CHRIST.
RIGHT? I MEAN, NO SHIT. NO SHIT AT ALL.
I'LL GET TO WORK ON THE USUAL SNITCHES. AND WE SHOULD FIND THAT HOOKER.
LET'S KEEP HIS MISSING CREDIT CARDS OPEN. MAYBE HOOK US A FISH.
YOU STEP IN GRANGE'S BLOOD? NEED YOU TO BE MORE CAREFUL.
HOLY FUCKING CHRIST.

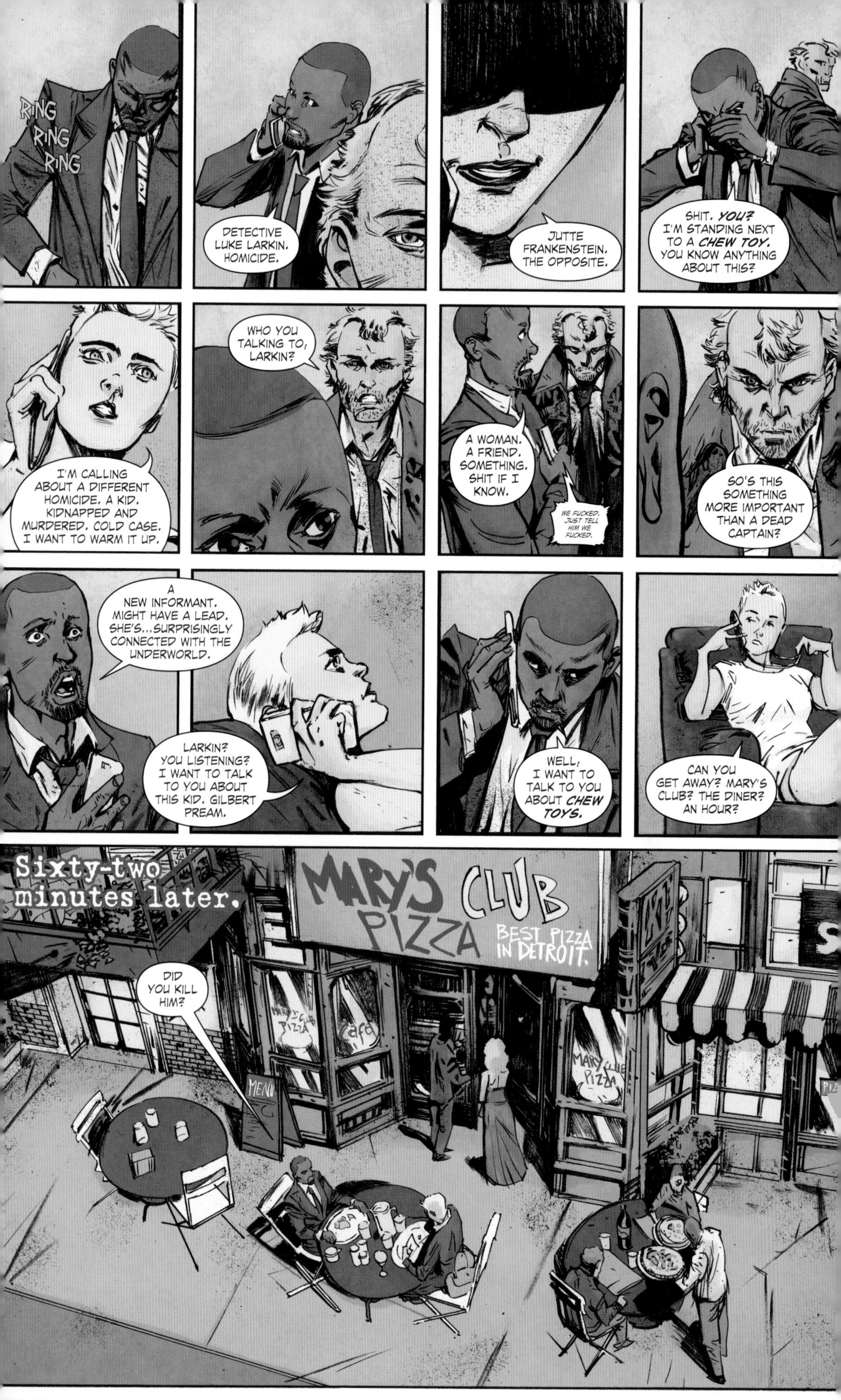
RING RING RING
DETECTIVE LUKE LARKIN. HOMICIDE.
JUTTE FRANKENSTEIN. THE OPPOSITE.
SHIT. YOU? I'M STANDING NEXT TO A CHEW TOY. YOU KNOW ANYTHING ABOUT THIS?
I'M CALLING ABOUT A DIFFERENT HOMICIDE. A KID. KIDNAPPED AND MURDERED. COLD CASE. I WANT TO WARM IT UP.
WHO YOU TALKING TO, LARKIN?
A WOMAN. A FRIEND. SOMETHING. SHIT IF I KNOW.
WE FUCKED. JUST TELL HIM WE FUCKED.
SO'S THIS SOMETHING MORE IMPORTANT THAN A DEAD CAPTAIN?
A NEW INFORMANT. MIGHT HAVE A LEAD. SHE'S...SURPRISINGLY CONNECTED WITH THE UNDERWORLD.
LARKIN? YOU LISTENING? I WANT TO TALK TO YOU ABOUT THIS KID. GILBERT PREAM.
WELL, I WANT TO TALK TO YOU ABOUT CHEW TOYS.
CAN YOU GET AWAY? MARY'S CLUB? THE DINER? AN HOUR?
Sixty-two minutes later.
MARY'S CLUB PIZZA
BEST PIZZA IN DETROIT.
DID YOU KILL HIM?
MENU

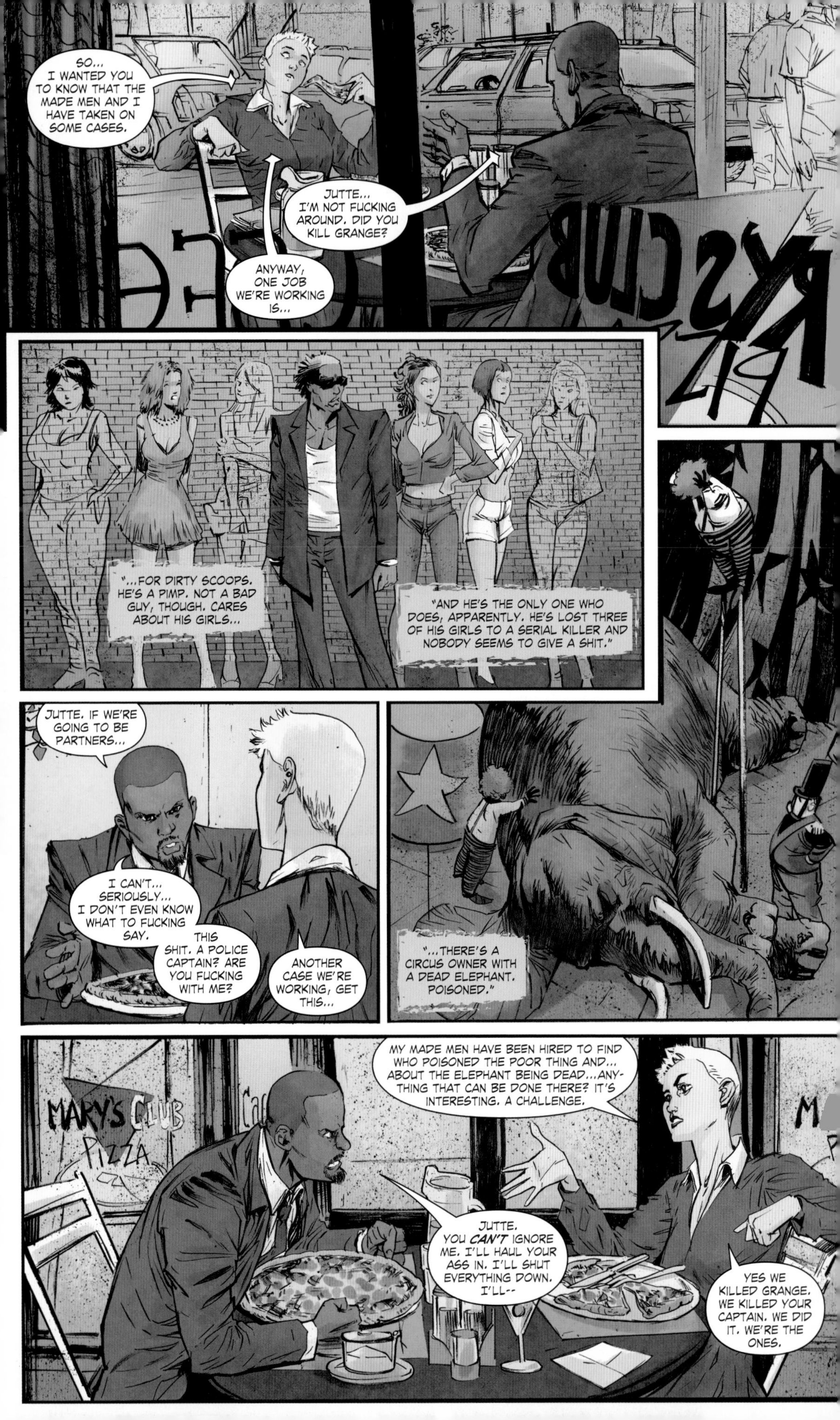
SO... I WANTED YOU TO KNOW THAT THE MADE MEN AND I HAVE TAKEN ON SOME CASES.
JUTTE... I'M NOT FUCKING AROUND. DID YOU KILL GRANGE?
ANYWAY, ONE JOB WE'RE WORKING IS...
"...FOR DIRTY SCOOPS. HE'S A PIMP. NOT A BAD GUY, THOUGH. CARES ABOUT HIS GIRLS...
"AND HE'S THE ONLY ONE WHO DOES, APPARENTLY. HE'S LOST THREE OF HIS GIRLS TO A SERIAL KILLER AND NOBODY SEEMS TO GIVE A SHIT."
JUTTE. IF WE'RE GOING TO BE PARTNERS...
I CAN'T... SERIOUSLY... I DON'T EVEN KNOW WHAT TO FUCKING SAY.
THIS SHIT. A POLICE CAPTAIN? ARE YOU FUCKING WITH ME?
ANOTHER CASE WE'RE WORKING, GET THIS...
"...THERE'S A CIRCUS OWNER WITH A DEAD ELEPHANT. POISONED."
MARY'S CLUB PIZZA
MY MADE MEN HAVE BEEN HIRED TO FIND WHO POISONED THE POOR THING AND... ABOUT THE ELEPHANT BEING DEAD...ANYTHING THAT CAN BE DONE THERE? IT'S INTERESTING. A CHALLENGE.
JUTTE. YOU ***CAN'T*** IGNORE ME. I'LL HAUL YOUR ASS IN. I'LL SHUT EVERYTHING DOWN. I'LL--
YES WE KILLED GRANGE. WE KILLED YOUR CAPTAIN. WE DID IT. WE'RE THE ONES.

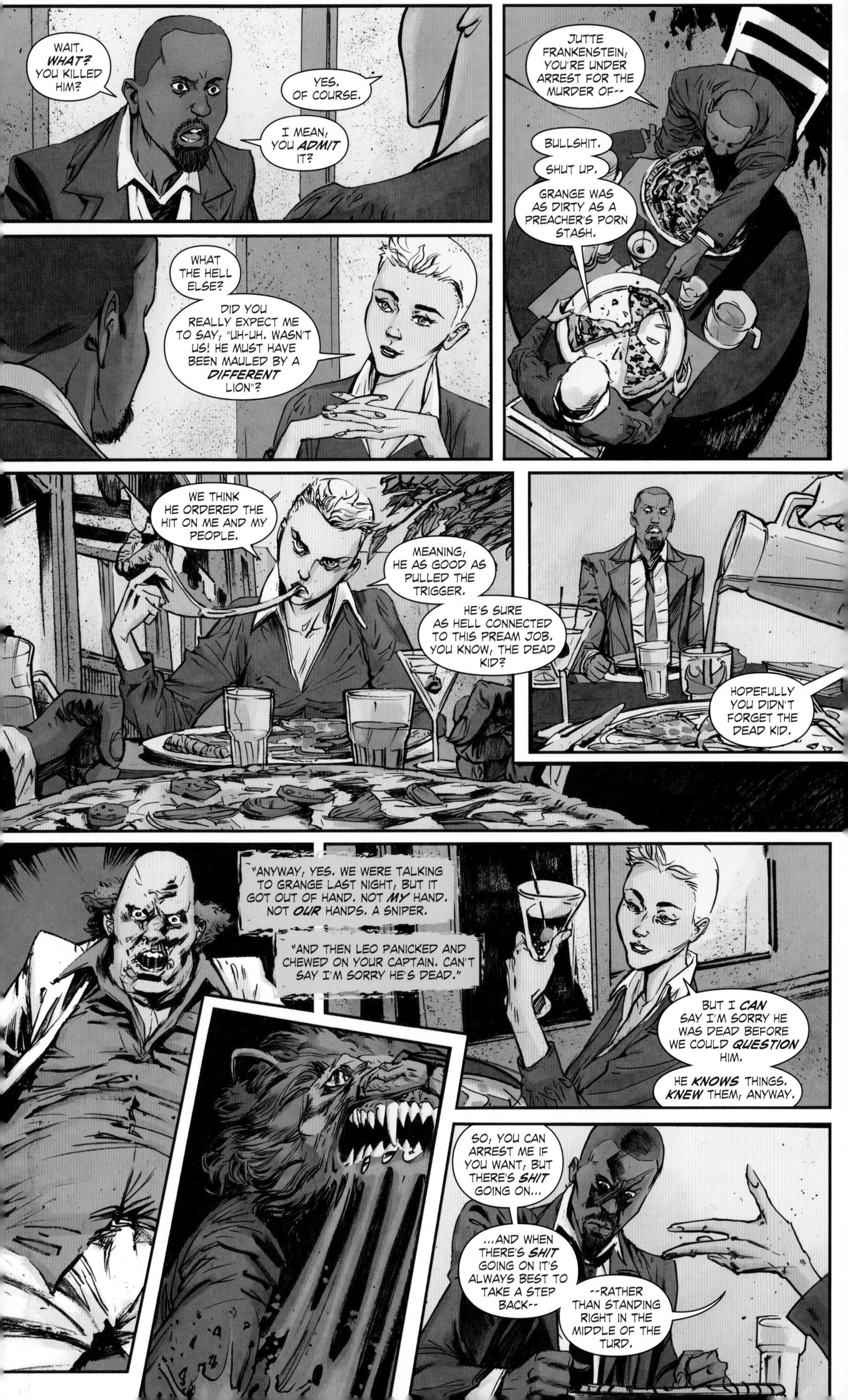

WAIT. WHAT? YOU KILLED HIM?
YES. OF COURSE.
I MEAN, YOU ADMIT IT?
JUTTE FRANKENSTEIN, YOU'RE UNDER ARREST FOR THE MURDER OF--
BULLSHIT.
SHUT UP.
GRANGE WAS AS DIRTY AS A PREACHER'S PORN STASH.
WHAT THE HELL ELSE?
DID YOU REALLY EXPECT ME TO SAY, "UH-UH. WASN'T US! HE MUST HAVE BEEN MAULED BY A DIFFERENT LION"?
WE THINK HE ORDERED THE HIT ON ME AND MY PEOPLE.
MEANING, HE AS GOOD AS PULLED THE TRIGGER.
HE'S SURE AS HELL CONNECTED TO THIS PREAM JOB. YOU KNOW, THE DEAD KID?
HOPEFULLY YOU DIDN'T FORGET THE DEAD KID.
"ANYWAY, YES. WE WERE TALKING TO GRANGE LAST NIGHT, BUT IT GOT OUT OF HAND. NOT MY HAND. NOT OUR HANDS. A SNIPER.
"AND THEN LEO PANICKED AND CHEWED ON YOUR CAPTAIN. CAN'T SAY I'M SORRY HE'S DEAD."
BUT I CAN SAY I'M SORRY HE WAS DEAD BEFORE WE COULD QUESTION HIM.
HE KNOWS THINGS. KNEW THEM, ANYWAY.
SO, YOU CAN ARREST ME IF YOU WANT, BUT THERE'S SHIT GOING ON...
...AND WHEN THERE'S SHIT GOING ON IT'S ALWAYS BEST TO TAKE A STEP BACK--
--RATHER THAN STANDING RIGHT IN THE MIDDLE OF THE TURD.

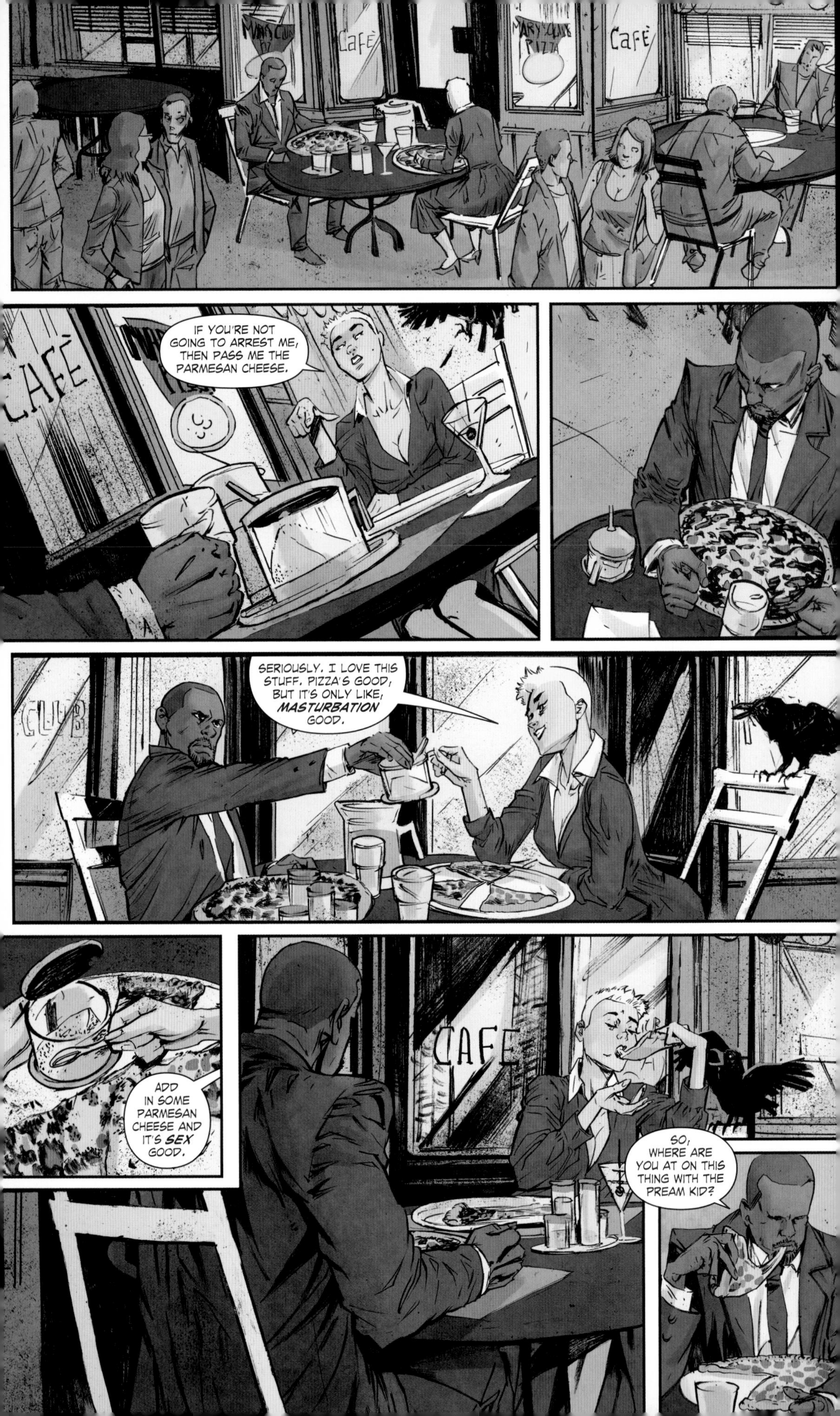
MARY'S CLUB PIZZA
CAFÉ
IF YOU'RE NOT GOING TO ARREST ME, THEN PASS ME THE PARMESAN CHEESE.
CAFÉ
SERIOUSLY. I LOVE THIS STUFF. PIZZA'S GOOD, BUT IT'S ONLY LIKE, MASTURBATION GOOD.
CLUB
ADD IN SOME PARMESAN CHEESE AND IT'S SEX GOOD.
CAFÉ
SO, WHERE ARE YOU AT ON THIS THING WITH THE PREAM KID?

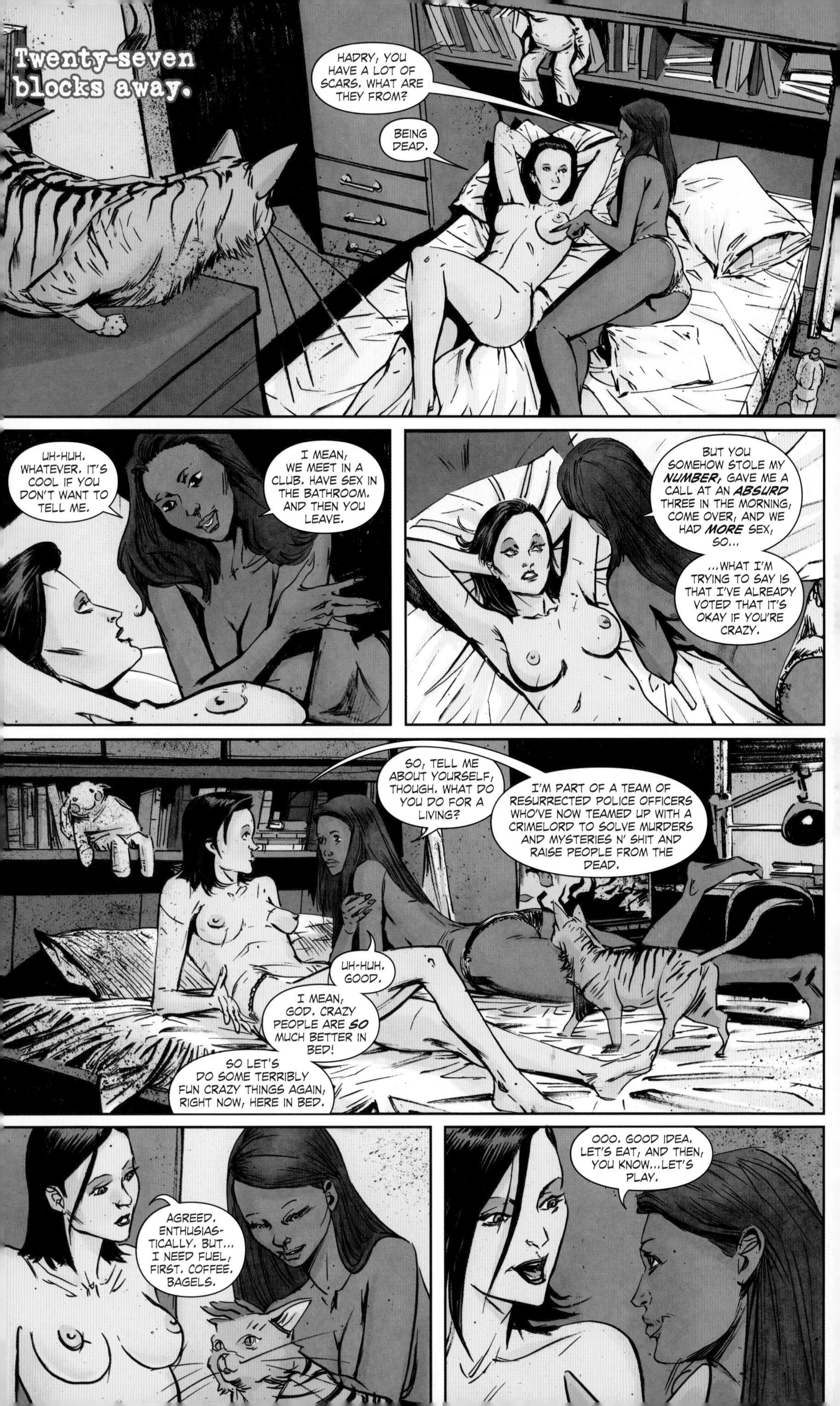
Twenty-seven blocks away.
HADRY, YOU HAVE A LOT OF SCARS. WHAT ARE THEY FROM?
BEING DEAD.
UH-HUH. WHATEVER. IT'S COOL IF YOU DON'T WANT TO TELL ME.
I MEAN, WE MEET IN A CLUB. HAVE SEX IN THE BATHROOM. AND THEN YOU LEAVE.
BUT YOU SOMEHOW STOLE MY NUMBER, GAVE ME A CALL AT AN ABSURD THREE IN THE MORNING, COME OVER, AND WE HAD MORE SEX, SO...
...WHAT I'M TRYING TO SAY IS THAT I'VE ALREADY VOTED THAT IT'S OKAY IF YOU'RE CRAZY.
SO, TELL ME ABOUT YOURSELF, THOUGH. WHAT DO YOU DO FOR A LIVING?
I'M PART OF A TEAM OF RESURRECTED POLICE OFFICERS WHO'VE NOW TEAMED UP WITH A CRIMELORD TO SOLVE MURDERS AND MYSTERIES N' SHIT AND RAISE PEOPLE FROM THE DEAD.
UH-HUH. GOOD.
I MEAN, GOD. CRAZY PEOPLE ARE SO MUCH BETTER IN BED!
SO LET'S DO SOME TERRIBLY FUN CRAZY THINGS AGAIN, RIGHT NOW, HERE IN BED.
AGREED. ENTHUSIAS-TICALLY. BUT... I NEED FUEL, FIRST. COFFEE. BAGELS.
OOO. GOOD IDEA. LET'S EAT, AND THEN, YOU KNOW...LET'S PLAY.

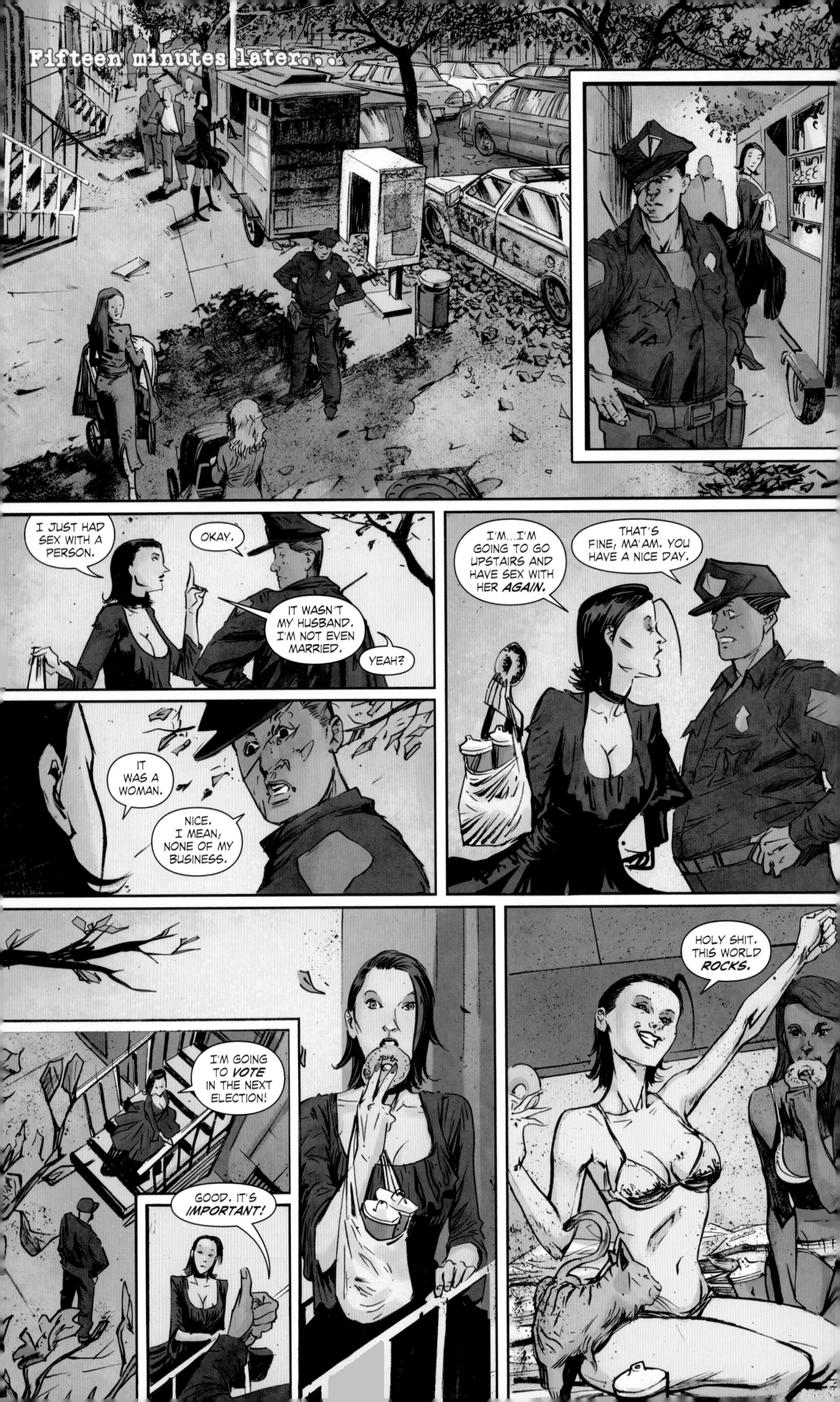
Fifteen minutes later...
I JUST HAD SEX WITH A PERSON.
OKAY.
IT WASN'T MY HUSBAND. I'M NOT EVEN MARRIED.
YEAH?
IT WAS A WOMAN.
NICE. I MEAN, NONE OF MY BUSINESS.
I'M...I'M GOING TO GO UPSTAIRS AND HAVE SEX WITH HER AGAIN.
THAT'S FINE, MA'AM. YOU HAVE A NICE DAY.
I'M GOING TO VOTE IN THE NEXT ELECTION!
GOOD. IT'S IMPORTANT!
HOLY SHIT. THIS WORLD ROCKS.

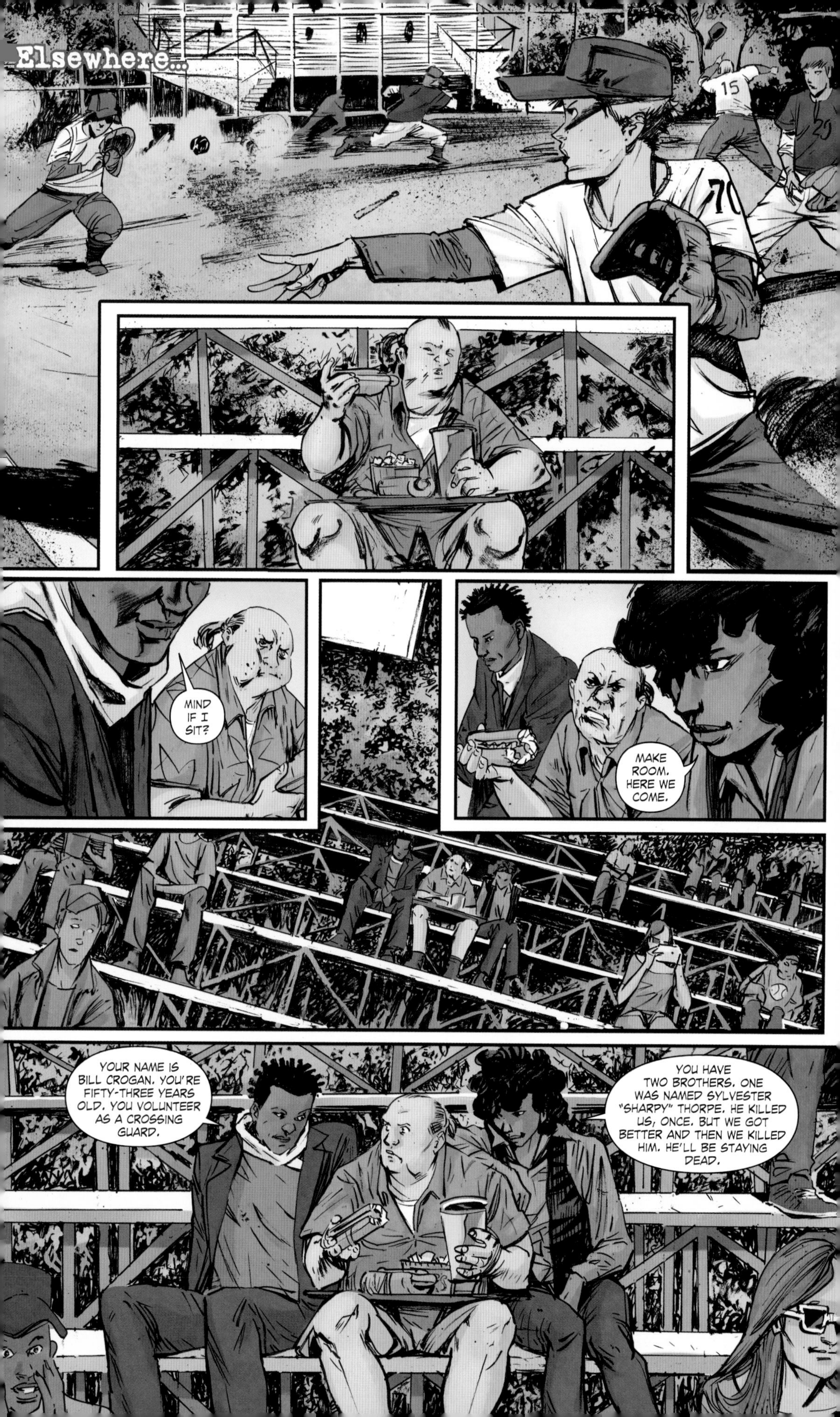
Elsewhere...
MIND IF I SIT?
MAKE ROOM. HERE WE COME.
YOUR NAME IS BILL CROGAN. YOU'RE FIFTY-THREE YEARS OLD. YOU VOLUNTEER AS A CROSSING GUARD.
YOU HAVE TWO BROTHERS. ONE WAS NAMED SYLVESTER "SHARPY" THORPE. HE KILLED US, ONCE. BUT WE GOT BETTER AND THEN WE KILLED HIM. HE'LL BE STAYING DEAD.

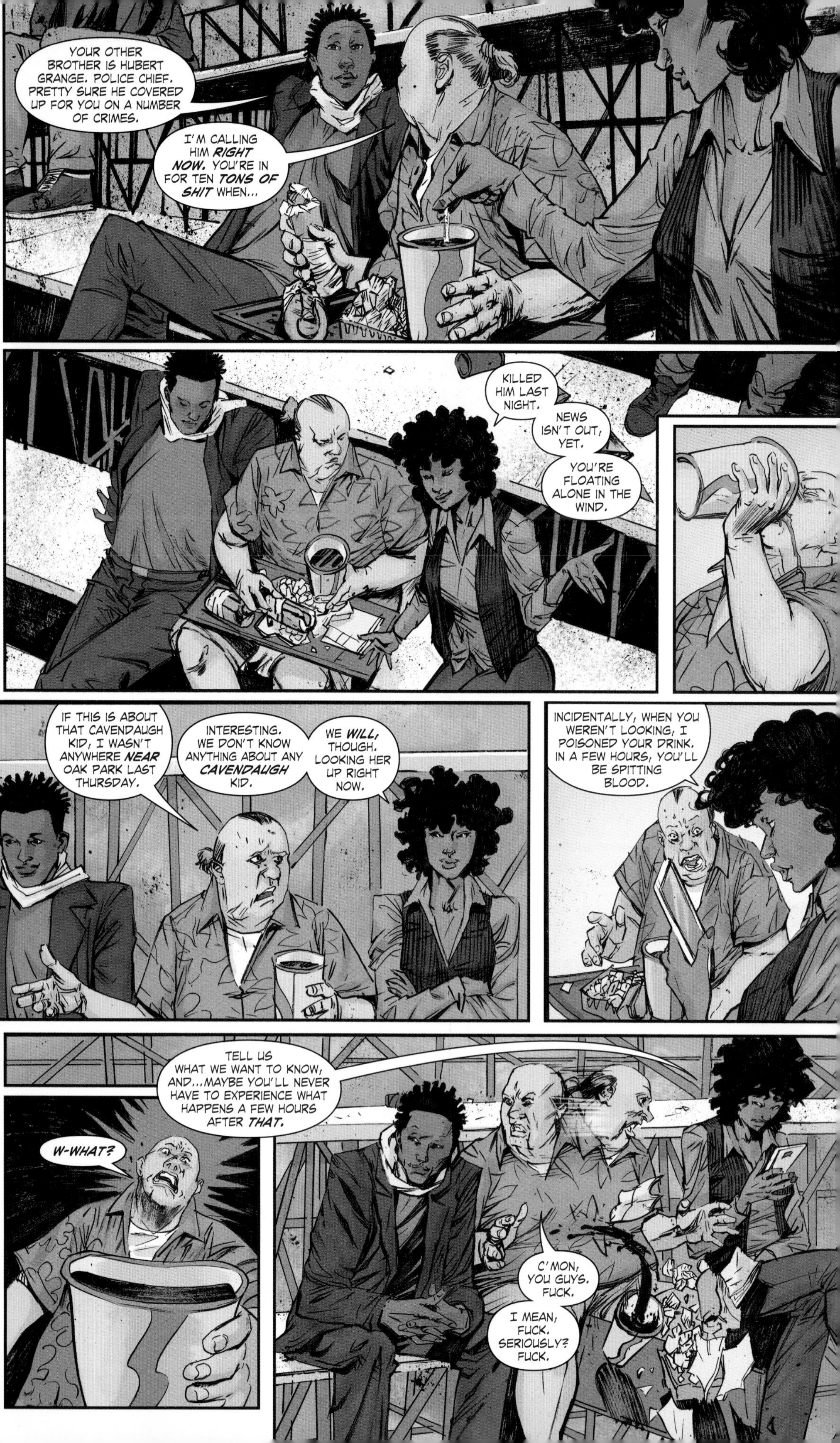
YOUR OTHER BROTHER IS HUBERT GRANGE. POLICE CHIEF. PRETTY SURE HE COVERED UP FOR YOU ON A NUMBER OF CRIMES.
I'M CALLING HIM RIGHT NOW. YOU'RE IN FOR TEN TONS OF SHIT WHEN...
KILLED HIM LAST NIGHT.
NEWS ISN'T OUT, YET.
YOU'RE FLOATING ALONE IN THE WIND.
IF THIS IS ABOUT THAT CAVENDAUGH KID, I WASN'T ANYWHERE NEAR OAK PARK LAST THURSDAY.
INTERESTING. WE DON'T KNOW ANYTHING ABOUT ANY CAVENDAUGH KID.
WE WILL, THOUGH. LOOKING HER UP RIGHT NOW.
INCIDENTALLY, WHEN YOU WEREN'T LOOKING, I POISONED YOUR DRINK. IN A FEW HOURS, YOU'LL BE SPITTING BLOOD.
TELL US WHAT WE WANT TO KNOW, AND...MAYBE YOU'LL NEVER HAVE TO EXPERIENCE WHAT HAPPENS A FEW HOURS AFTER THAT.
W-WHAT?
C'MON, YOU GUYS. FUCK.
I MEAN, FUCK. SERIOUSLY? FUCK.

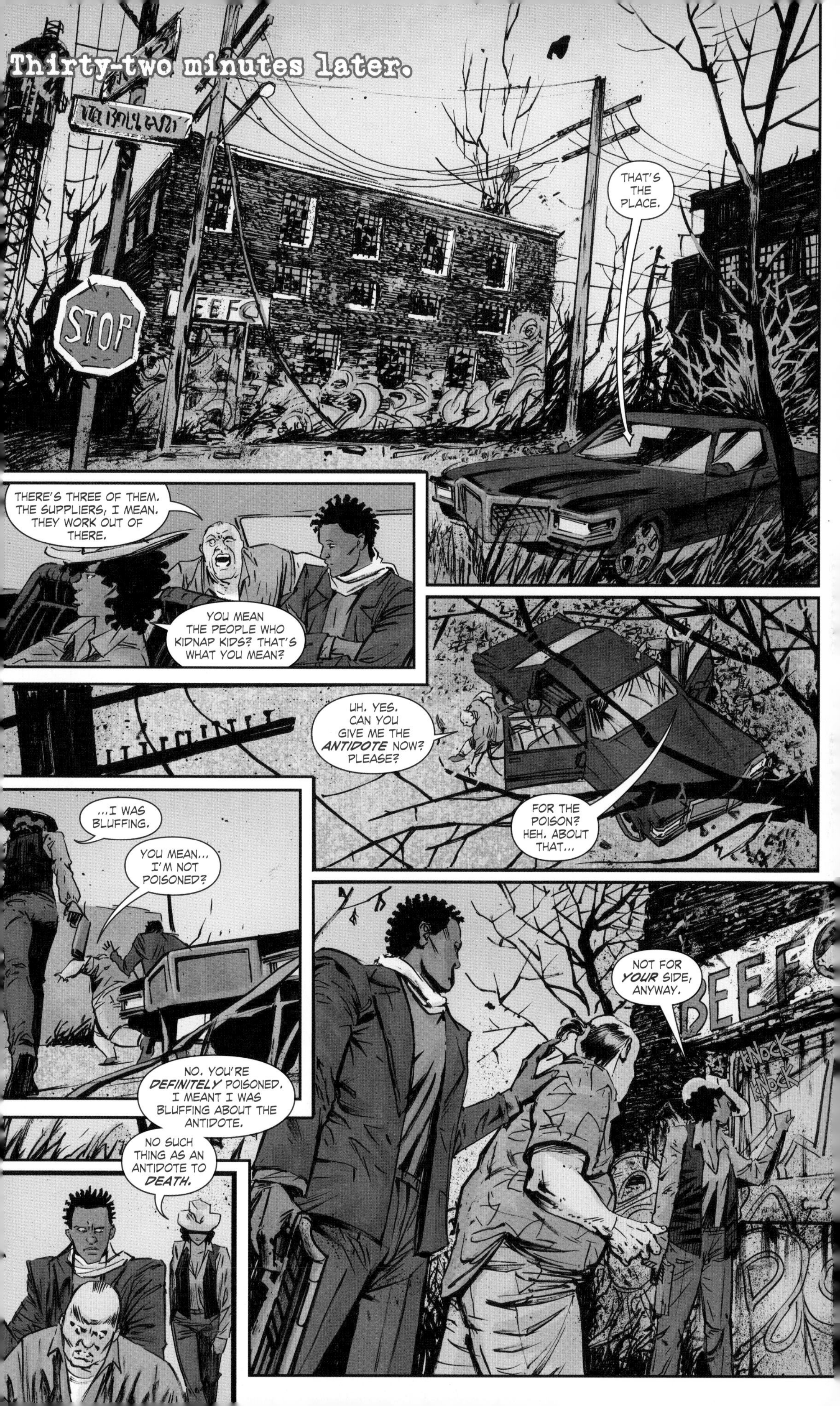
Thirty-two minutes later.
STOP
BEEF
THAT'S THE PLACE.
THERE'S THREE OF THEM. THE SUPPLIERS, I MEAN. THEY WORK OUT OF THERE.
YOU MEAN THE PEOPLE WHO KIDNAP KIDS? THAT'S WHAT YOU MEAN?
UH. YES. CAN YOU GIVE ME THE *ANTIDOTE* NOW? PLEASE?
FOR THE POISON? HEH. ABOUT THAT...
...I WAS BLUFFING.
YOU MEAN... I'M NOT POISONED?
NO. YOU'RE *DEFINITELY* POISONED. I MEANT I WAS BLUFFING ABOUT THE ANTIDOTE.
NO SUCH THING AS AN ANTIDOTE TO *DEATH.*
NOT FOR *YOUR* SIDE, ANYWAY.
BEEF
KNOCK KNOCK

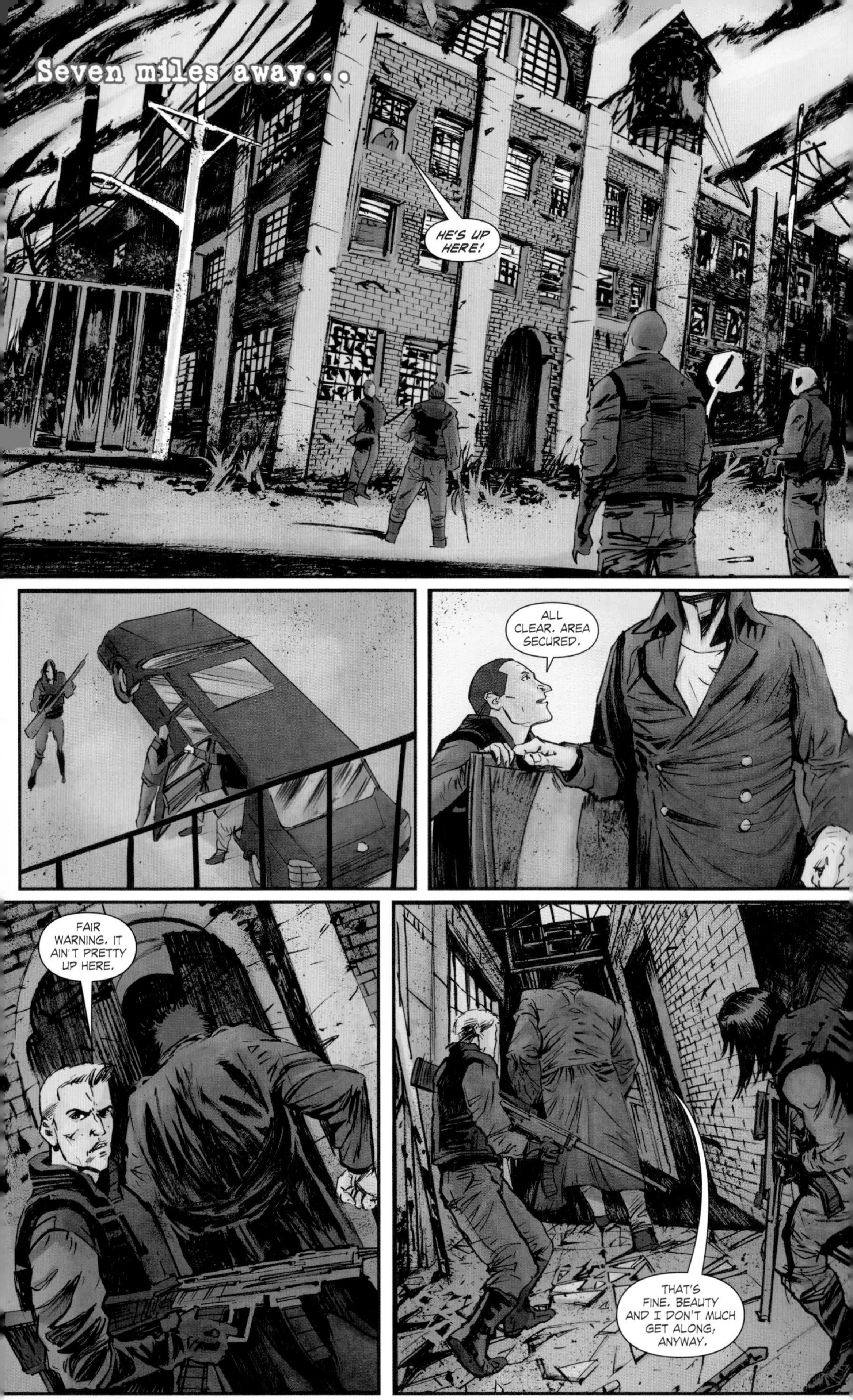

Seven miles away...
HE'S UP HERE!
ALL CLEAR. AREA SECURED.
FAIR WARNING. IT AIN'T PRETTY UP HERE.
THAT'S FINE. BEAUTY AND I DON'T MUCH GET ALONG, ANYWAY.

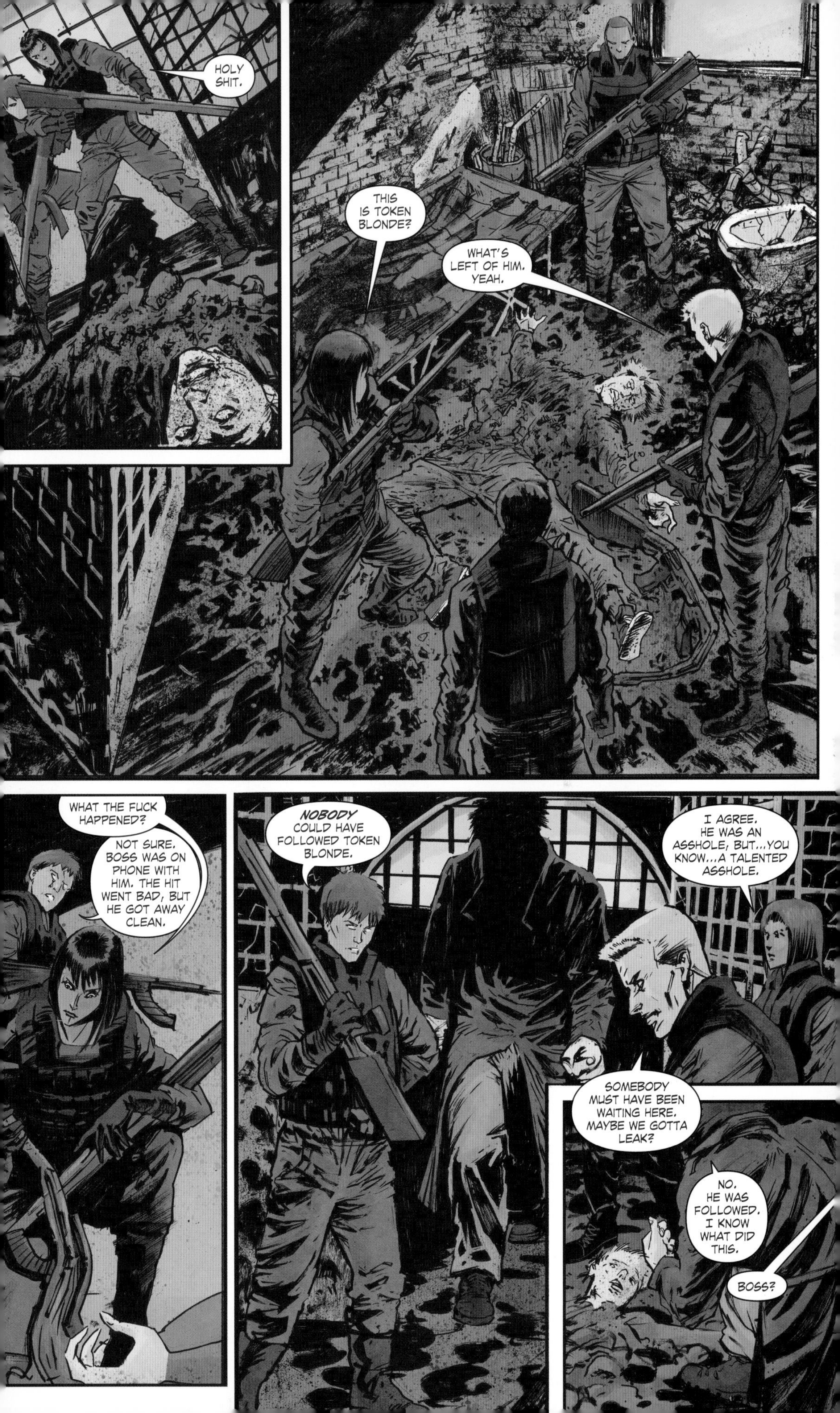
HOLY SHIT.
THIS IS TOKEN BLONDE?
WHAT'S LEFT OF HIM. YEAH.
WHAT THE FUCK HAPPENED?
NOT SURE. BOSS WAS ON PHONE WITH HIM. THE HIT WENT BAD, BUT HE GOT AWAY CLEAN.
NOBODY COULD HAVE FOLLOWED TOKEN BLONDE.
I AGREE. HE WAS AN ASSHOLE, BUT...YOU KNOW...A TALENTED ASSHOLE.
SOMEBODY MUST HAVE BEEN WAITING HERE. MAYBE WE GOTTA LEAK?
NO. HE WAS FOLLOWED. I KNOW WHAT DID THIS.
BOSS?

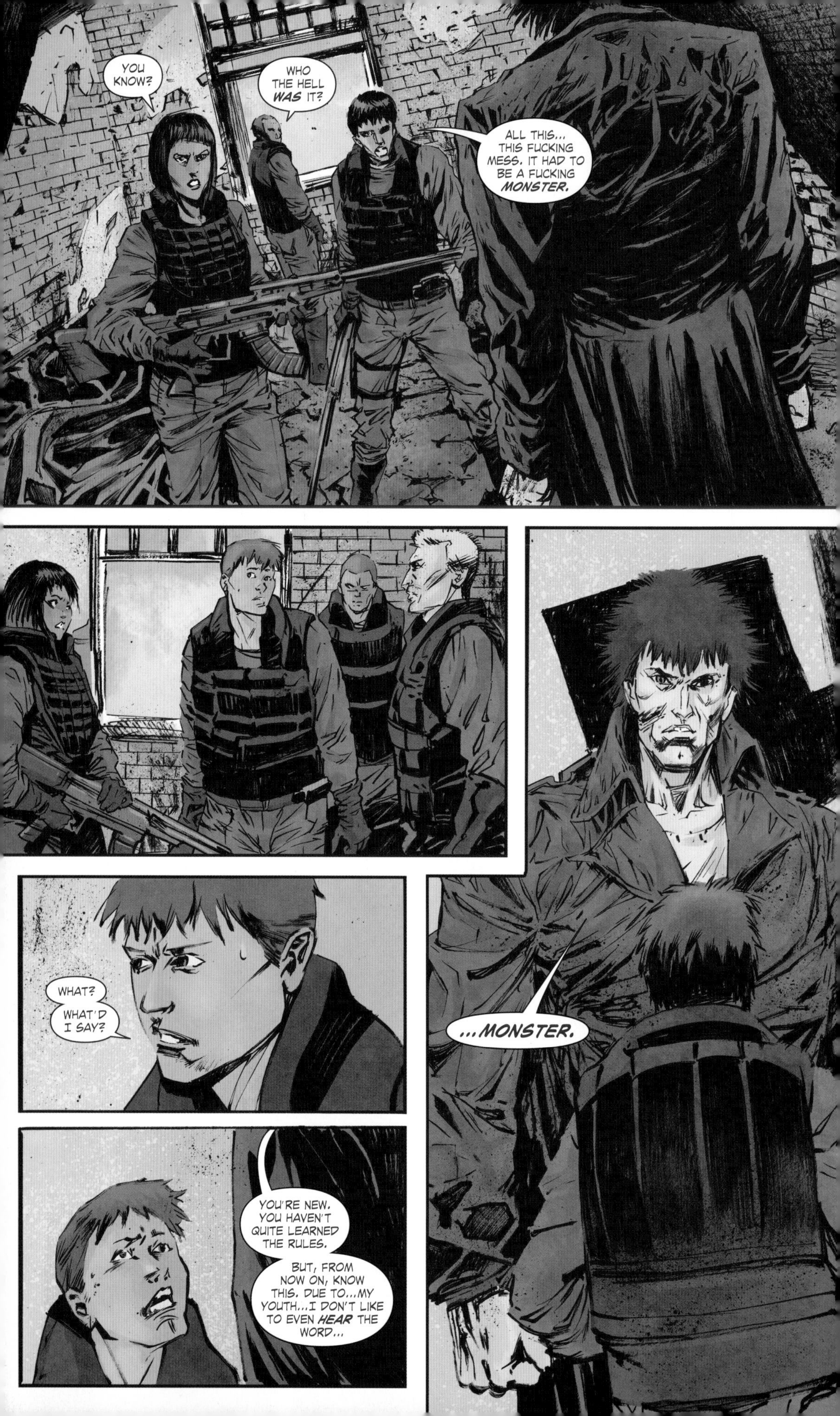
YOU KNOW?
WHO THE HELL WAS IT?
ALL THIS... THIS FUCKING MESS. IT HAD TO BE A FUCKING MONSTER.
WHAT?
WHAT'D I SAY?
YOU'RE NEW. YOU HAVEN'T QUITE LEARNED THE RULES.
BUT, FROM NOW ON, KNOW THIS. DUE TO...MY YOUTH...I DON'T LIKE TO EVEN HEAR THE WORD...
...MONSTER.

CHAPTER FIVE

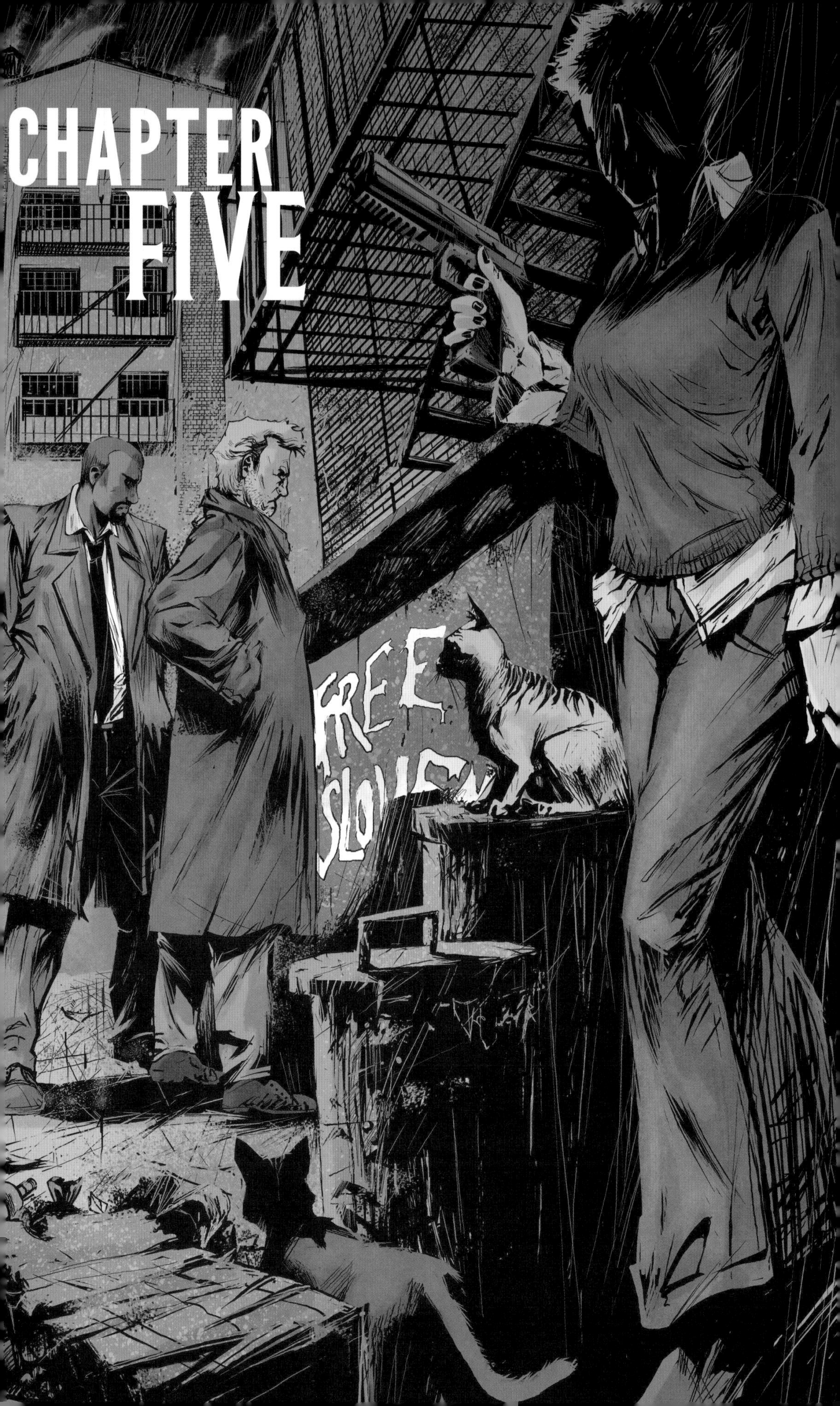

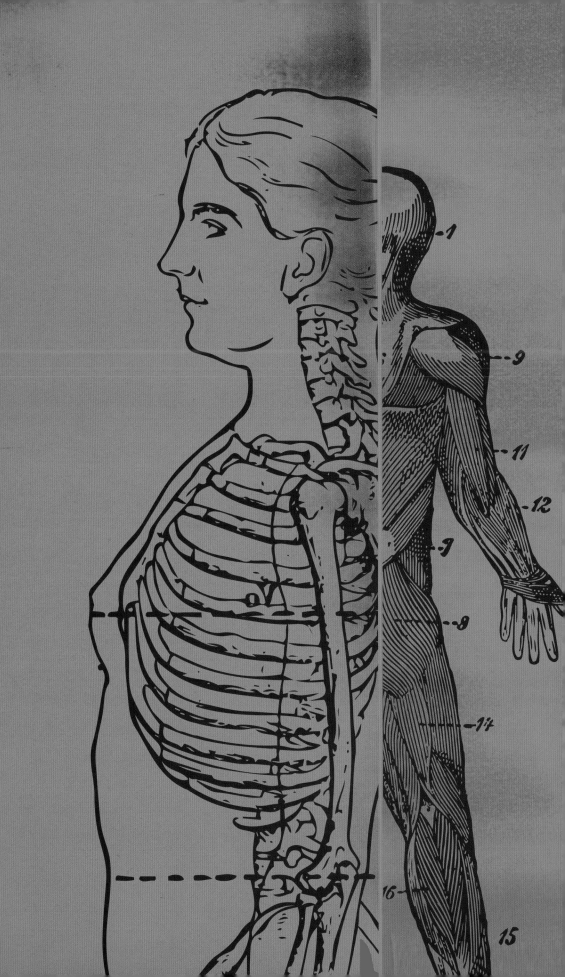

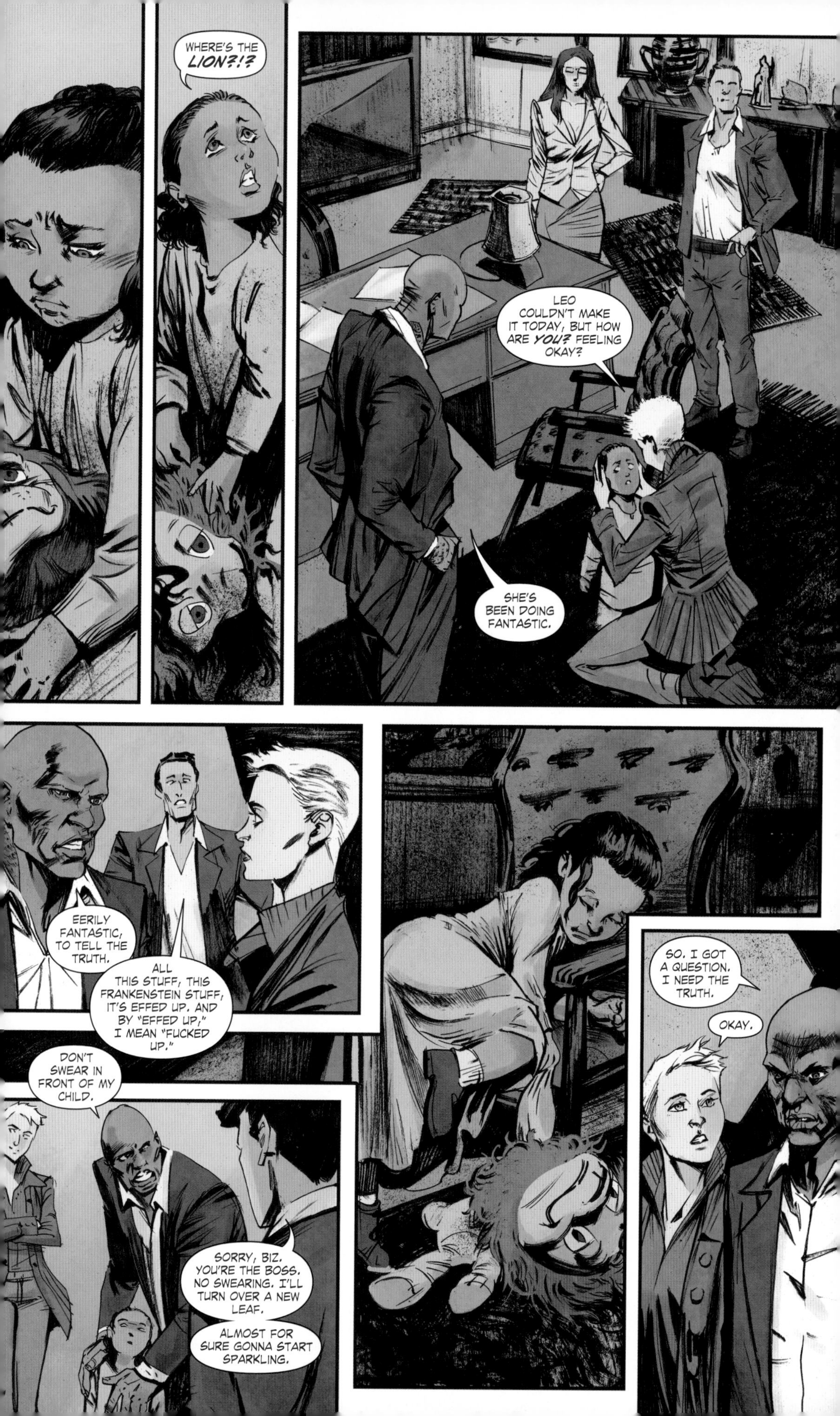
WHERE'S THE LION?!?
LEO COULDN'T MAKE IT TODAY, BUT HOW ARE YOU? FEELING OKAY?
SHE'S BEEN DOING FANTASTIC.
EERILY FANTASTIC, TO TELL THE TRUTH.
ALL THIS STUFF, THIS FRANKENSTEIN STUFF, IT'S EFFED UP. AND BY "EFFED UP," I MEAN "FUCKED UP."
DON'T SWEAR IN FRONT OF MY CHILD.
SORRY, BIZ. YOU'RE THE BOSS. NO SWEARING. I'LL TURN OVER A NEW LEAF.
ALMOST FOR SURE GONNA START SPARKLING.
SO. I GOT A QUESTION. I NEED THE TRUTH.
OKAY.

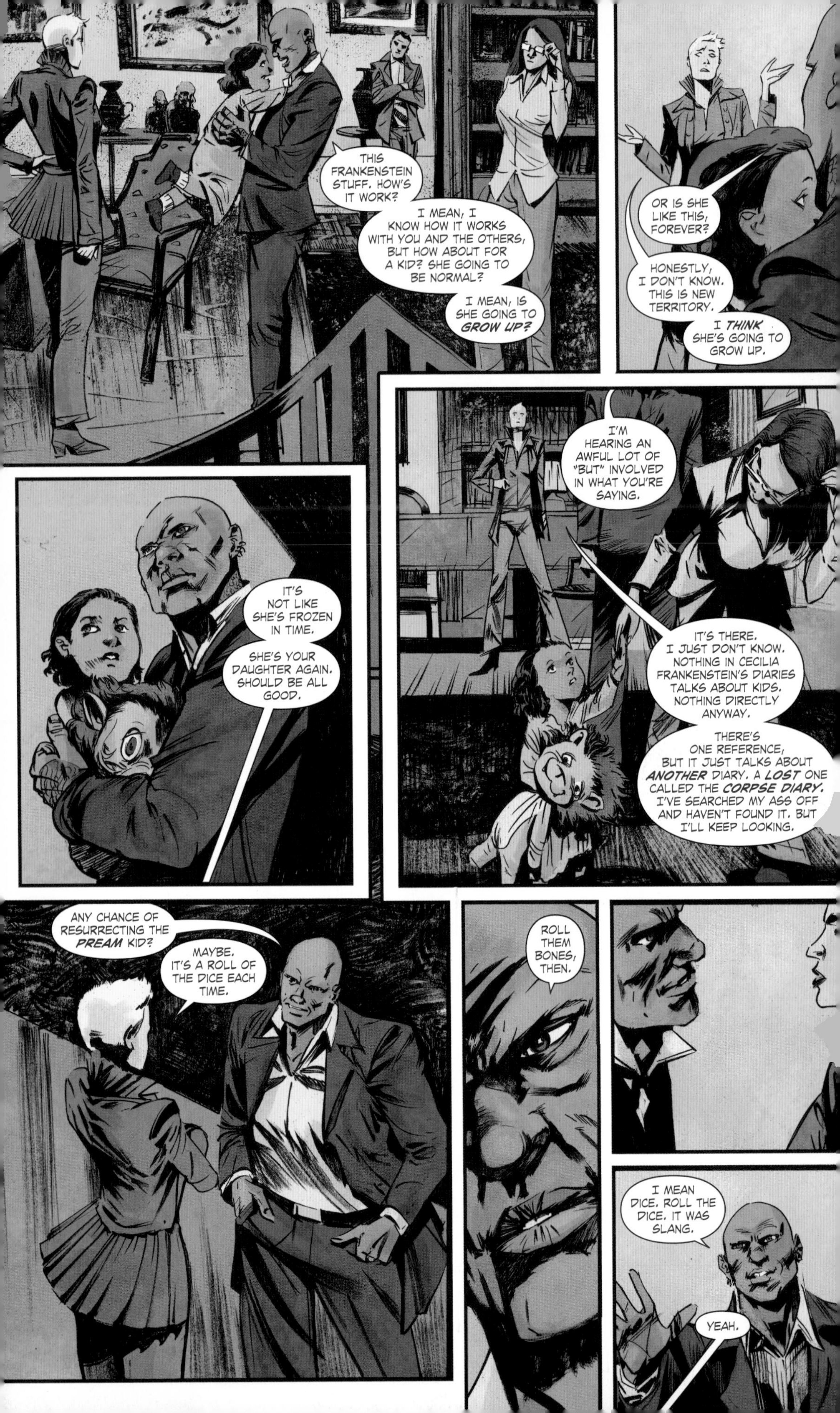
THIS FRANKENSTEIN STUFF. HOW'S IT WORK?
I MEAN, I KNOW HOW IT WORKS WITH YOU AND THE OTHERS, BUT HOW ABOUT FOR A KID? SHE GOING TO BE NORMAL?
I MEAN, IS SHE GOING TO GROW UP?
OR IS SHE LIKE THIS, FOREVER?
HONESTLY, I DON'T KNOW. THIS IS NEW TERRITORY.
I THINK SHE'S GOING TO GROW UP.
IT'S NOT LIKE SHE'S FROZEN IN TIME.
SHE'S YOUR DAUGHTER AGAIN. SHOULD BE ALL GOOD.
I'M HEARING AN AWFUL LOT OF "BUT" INVOLVED IN WHAT YOU'RE SAYING.
IT'S THERE. I JUST DON'T KNOW. NOTHING IN CECILIA FRANKENSTEIN'S DIARIES TALKS ABOUT KIDS. NOTHING DIRECTLY ANYWAY.
THERE'S ONE REFERENCE, BUT IT JUST TALKS ABOUT ANOTHER DIARY. A LOST ONE CALLED THE CORPSE DIARY. I'VE SEARCHED MY ASS OFF AND HAVEN'T FOUND IT. BUT I'LL KEEP LOOKING.
ANY CHANCE OF RESURRECTING THE PREAM KID?
MAYBE. IT'S A ROLL OF THE DICE EACH TIME.
ROLL THEM BONES, THEN.
I MEAN DICE. ROLL THE DICE. IT WAS SLANG.
YEAH.

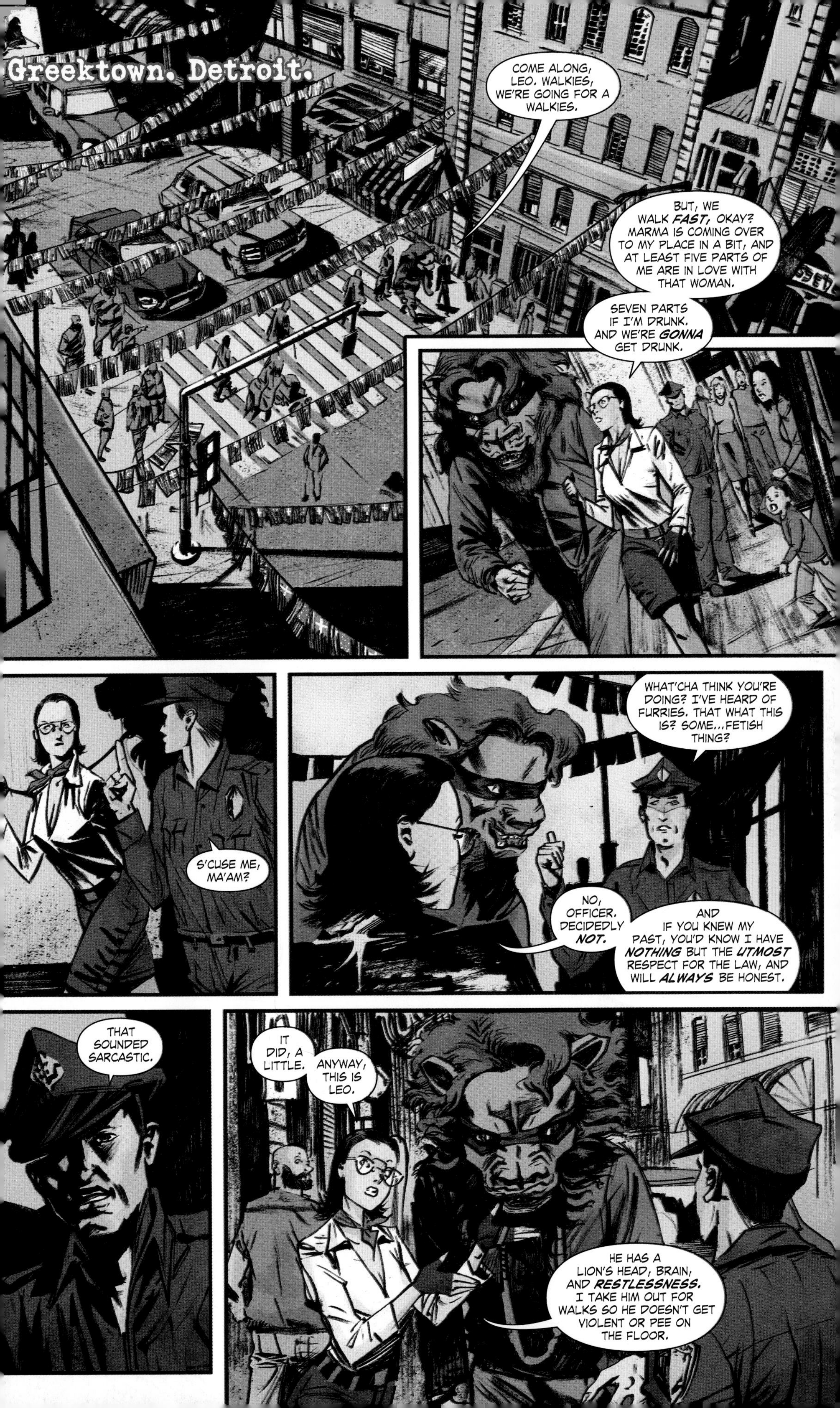

Greektown. Detroit.
COME ALONG, LEO. WALKIES, WE'RE GOING FOR A WALKIES.
BUT, WE WALK FAST, OKAY? MARMA IS COMING OVER TO MY PLACE IN A BIT, AND AT LEAST FIVE PARTS OF ME ARE IN LOVE WITH THAT WOMAN.
SEVEN PARTS IF I'M DRUNK. AND WE'RE GONNA GET DRUNK.
S'CUSE ME, MA'AM?
WHAT'CHA THINK YOU'RE DOING? I'VE HEARD OF FURRIES. THAT WHAT THIS IS? SOME...FETISH THING?
NO, OFFICER. DECIDEDLY NOT.
AND IF YOU KNEW MY PAST, YOU'D KNOW I HAVE NOTHING BUT THE UTMOST RESPECT FOR THE LAW, AND WILL ALWAYS BE HONEST.
THAT SOUNDED SARCASTIC.
IT DID, A LITTLE.
ANYWAY, THIS IS LEO.
HE HAS A LION'S HEAD, BRAIN, AND RESTLESSNESS. I TAKE HIM OUT FOR WALKS SO HE DOESN'T GET VIOLENT OR PEE ON THE FLOOR.

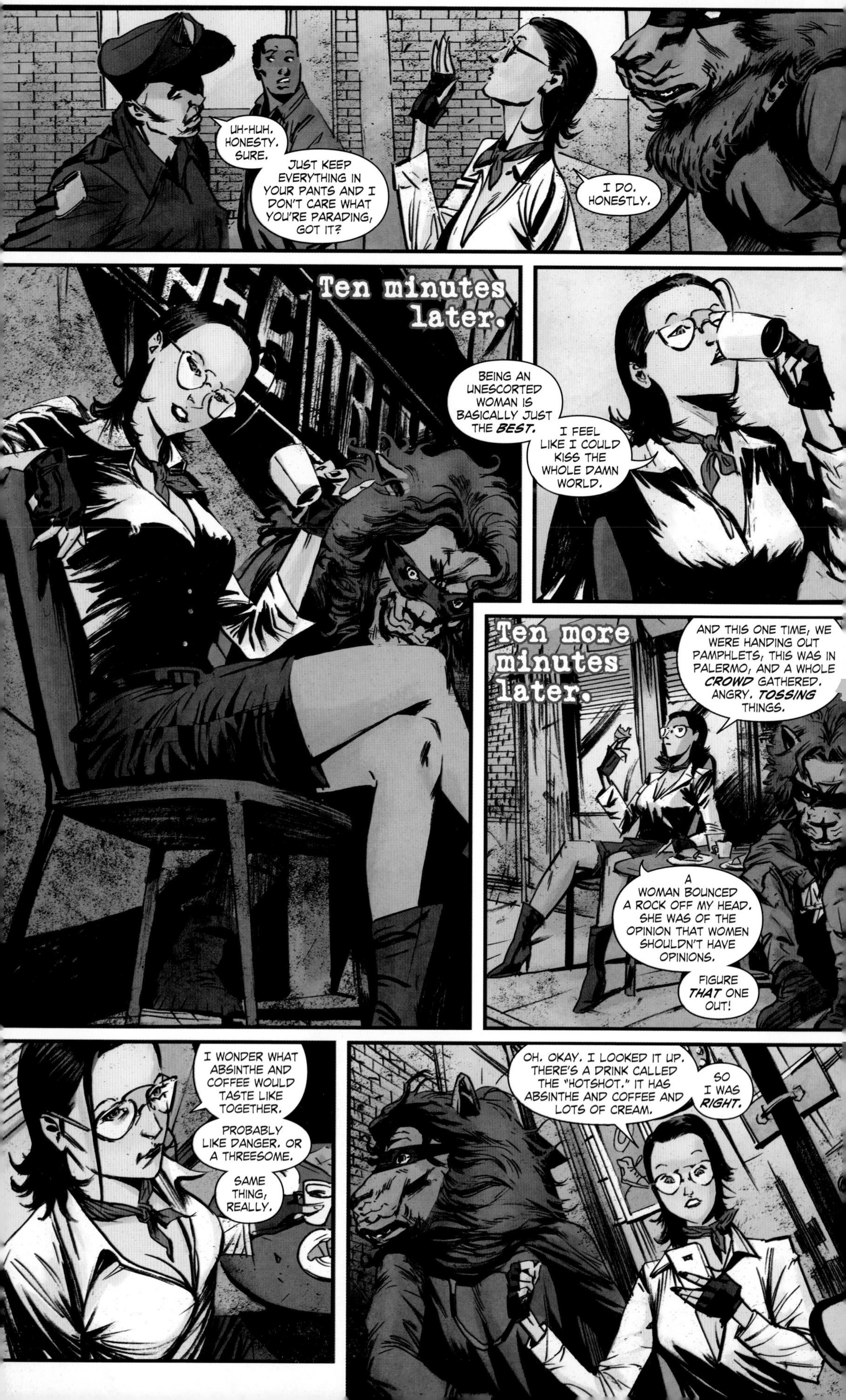
UH-HUH. HONESTY. SURE.
JUST KEEP EVERYTHING IN YOUR PANTS AND I DON'T CARE WHAT YOU'RE PARADING, GOT IT?
I DO. HONESTLY.
Ten minutes later.
BEING AN UNESCORTED WOMAN IS BASICALLY JUST THE *BEST.*
I FEEL LIKE I COULD KISS THE WHOLE DAMN WORLD.
Ten more minutes later.
AND THIS ONE TIME, WE WERE HANDING OUT PAMPHLETS, THIS WAS IN PALERMO, AND A WHOLE *CROWD* GATHERED. ANGRY. *TOSSING* THINGS.
A WOMAN BOUNCED A ROCK OFF MY HEAD. SHE WAS OF THE OPINION THAT WOMEN SHOULDN'T HAVE OPINIONS.
FIGURE *THAT* ONE OUT!
I WONDER WHAT ABSINTHE AND COFFEE WOULD TASTE LIKE TOGETHER.
PROBABLY LIKE DANGER. OR A THREESOME.
SAME THING, REALLY.
OH. OKAY. I LOOKED IT UP. THERE'S A DRINK CALLED THE "HOTSHOT." IT HAS ABSINTHE AND COFFEE AND LOTS OF CREAM.
SO I WAS *RIGHT.*

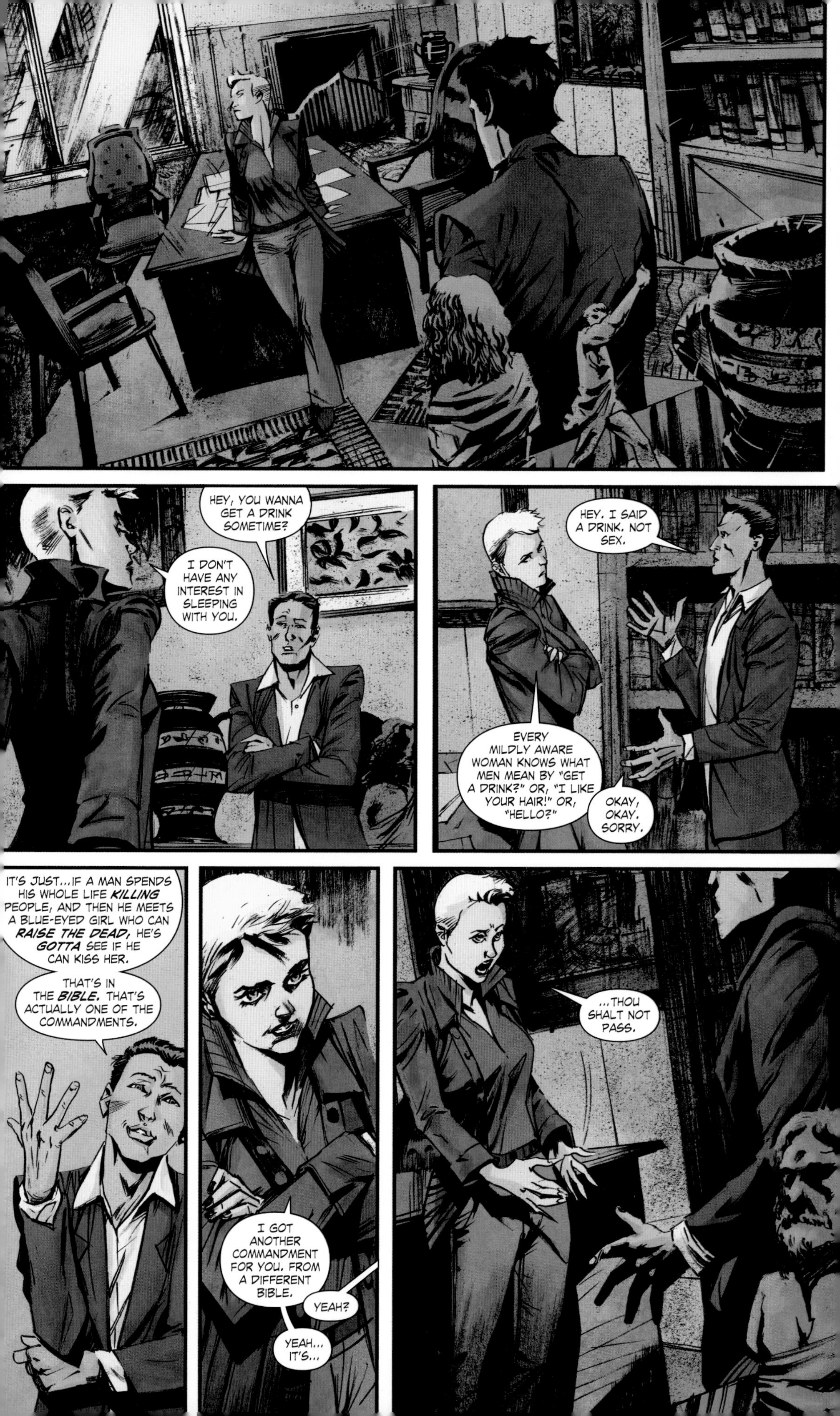
HEY, YOU WANNA GET A DRINK SOMETIME?
I DON'T HAVE ANY INTEREST IN SLEEPING WITH YOU.
HEY. I SAID A DRINK. NOT SEX.
EVERY MILDLY AWARE WOMAN KNOWS WHAT MEN MEAN BY "GET A DRINK?" OR, "I LIKE YOUR HAIR!" OR, "HELLO?"
OKAY, OKAY. SORRY.
IT'S JUST...IF A MAN SPENDS HIS WHOLE LIFE KILLING PEOPLE, AND THEN HE MEETS A BLUE-EYED GIRL WHO CAN RAISE THE DEAD, HE'S GOTTA SEE IF HE CAN KISS HER.
THAT'S IN THE BIBLE. THAT'S ACTUALLY ONE OF THE COMMANDMENTS.
I GOT ANOTHER COMMANDMENT FOR YOU. FROM A DIFFERENT BIBLE.
YEAH?
YEAH... IT'S...
...THOU SHALT NOT PASS.

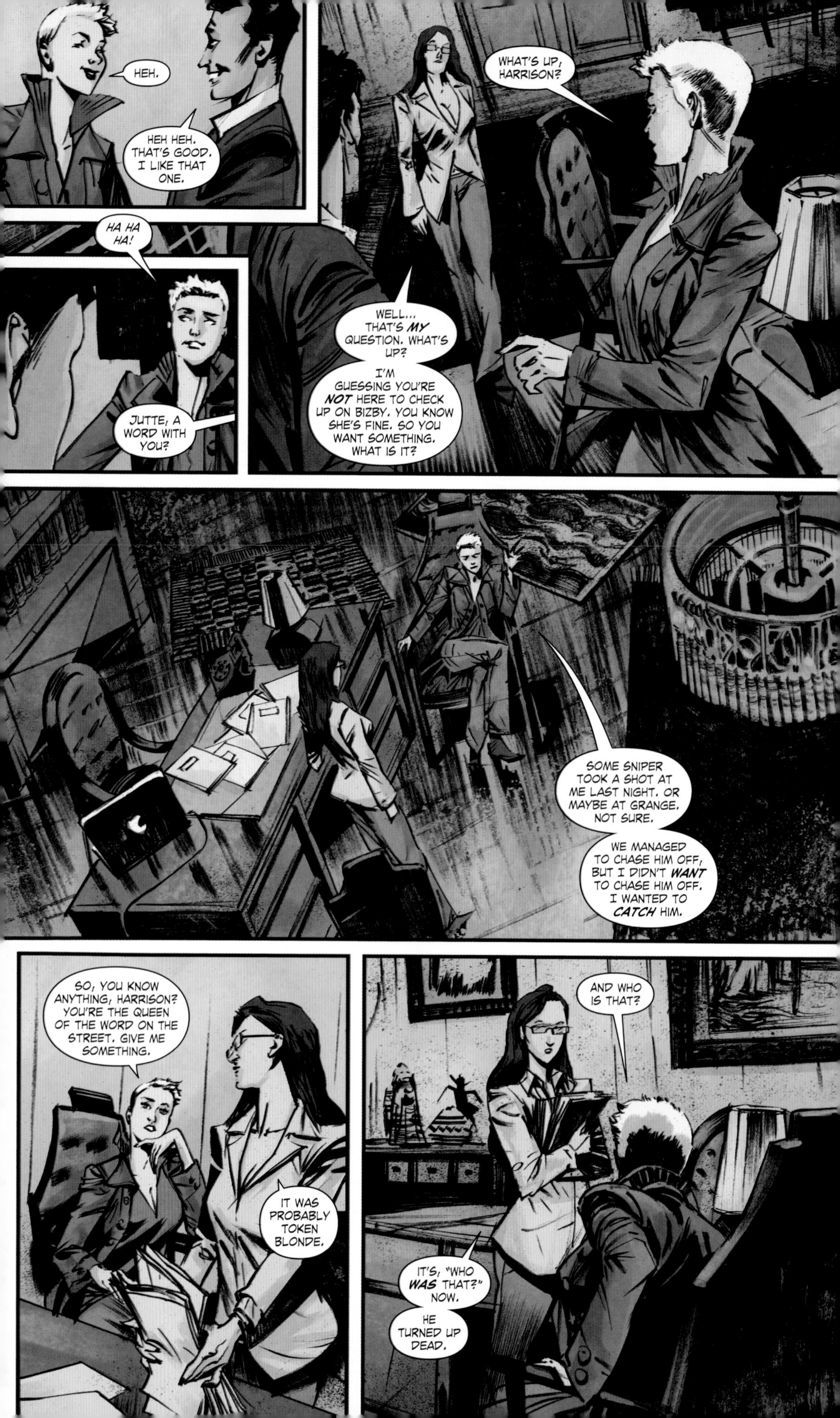
HEH.
HEH HEH. THAT'S GOOD. I LIKE THAT ONE.
WHAT'S UP, HARRISON?
HA HA HA!
JUTTE, A WORD WITH YOU?
WELL... THAT'S *MY* QUESTION. WHAT'S UP?
I'M GUESSING YOU'RE *NOT* HERE TO CHECK UP ON BIZBY. YOU KNOW SHE'S FINE. SO YOU WANT SOMETHING. WHAT IS IT?
SOME SNIPER TOOK A SHOT AT ME LAST NIGHT. OR MAYBE AT GRANGE. NOT SURE.
WE MANAGED TO CHASE HIM OFF, BUT I DIDN'T *WANT* TO CHASE HIM OFF. I WANTED TO *CATCH* HIM.
SO, YOU KNOW ANYTHING, HARRISON? YOU'RE THE QUEEN OF THE WORD ON THE STREET. GIVE ME SOMETHING.
IT WAS PROBABLY TOKEN BLONDE.
AND WHO IS THAT?
IT'S, "WHO *WAS* THAT?" NOW.
HE TURNED UP DEAD.

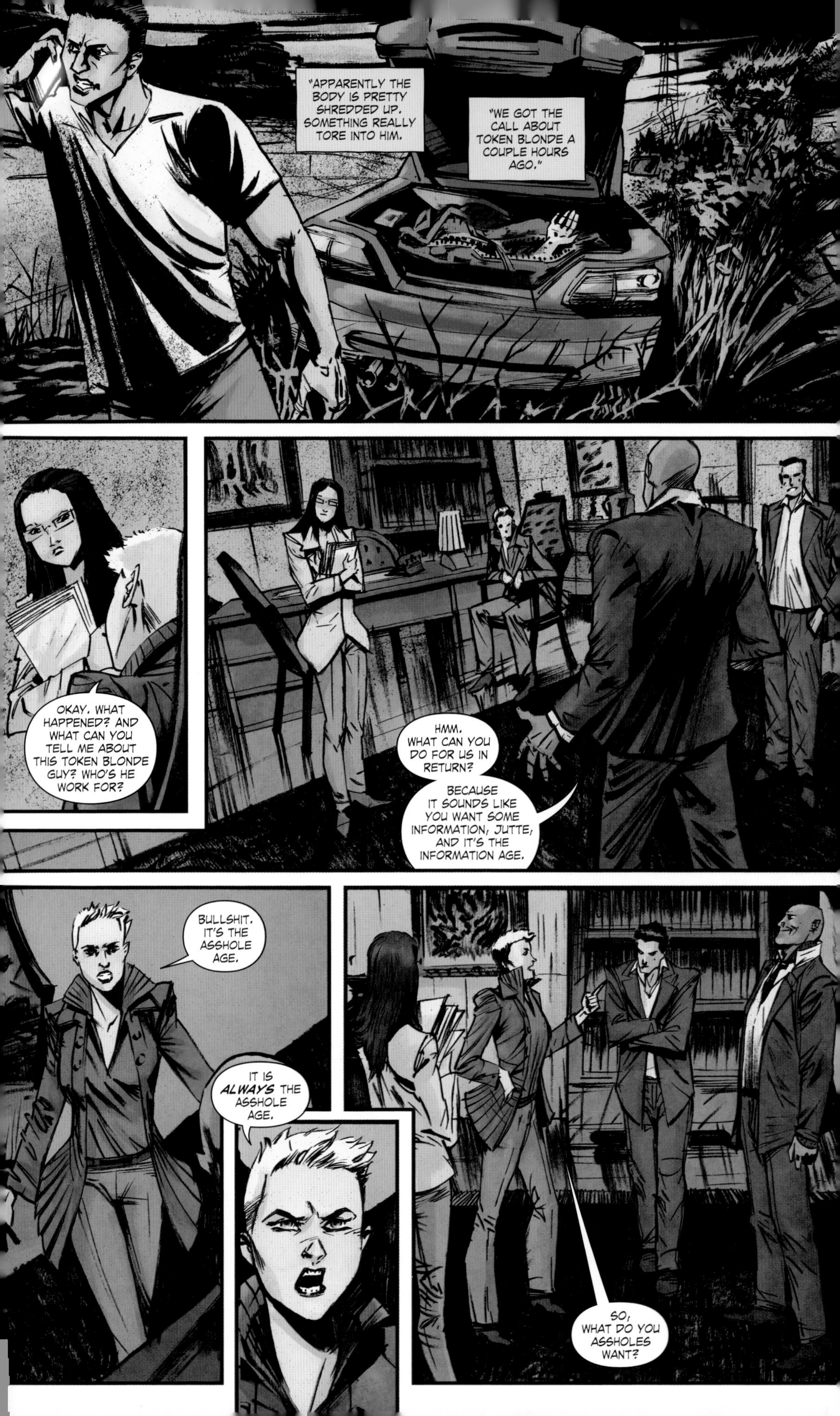
"APPARENTLY THE BODY IS PRETTY SHREDDED UP. SOMETHING REALLY TORE INTO HIM.
"WE GOT THE CALL ABOUT TOKEN BLONDE A COUPLE HOURS AGO."
OKAY. WHAT HAPPENED? AND WHAT CAN YOU TELL ME ABOUT THIS TOKEN BLONDE GUY? WHO'S HE WORK FOR?
HMM. WHAT CAN YOU DO FOR US IN RETURN?
BECAUSE IT SOUNDS LIKE YOU WANT SOME INFORMATION, JUTTE, AND IT'S THE INFORMATION AGE.
BULLSHIT. IT'S THE ASSHOLE AGE.
IT IS ALWAYS THE ASSHOLE AGE.
SO, WHAT DO YOU ASSHOLES WANT?

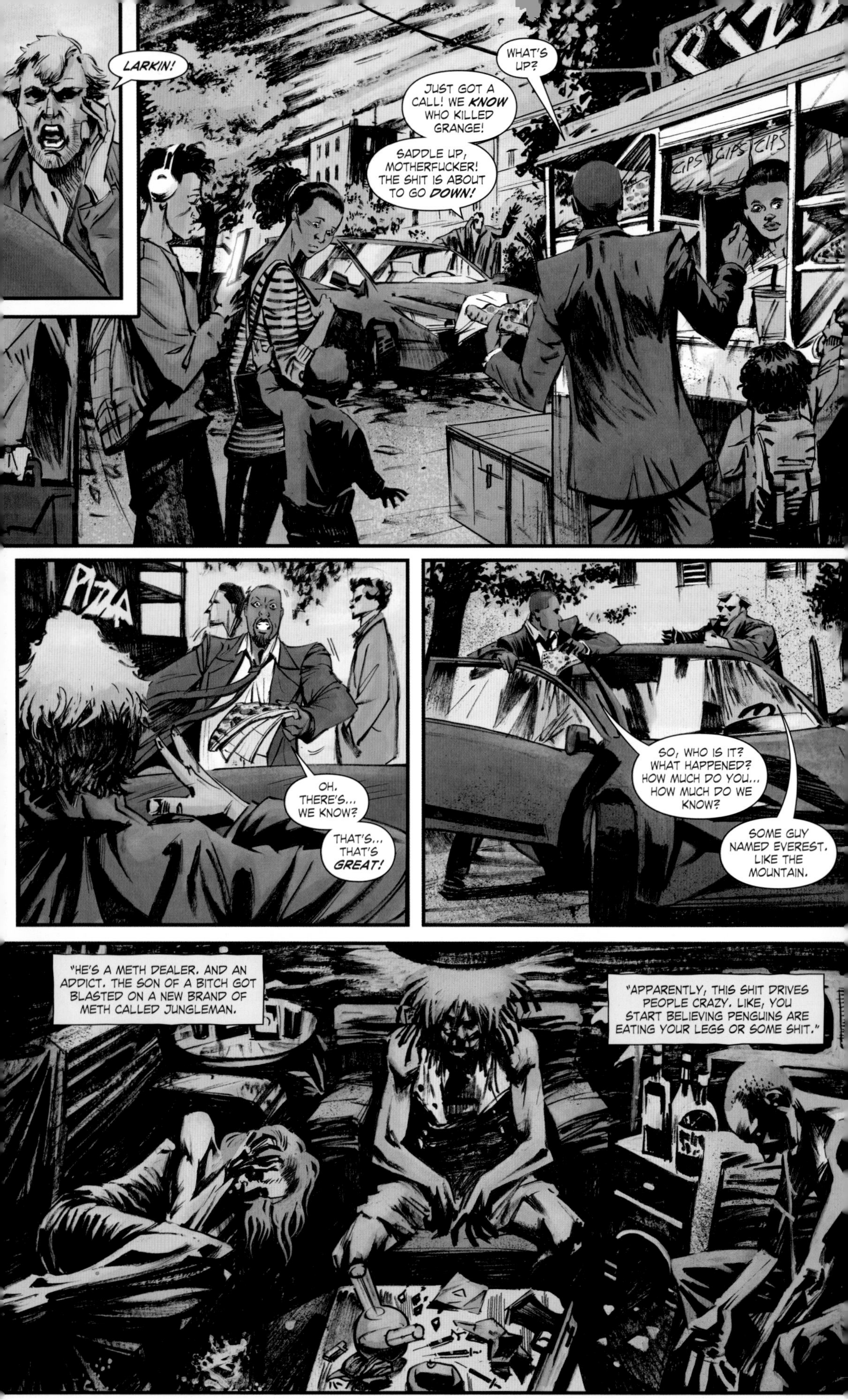
LARKIN!
WHAT'S UP?
JUST GOT A CALL! WE KNOW WHO KILLED GRANGE!
SADDLE UP, MOTHERFUCKER! THE SHIT IS ABOUT TO GO DOWN!
CIPS CIPS CIPS
PIZZA
OH. THERE'S... WE KNOW?
THAT'S... THAT'S GREAT!
SO, WHO IS IT? WHAT HAPPENED? HOW MUCH DO YOU... HOW MUCH DO WE KNOW?
SOME GUY NAMED EVEREST. LIKE THE MOUNTAIN.
"HE'S A METH DEALER. AND AN ADDICT. THE SON OF A BITCH GOT BLASTED ON A NEW BRAND OF METH CALLED JUNGLEMAN.
"APPARENTLY, THIS SHIT DRIVES PEOPLE CRAZY. LIKE, YOU START BELIEVING PENGUINS ARE EATING YOUR LEGS OR SOME SHIT."

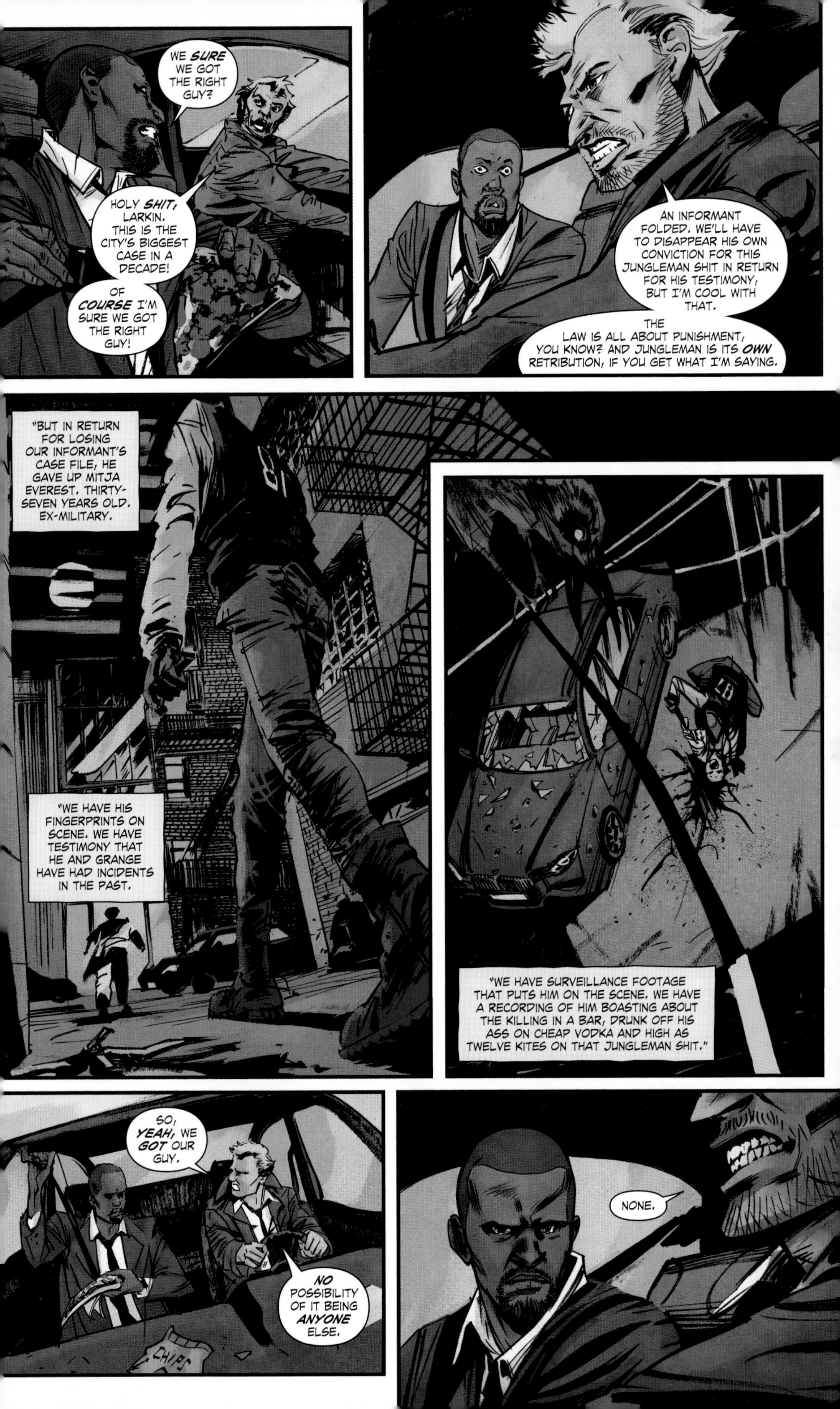
WE SURE WE GOT THE RIGHT GUY?
HOLY SHIT, LARKIN. THIS IS THE CITY'S BIGGEST CASE IN A DECADE!
OF COURSE I'M SURE WE GOT THE RIGHT GUY!
AN INFORMANT FOLDED. WE'LL HAVE TO DISAPPEAR HIS OWN CONVICTION FOR THIS JUNGLEMAN SHIT IN RETURN FOR HIS TESTIMONY, BUT I'M COOL WITH THAT.
THE LAW IS ALL ABOUT PUNISHMENT, YOU KNOW? AND JUNGLEMAN IS ITS OWN RETRIBUTION, IF YOU GET WHAT I'M SAYING.
"BUT IN RETURN FOR LOSING OUR INFORMANT'S CASE FILE, HE GAVE UP MITJA EVEREST. THIRTY-SEVEN YEARS OLD. EX-MILITARY.
"WE HAVE HIS FINGERPRINTS ON SCENE. WE HAVE TESTIMONY THAT HE AND GRANGE HAVE HAD INCIDENTS IN THE PAST.
"WE HAVE SURVEILLANCE FOOTAGE THAT PUTS HIM ON THE SCENE. WE HAVE A RECORDING OF HIM BOASTING ABOUT THE KILLING IN A BAR, DRUNK OFF HIS ASS ON CHEAP VODKA AND HIGH AS TWELVE KITES ON THAT JUNGLEMAN SHIT."
SO, YEAH, WE GOT OUR GUY.
NO POSSIBILITY OF IT BEING ANYONE ELSE.
NONE.

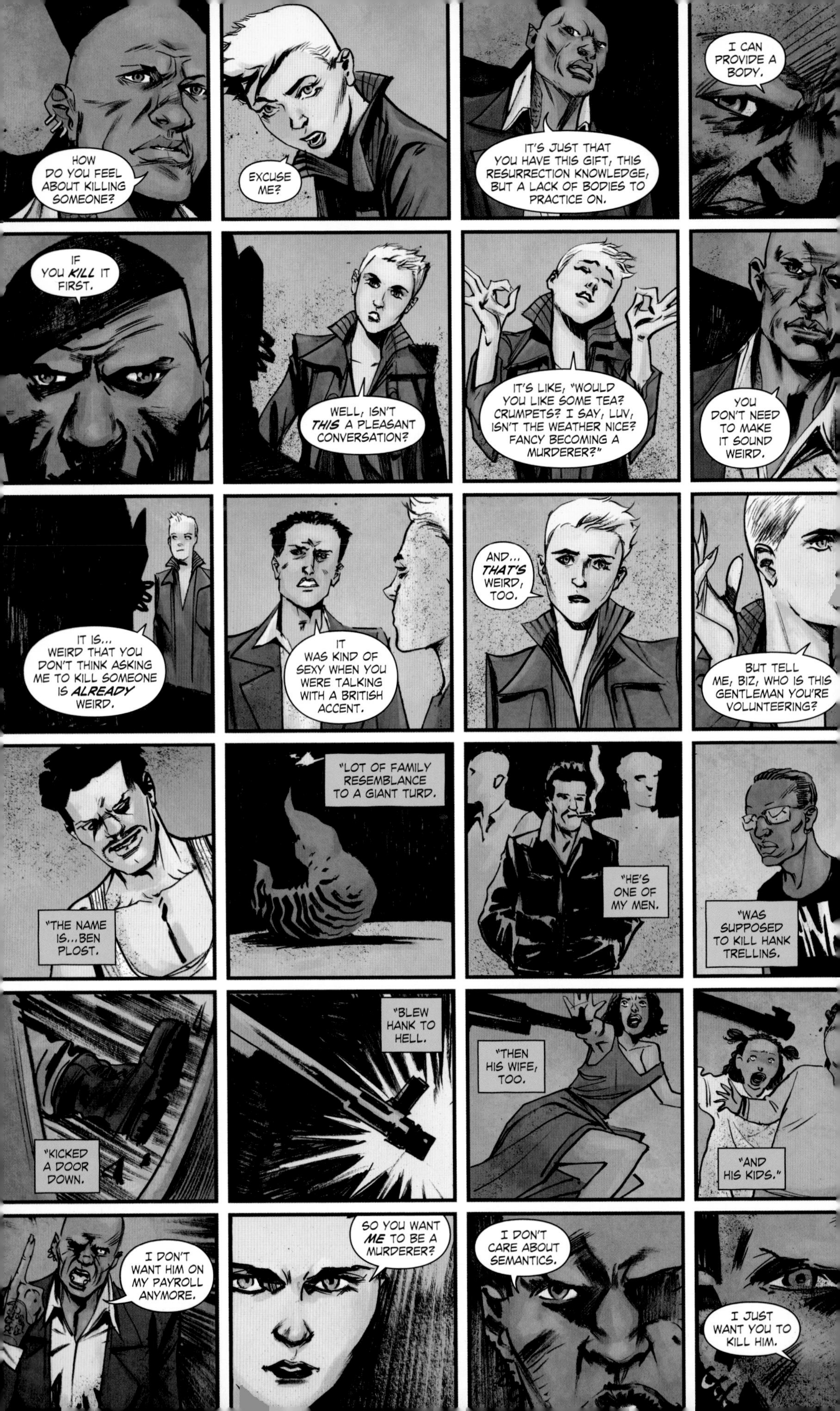

HOW DO YOU FEEL ABOUT KILLING SOMEONE?
EXCUSE ME?
IT'S JUST THAT YOU HAVE THIS GIFT, THIS RESURRECTION KNOWLEDGE, BUT A LACK OF BODIES TO PRACTICE ON.
I CAN PROVIDE A BODY.
IF YOU *KILL* IT FIRST.
WELL, ISN'T *THIS* A PLEASANT CONVERSATION?
IT'S LIKE, "WOULD YOU LIKE SOME TEA? CRUMPETS? I SAY, LUV, ISN'T THE WEATHER NICE? FANCY BECOMING A MURDERER?"
YOU DON'T NEED TO MAKE IT SOUND WEIRD.
IT IS... WEIRD THAT YOU DON'T THINK ASKING ME TO KILL SOMEONE IS *ALREADY* WEIRD.
IT WAS KIND OF SEXY WHEN YOU WERE TALKING WITH A BRITISH ACCENT.
AND... *THAT'S* WEIRD, TOO.
BUT TELL ME, BIZ, WHO IS THIS GENTLEMAN YOU'RE VOLUNTEERING?
"THE NAME IS...BEN PLOST.
"LOT OF FAMILY RESEMBLANCE TO A GIANT TURD.
"HE'S ONE OF MY MEN.
"WAS SUPPOSED TO KILL HANK TRELLINS.
"KICKED A DOOR DOWN.
"BLEW HANK TO HELL.
"THEN HIS WIFE, TOO.
"AND HIS KIDS."
I DON'T WANT HIM ON MY PAYROLL ANYMORE.
SO YOU WANT *ME* TO BE A MURDERER?
I DON'T CARE ABOUT SEMANTICS.
I JUST WANT YOU TO KILL HIM.

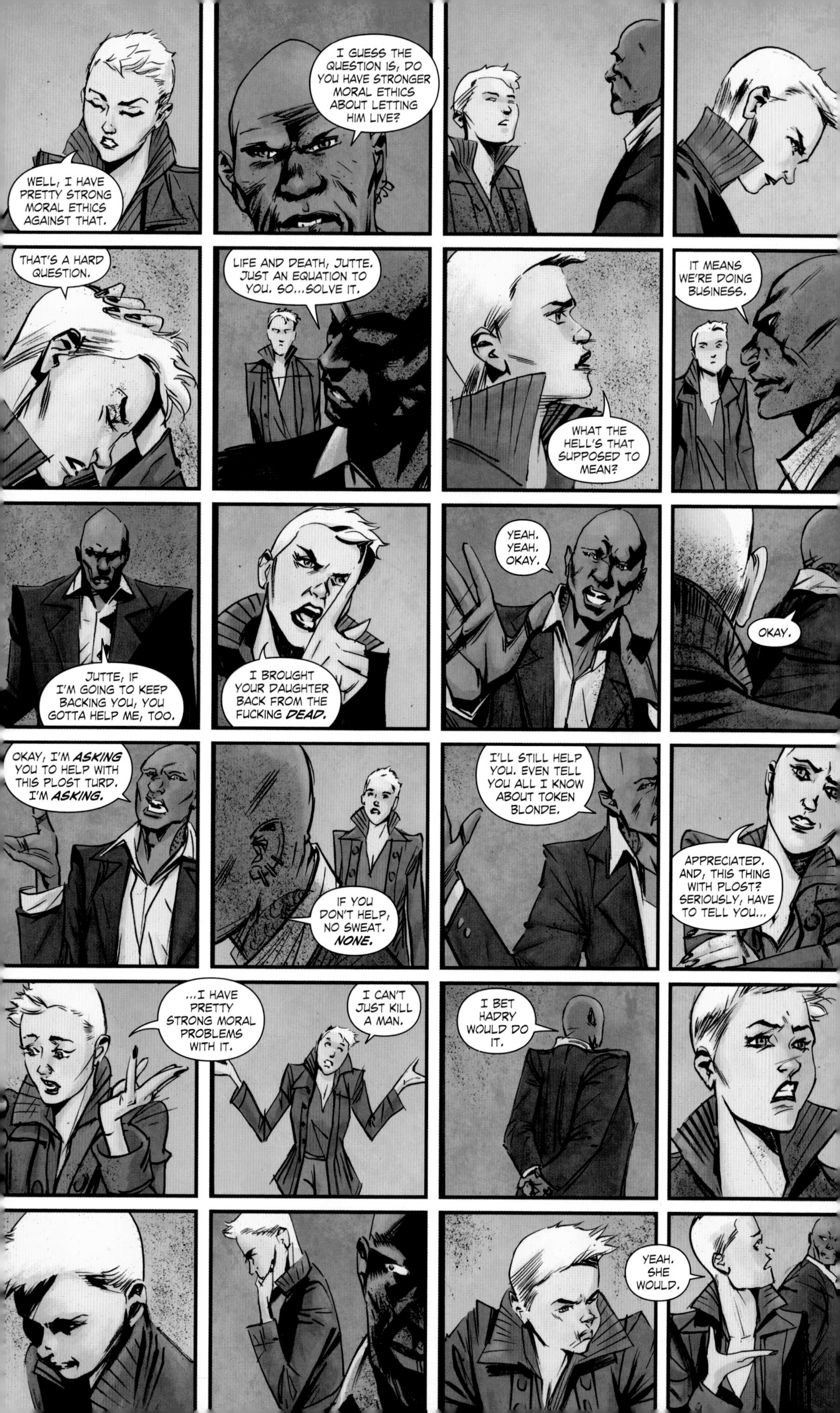
WELL, I HAVE PRETTY STRONG MORAL ETHICS AGAINST THAT.
I GUESS THE QUESTION IS, DO YOU HAVE STRONGER MORAL ETHICS ABOUT LETTING HIM LIVE?
THAT'S A HARD QUESTION.
LIFE AND DEATH, JUTTE. JUST AN EQUATION TO YOU. SO...SOLVE IT.
WHAT THE HELL'S THAT SUPPOSED TO MEAN?
IT MEANS WE'RE DOING BUSINESS.
JUTTE, IF I'M GOING TO KEEP BACKING YOU, YOU GOTTA HELP ME, TOO.
I BROUGHT YOUR DAUGHTER BACK FROM THE FUCKING ***DEAD.***
YEAH. YEAH. OKAY.
OKAY.
OKAY, I'M ***ASKING*** YOU TO HELP WITH THIS PLOST TURD. I'M ***ASKING.***
IF YOU DON'T HELP, NO SWEAT. ***NONE.***
I'LL STILL HELP YOU. EVEN TELL YOU ALL I KNOW ABOUT TOKEN BLONDE.
APPRECIATED. AND, THIS THING WITH PLOST? SERIOUSLY, HAVE TO TELL YOU...
...I HAVE PRETTY STRONG MORAL PROBLEMS WITH IT.
I CAN'T JUST KILL A MAN.
I BET HADRY WOULD DO IT.
YEAH. SHE WOULD.

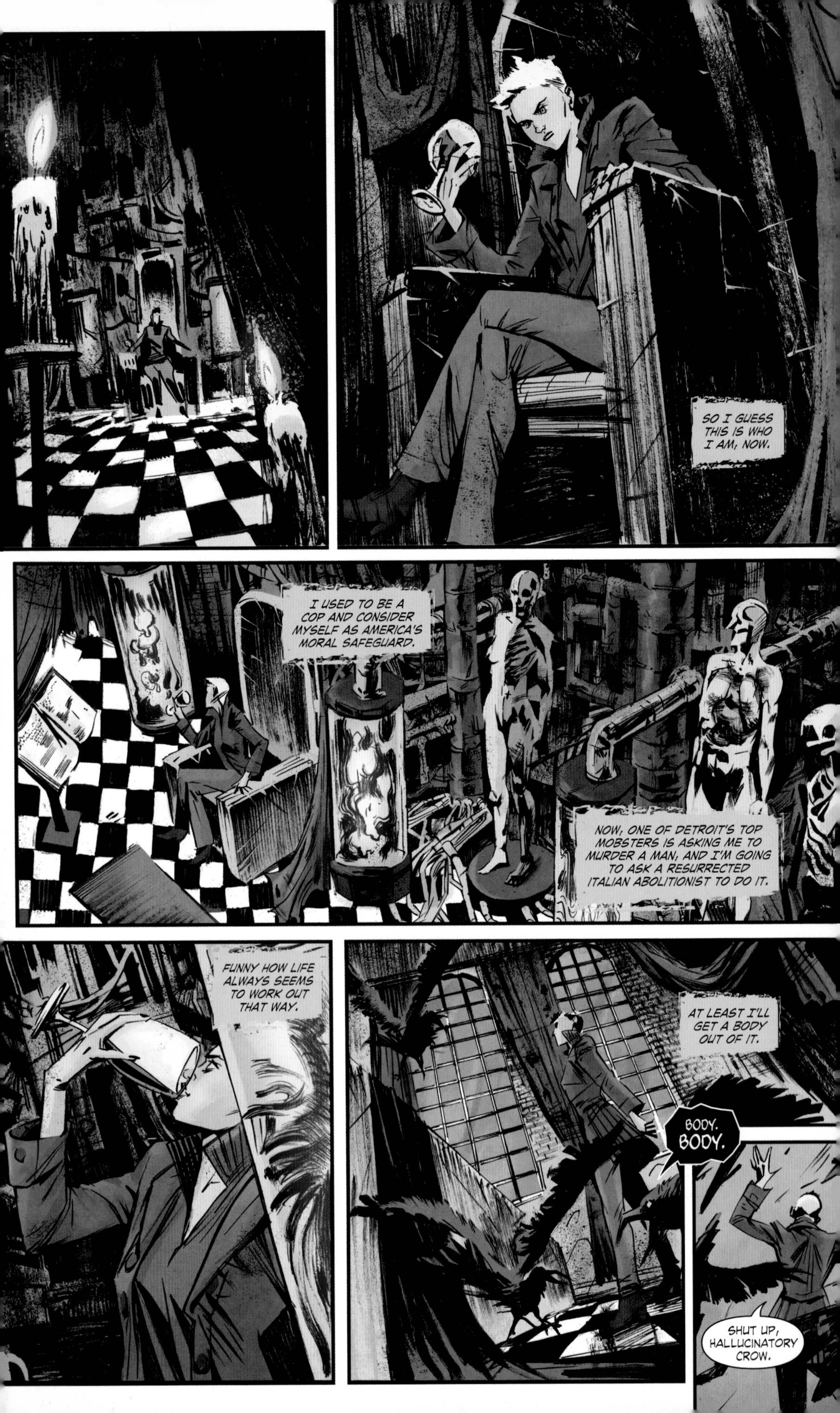
SO I GUESS THIS IS WHO I AM, NOW.
I USED TO BE A COP AND CONSIDER MYSELF AS AMERICA'S MORAL SAFEGUARD.
NOW, ONE OF DETROIT'S TOP MOBSTERS IS ASKING ME TO MURDER A MAN, AND I'M GOING TO ASK A RESURRECTED ITALIAN ABOLITIONIST TO DO IT.
FUNNY HOW LIFE ALWAYS SEEMS TO WORK OUT THAT WAY.
AT LEAST I'LL GET A BODY OUT OF IT.
BODY. BODY.
SHUT UP, HALLUCINATORY CROW.

MY GRANDMOTHER CECILIA SEEMED TO HAVE A NEVER-ENDING SUPPLY OF BODIES.

I STILL HAVE A SMORGASBORD OF LEFTOVER BODY PARTS FROM HER STOCK, PRESERVED IN CHEMICALS SHE CONCOCTED; BUT...

...CECILIA SEEMED TO ACQUIRE BODIES FROM STRANGE PLACES.

KIRKLEES ASYLUM TROUBLED INDIVIDUALS
For those unfortunates impaired or diminished mental capacity. God be praised.

OFTEN BY UNFORTUNATE MEANS.

LAMBETH ANTI-FEMINIST LEAGUE
Keep women where God intended.

AND SHE WAS... WHIMSICAL.

REGARDLESS, THE MODERN AGE HAS BROUGHT ABOUT A WEALTH OF CHANGES IN OUR BODIES. A WHOLE NEW ERA OF EVOLUTION. I NEED TO ADD A FEW RECENT BODIES, FLESH OUT MY STOCK OF FLESH, SO TO SPEAK.

SPEAK! SPEAK!

NO, *DON'T* SPEAK. SHUT UP.

HALLUCINATIONS ARE SUPPOSED TO KEEP THEIR BEAKS SHUT.

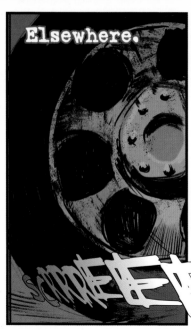

Elsewhere.

SCRREEEE THUMP

LET'S GO! *LET'S GO!*

WE'RE IN POSITION, DETECTIVE!

DO IT!

CRAASH!

STILL NOT SURE ABOUT THIS BEING OUR GUY. ALL SOUNDS TOO *EASY.*

LIKE, ALL THAT INFORMATION FITTING TOGETHER? LEAVING ALL THAT *EVIDENCE* BEHIND? THAT *NEVER* HAPPENS.

YEAH, WELL PEOPLE WHO KILL POLICE CAPTAINS WHEN THEY'RE STUFFED FULL OF METH--

--AREN'T EXACTLY KNOWN FOR THEIR *FUCKIN' SUBTLETY!*

ALL I'M SAYING IS, WE *FIND* THIS GUY, WE *CUFF* HIM. UNTIL WE KNOW WHAT'S WHAT.

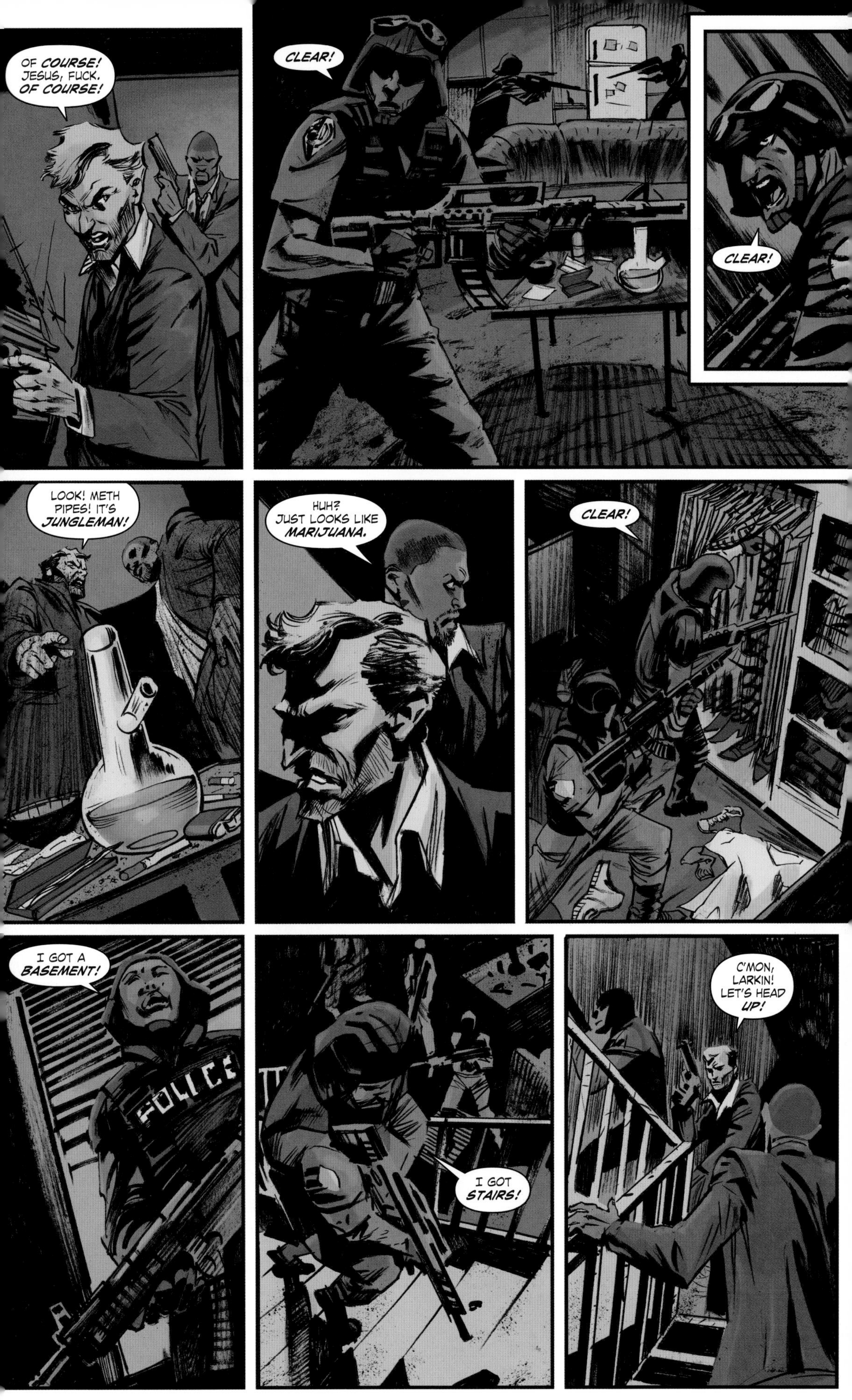
OF COURSE! JESUS, FUCK. OF COURSE!
CLEAR!
CLEAR!
LOOK! METH PIPES! IT'S JUNGLEMAN!
HUH? JUST LOOKS LIKE MARIJUANA.
CLEAR!
I GOT A BASEMENT!
POLICE
I GOT STAIRS!
C'MON, LARKIN! LET'S HEAD UP!

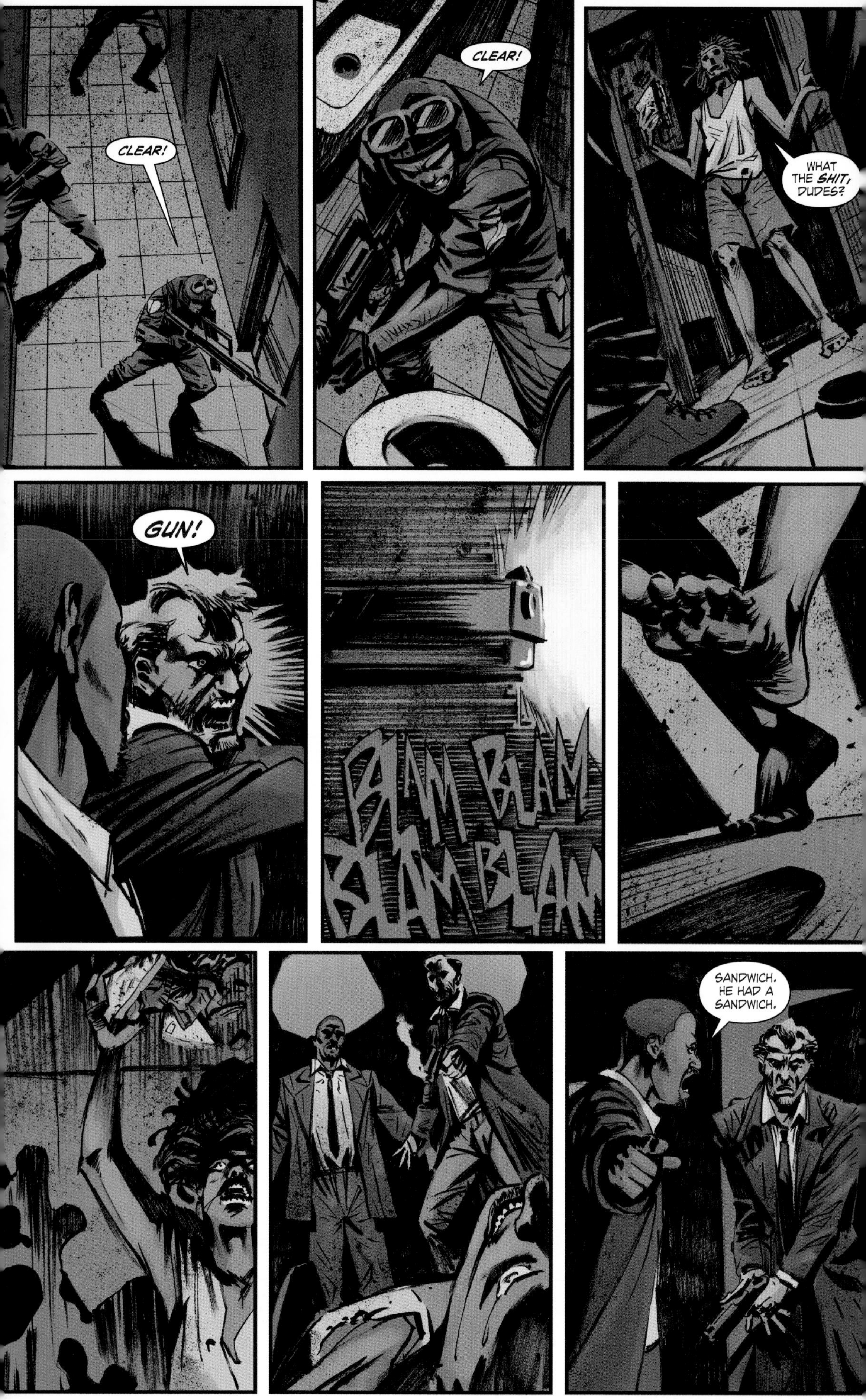
CLEAR!
CLEAR!
WHAT THE SHIT, DUDES?
GUN!
BLAM BLAM
BLAM BLAM
SANDWICH. HE HAD A SANDWICH.

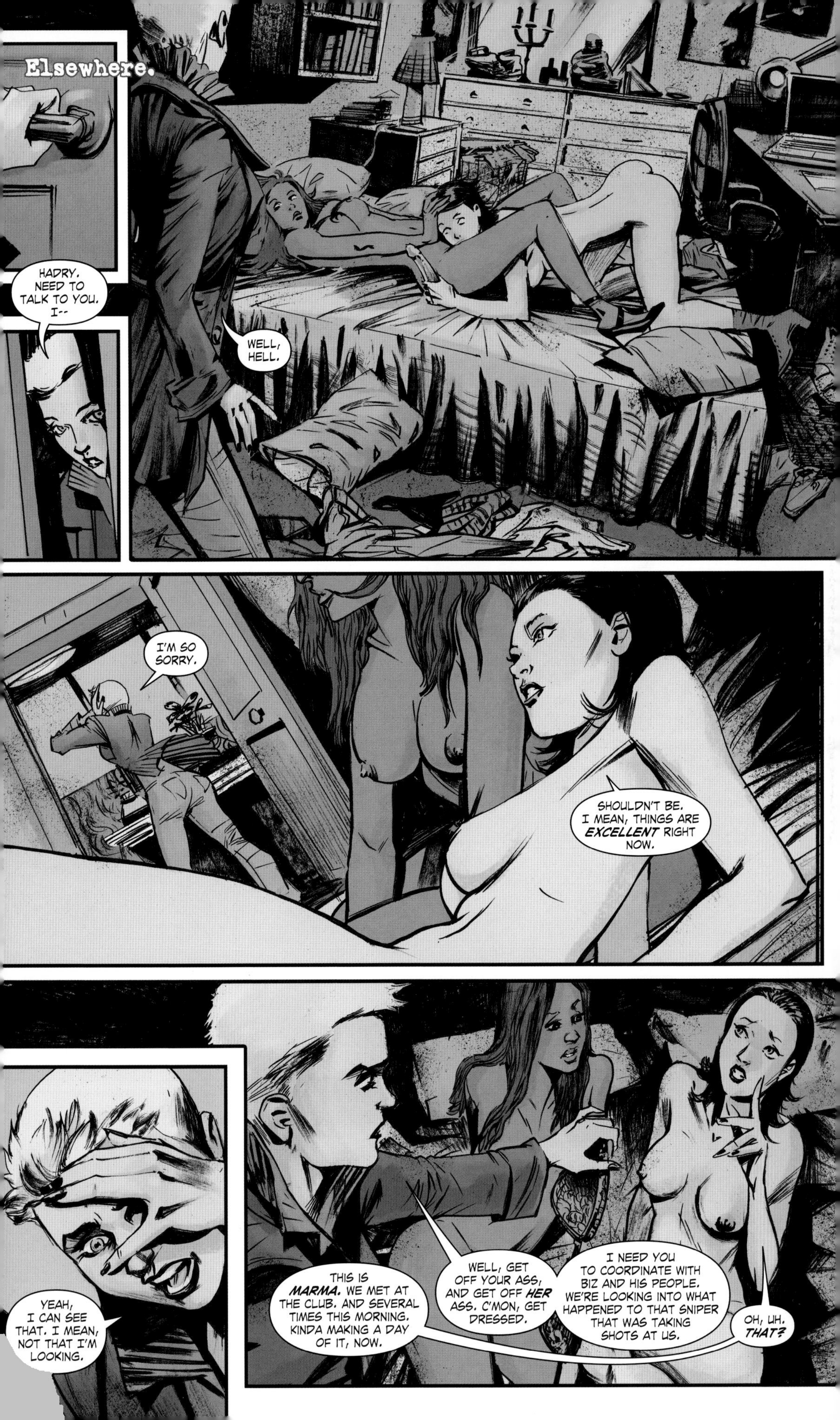
Elsewhere.
HADRY. NEED TO TALK TO YOU. I--
WELL, HELL.
I'M SO SORRY.
SHOULDN'T BE. I MEAN, THINGS ARE EXCELLENT RIGHT NOW.
YEAH, I CAN SEE THAT. I MEAN, NOT THAT I'M LOOKING.
THIS IS MARMA. WE MET AT THE CLUB. AND SEVERAL TIMES THIS MORNING. KINDA MAKING A DAY OF IT, NOW.
WELL, GET OFF YOUR ASS, AND GET OFF HER ASS. C'MON, GET DRESSED.
I NEED YOU TO COORDINATE WITH BIZ AND HIS PEOPLE. WE'RE LOOKING INTO WHAT HAPPENED TO THAT SNIPER THAT WAS TAKING SHOTS AT US.
OH, UH. THAT?

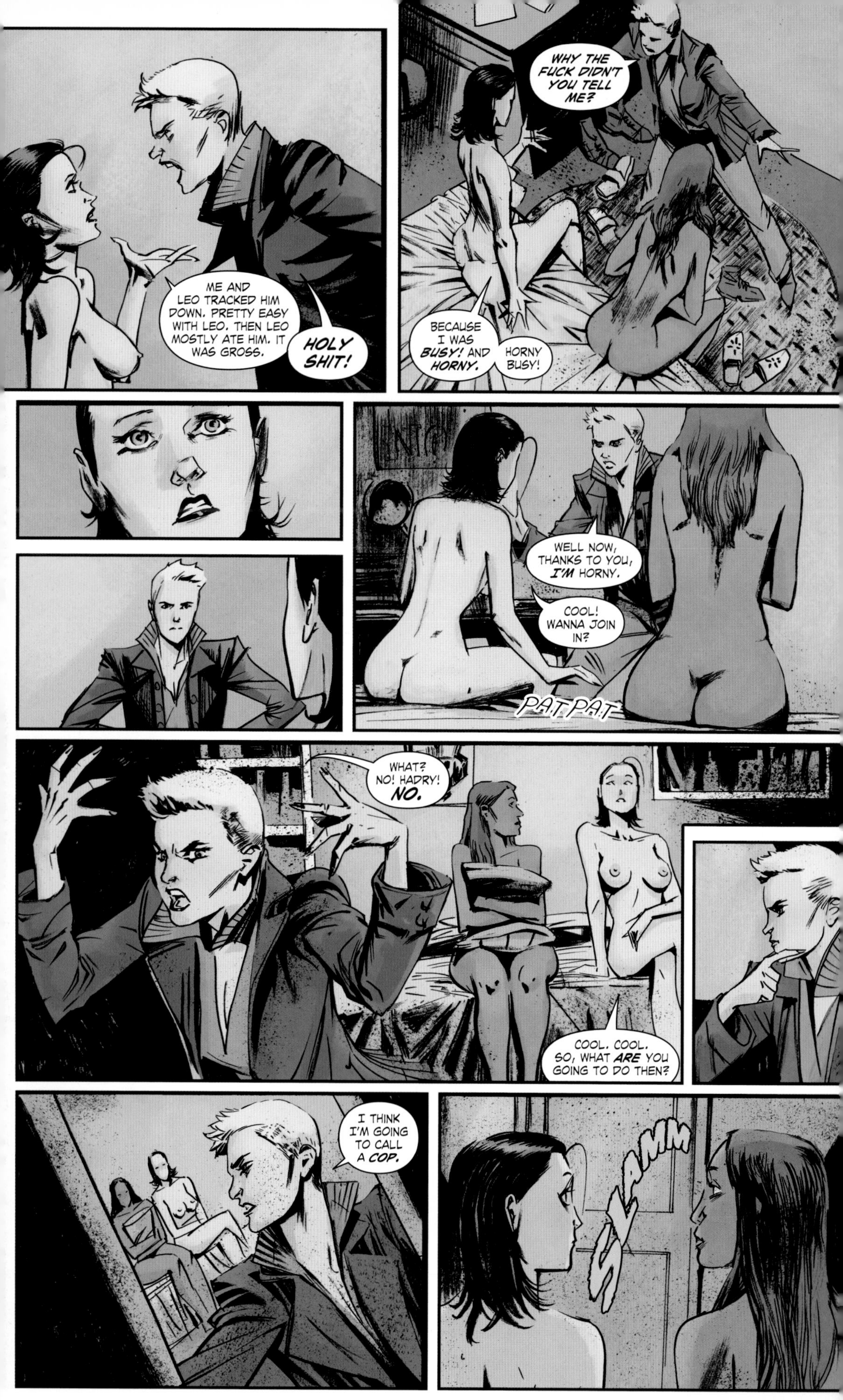
ME AND LEO TRACKED HIM DOWN. PRETTY EASY WITH LEO. THEN LEO MOSTLY ATE HIM. IT WAS GROSS.
HOLY SHIT!
WHY THE FUCK DIDN'T YOU TELL ME?
BECAUSE I WAS BUSY! AND HORNY.
HORNY BUSY!
WELL NOW, THANKS TO YOU, I'M HORNY.
COOL! WANNA JOIN IN?
PAT PAT
WHAT? NO! HADRY! NO.
COOL. COOL. SO, WHAT ARE YOU GOING TO DO THEN?
I THINK I'M GOING TO CALL A COP.
SLAMM

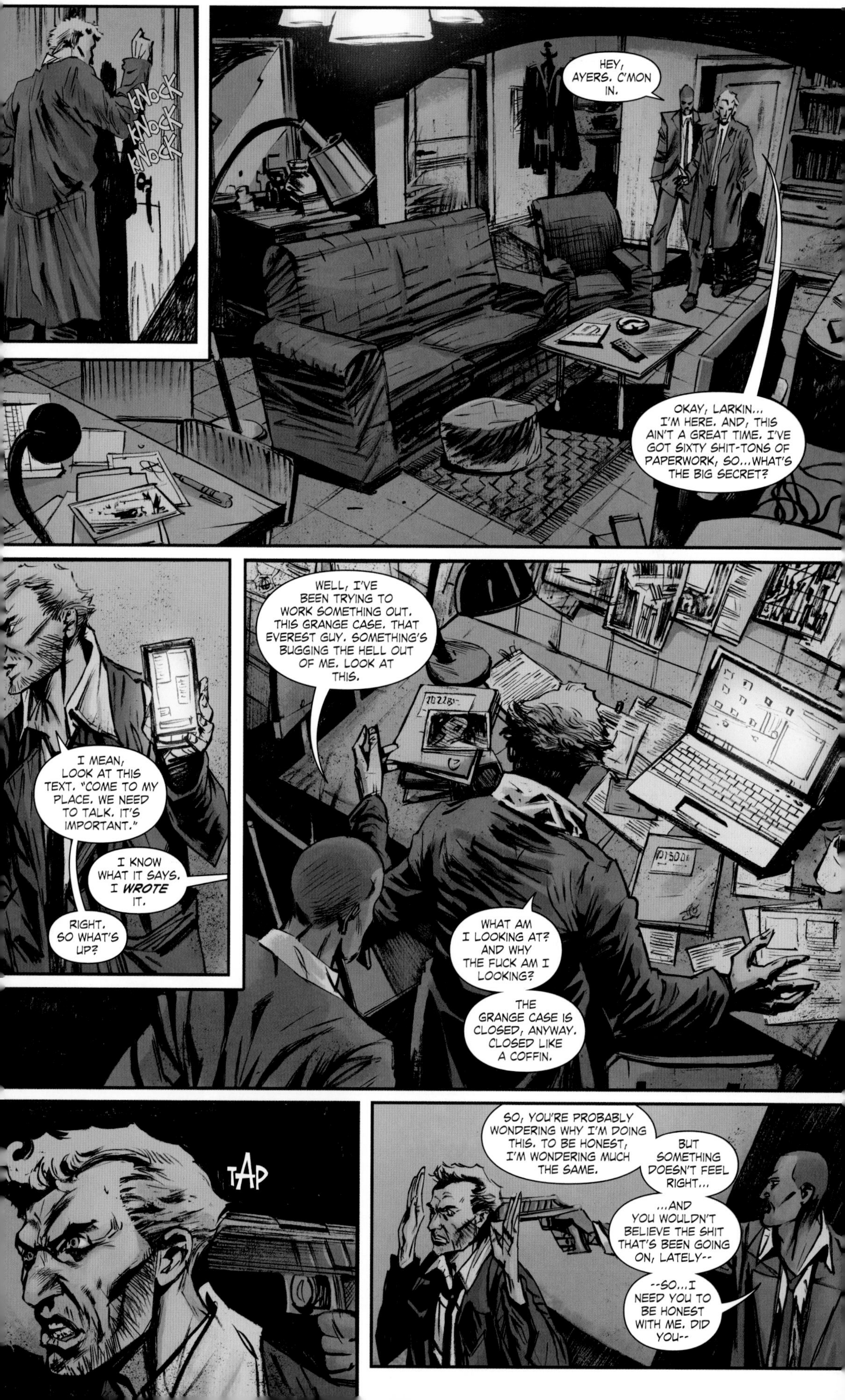
KNOCK KNOCK KNOCK
HEY, AYERS. C'MON IN.
OKAY, LARKIN... I'M HERE. AND, THIS AIN'T A GREAT TIME. I'VE GOT SIXTY SHIT-TONS OF PAPERWORK, SO...WHAT'S THE BIG SECRET?
I MEAN, LOOK AT THIS TEXT. "COME TO MY PLACE. WE NEED TO TALK. IT'S IMPORTANT."
I KNOW WHAT IT SAYS. I *WROTE* IT.
RIGHT. SO WHAT'S UP?
WELL, I'VE BEEN TRYING TO WORK SOMETHING OUT. THIS GRANGE CASE. THAT EVEREST GUY. SOMETHING'S BUGGING THE HELL OUT OF ME. LOOK AT THIS.
WHAT AM I LOOKING AT? AND WHY THE FUCK AM I LOOKING?
THE GRANGE CASE IS CLOSED, ANYWAY. CLOSED LIKE A COFFIN.
TAP
SO, YOU'RE PROBABLY WONDERING WHY I'M DOING THIS. TO BE HONEST, I'M WONDERING MUCH THE SAME.
BUT SOMETHING DOESN'T FEEL RIGHT...
...AND YOU WOULDN'T BELIEVE THE SHIT THAT'S BEEN GOING ON, LATELY--
--SO...I NEED YOU TO BE HONEST WITH ME. DID YOU--

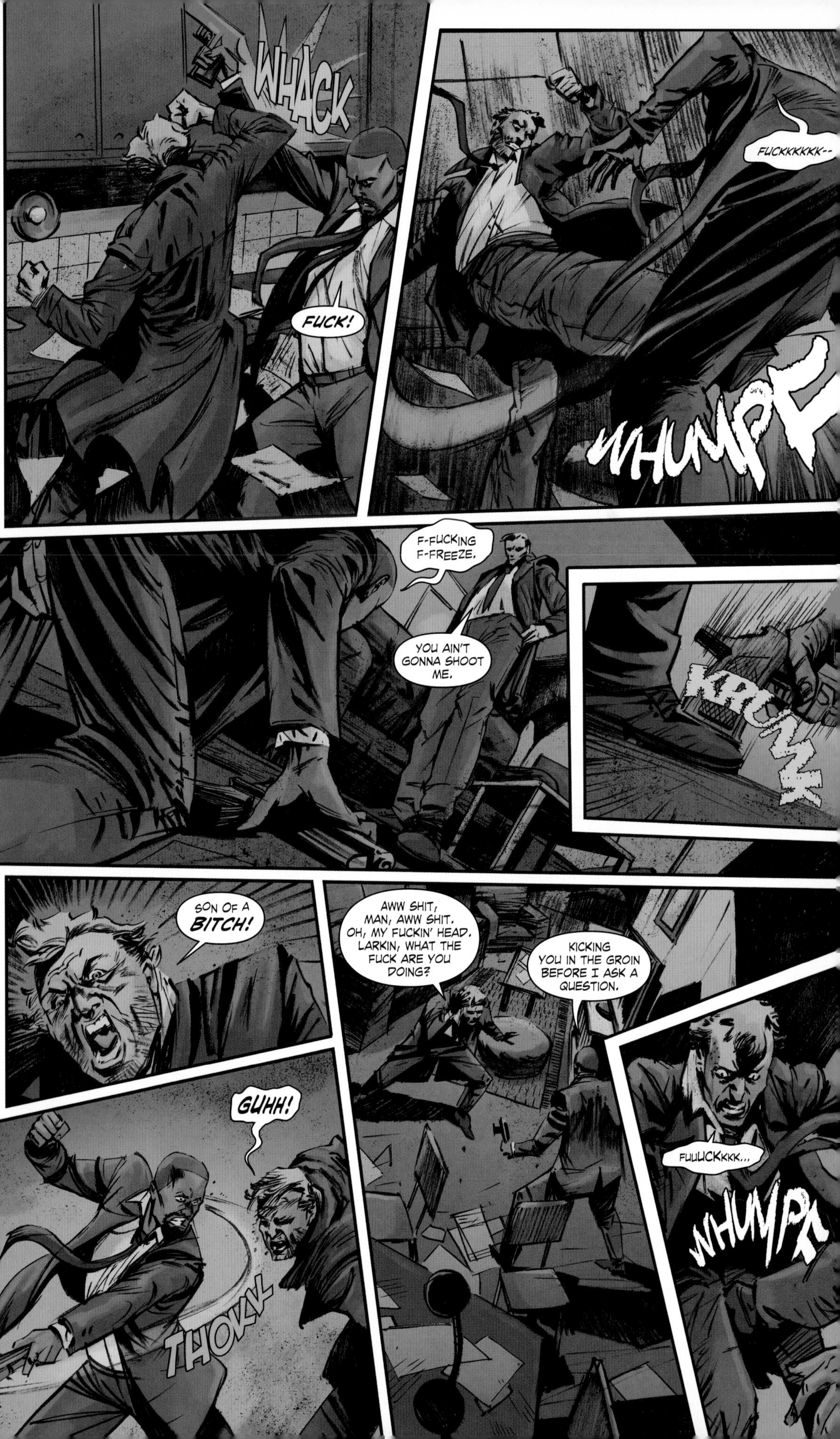
WHACK
FUCK!
FUCKKKKKK--
WHUMPF
F-FUCKING F-FREEZE.
YOU AIN'T GONNA SHOOT ME.
KRUNK
SON OF A BITCH!
GUHH!
THOKK
AWW SHIT, MAN, AWW SHIT. OH, MY FUCKIN' HEAD. LARKIN, WHAT THE FUCK ARE YOU DOING?
KICKING YOU IN THE GROIN BEFORE I ASK A QUESTION.
FUUUCKKKK...
WHUMPF

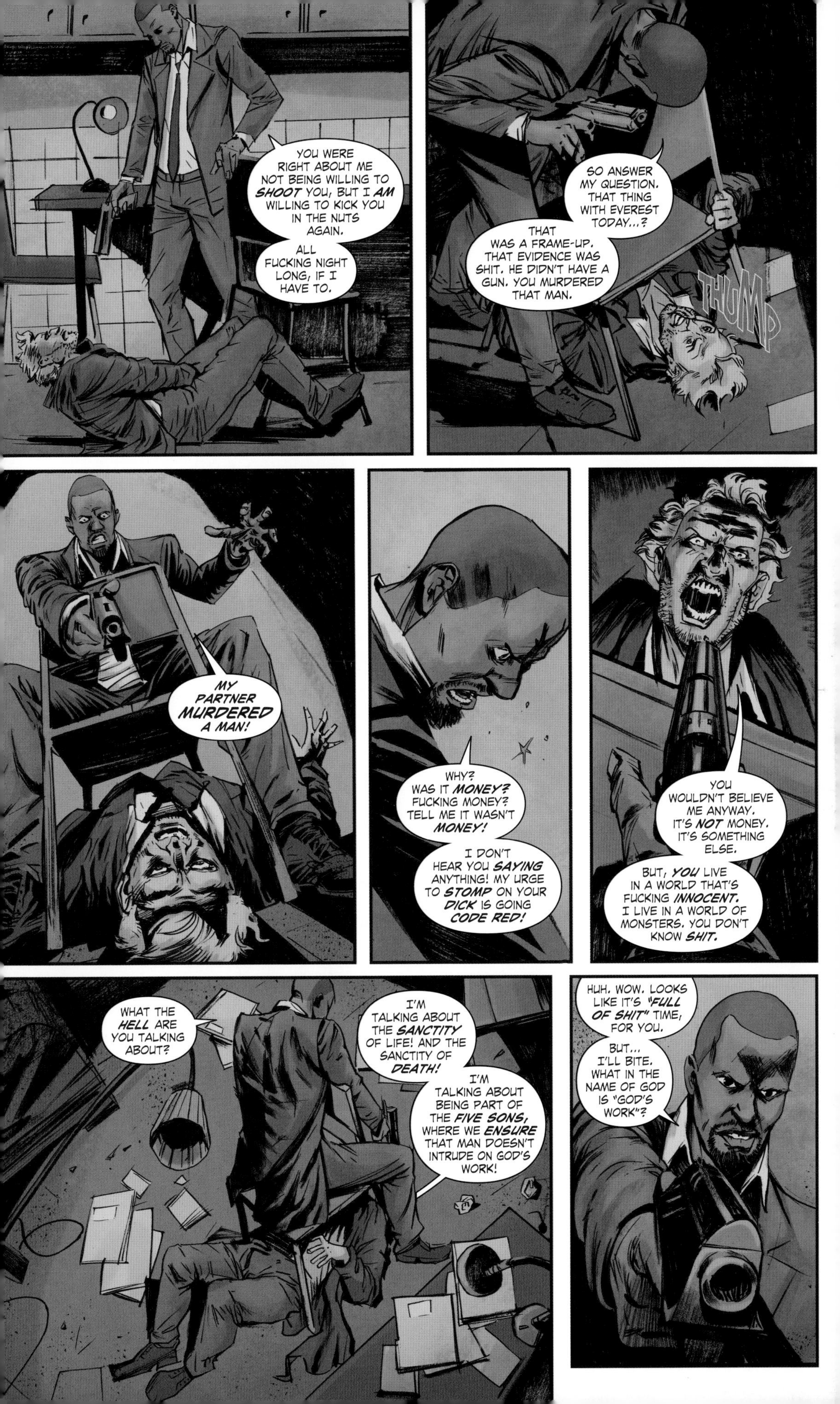
YOU WERE RIGHT ABOUT ME NOT BEING WILLING TO SHOOT YOU, BUT I AM WILLING TO KICK YOU IN THE NUTS AGAIN.
ALL FUCKING NIGHT LONG, IF I HAVE TO.
SO ANSWER MY QUESTION. THAT THING WITH EVEREST TODAY...?
THAT WAS A FRAME-UP. THAT EVIDENCE WAS SHIT. HE DIDN'T HAVE A GUN. YOU MURDERED THAT MAN.
THUMP
MY PARTNER MURDERED A MAN!
WHY? WAS IT MONEY? FUCKING MONEY? TELL ME IT WASN'T MONEY!
I DON'T HEAR YOU SAYING ANYTHING! MY URGE TO STOMP ON YOUR DICK IS GOING CODE RED!
YOU WOULDN'T BELIEVE ME ANYWAY. IT'S NOT MONEY. IT'S SOMETHING ELSE.
BUT, YOU LIVE IN A WORLD THAT'S FUCKING INNOCENT. I LIVE IN A WORLD OF MONSTERS. YOU DON'T KNOW SHIT.
WHAT THE HELL ARE YOU TALKING ABOUT?
I'M TALKING ABOUT THE SANCTITY OF LIFE! AND THE SANCTITY OF DEATH!
I'M TALKING ABOUT BEING PART OF THE FIVE SONS, WHERE WE ENSURE THAT MAN DOESN'T INTRUDE ON GOD'S WORK!
HUH. WOW. LOOKS LIKE IT'S "FULL OF SHIT" TIME, FOR YOU.
BUT... I'LL BITE. WHAT IN THE NAME OF GOD IS "GOD'S WORK"?

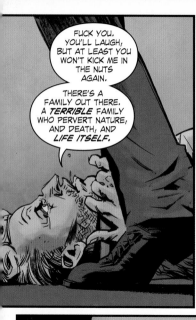

FUCK YOU. YOU'LL LAUGH, BUT AT LEAST YOU WON'T KICK ME IN THE NUTS AGAIN.

THERE'S A FAMILY OUT THERE. A *TERRIBLE* FAMILY WHO PERVERT NATURE, AND DEATH, AND *LIFE ITSELF.*

I'M TALKING ABOUT A FAMILY NAMED...

...FRANKENSTEIN.

AWW SHIT.

HELLO?

JUTTE?

DON'T LOOK AT *ME*. I JUST CAME HERE TO GET LAID.

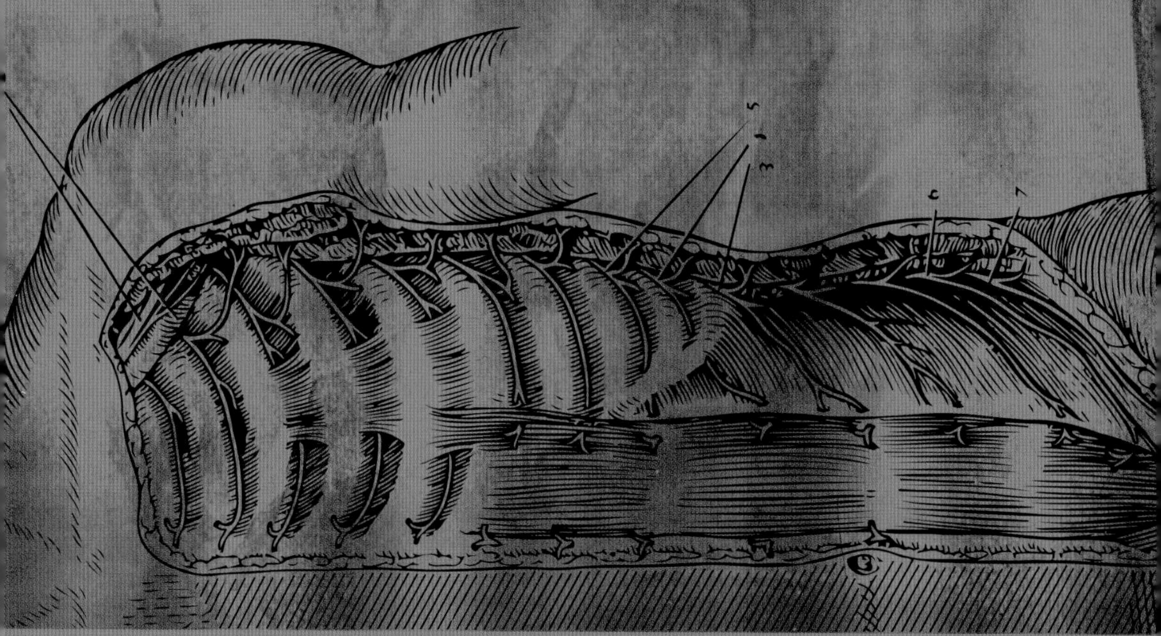

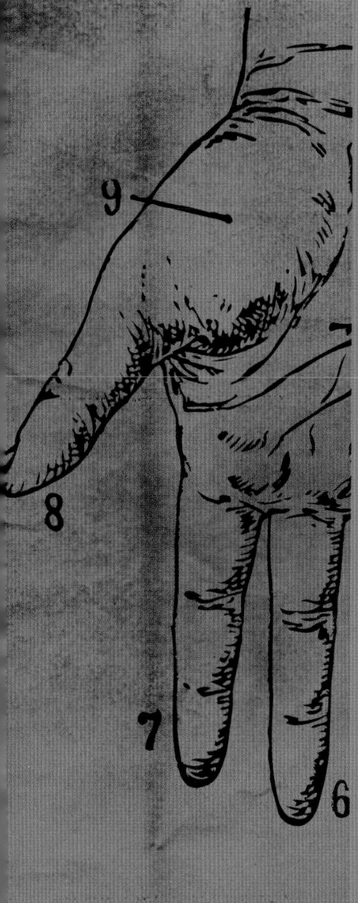
9
8
7
6

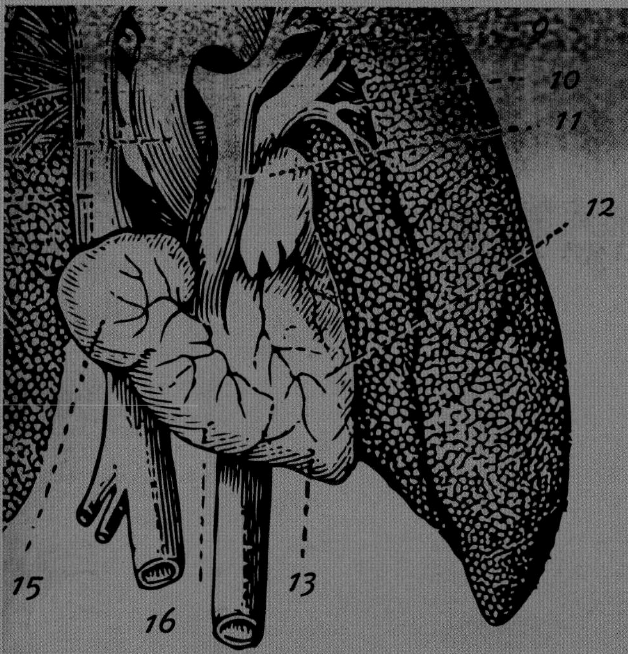
10
11
12
15
16
13

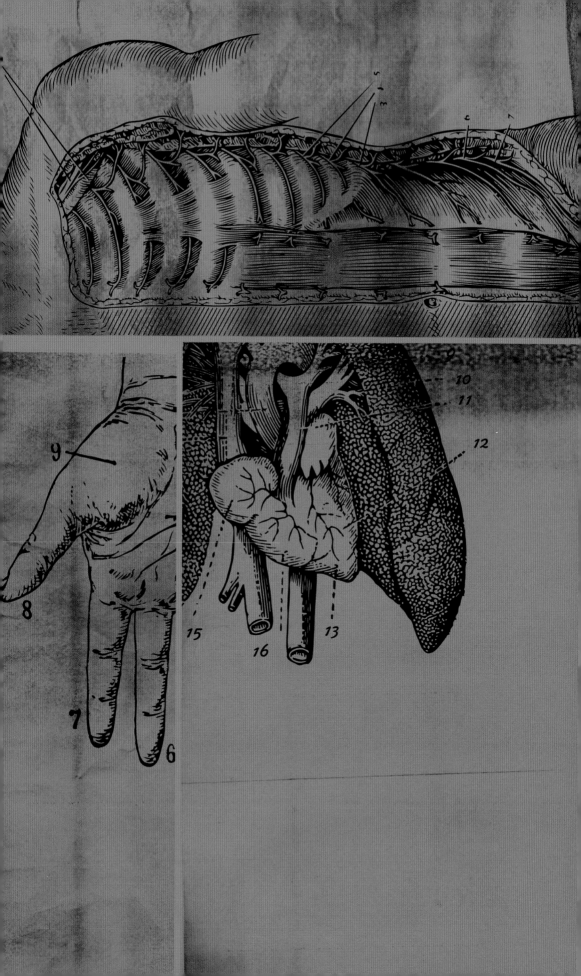

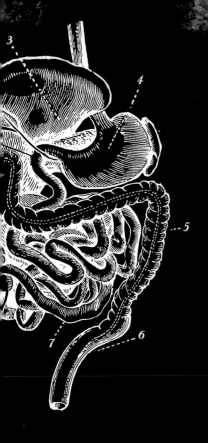

PAUL TOBIN lives in Portland, Oregon, and is the author of a multitude of comics in a wide variety of genres, having written hundreds of comics for such publishers as Marvel, Dark Horse, DC, Top Shelf, Fantagraphics, and Oni Press, including the multiple Eisner Award winning *BANDETTE* (in conjunction with his wife, artist Colleen Coover) and his wildly successful *PLANTS VS. ZOMBIES* series at Dark Horse. Other highlights include *COLDER*, a horror series nominated for both an Eisner and a Bram Stoker award, his *PREPARE TO DIE* novel, and his *GENIUS FACTOR* series of novels for middle grade readers. Current projects include more novels on the way, as well as further creator-owned comics for both print and digital publishers.

Paul enjoys burlesque shows, climbing various walls at the bouldering gym, dogs, fierce rainstorms, and video games where he gets to befriend all the talking animals in towns, or shoot various aliens right in the face, thank you very much.

ARJUNA SUSINI was born in Livorno, Italy, in 1984. He graduated from the International School of Comics in Florence in 2008. In 2011, his first comic, *BULLET BALLAD*, was published by BD Edizioni. In 2012 he worked with Graphic India on two series, *MISTRY P.I.* and *SHIKARY FORCE: HUNTERS*, while working as a concept artist for Mighty Box on the game *POSTHUMAN: SANCTUARY*. His newest work is *MADE MEN* from Oni Press, but he has other secret projects in the works.

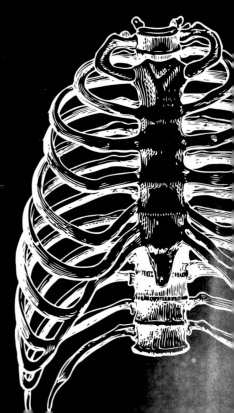

GONZALO DUARTE was born in Buenos Aires, Argentina, in 1986. After a couple of years working in the animation industry he made the jump to comic books, his lifelong passion. He's been working since 2009 as a writer in the Argentine comics scene on magazines such as *TERMINUS* and *PROXIMA*, and as a colorist on titles such as Boom! Studios' *BIG TROUBLE IN LITTLE CHINA* and Oni Press' *HELLBREAK*, *BRIK*, and *THE BUNKER*.

You can see more of his work at *gonzaloduarte.com*.

SAIDA TEMOFONTE is originally from Italy. She letters for DC Comics, Lion Forge, Kymera Press, Oni Press and IDW and calls Los Angeles her beloved home now.

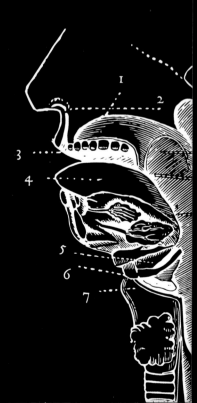

READ MORE FROM ONI PRESS

I WAS THE CAT
PAUL TOBIN
BENJAMIN DEWEY

I WAS THE CAT
By Paul Tobin &
Benjamin Dewey
192 pages, hardcover,
color interiors
ISBN 978-1-62010-139-1

REDLINE
HOLMAN · McCORMACK · FITZPATRICK · CRANK!

REDLINE
By Neal Holman,
Clayton McCormack,
and Kelly Fitzpatrick
128 pages, softcover,
color interiors
ISBN 978-1-62010-459-0

THE DAMNED
VOLUME 1. "THREE DAYS DEAD"
by Cullen Bunn and Brian Hurtt with Bill Crabtree
ONLY $9.99 U.S.

THE DAMNED, VOL 1: THREE DAYS DEAD
By Cullen Bunn, Brian Hurtt,
and Bill Crabtree
152 pages, softcover,
color interiors
ISBN 978-1-62010-385-2

Spectacle
MEGAN ROSE GEDRIS
BOOK ONE

SPECTACLE, BOOK ONE
By Megan Rose Gedris
136 pages, softcover,
color interiors
ISBN 978-1-62010-492-7

ZANDER CANNON
KAIJUMAX
SEASON ONE

KAIJUMAX SEASON ONE: TERROR AND RESPECT
By Zander Cannon
168 pages, softcover,
color interiors
ISBN 978-1-62010-270-1

HEARTTHROB
CHRISTOPHER SEBELA • ROBERT WILSON IV • NICK FILARDI
"Crime, romance and open heart surgery. Highly (cardiac) arresting."
-Kieron Gillen, The Wicked + The Divine
1

HEARTTHROB, VOL 1: NEVER GOING BACK AGAIN
By Christopher Sebela,
Robert Wilson IV,
and Nick Filardi
136 pages, softcover,
color interiors
ISBN 978-1-62010-338-8

For more information on these and other fine Oni Press comic books and graphic novels visit **www.onipress.com**.
To find a comic specialty store in your area visit **www.comicshops.us**.

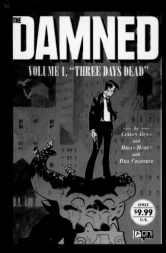